THE BATTLE FOR EUROPE

The Battle for Europe

How an Elite Hijacked a Continent – and How We Can Take it Back

Thomas Fazi

First published 2014 by Pluto Press
345 Archway Road, London N6 5AA

www.plutobooks.com

Distributed in the United States of America exclusively by
Palgrave Macmillan, a division of St. Martin's Press LLC,
175 Fifth Avenue, New York, NY 10010

British Library Cataloguing in Publication Data
A catalogue record for this book is available from the British Library

ISBN 978 0 7453 3451 6 Hardback
ISBN 978 0 7453 3450 9 Paperback
ISBN 978 1 7837 1022 5 PDF eBook
ISBN 978 1 7837 1024 9 Kindle eBook
ISBN 978 1 7837 1023 2 EPUB eBook

Library of Congress Cataloging in Publication Data applied for

This book is printed on paper suitable for recycling and made from fully managed and sustained forest sources. Logging, pulping and manufacturing processes are expected to conform to the environmental standards of the country of origin.

10 9 8 7 6 5 4 3 2 1

Typeset by Curran Publishing Services, Norwich
Simultaneously printed digitally by CPI Antony Rowe, Chippenham, UK and
Edwards Bros in the United States of America

Contents

Figures and tables

Figures

Tables

The motivation that underlay the Resistance was outrage. We, the veterans of the Resistance movements … call on the younger generations to revive and carry forward the tradition of the Resistance and its ideas. We say to you: take over, keep going, get angry!

Stéphane Hessel (1917–2013), former Resistance fighter*

* from *Time for Outrage!* trans. Damion Searls, London: Quartet Books, 2011, p. 16.

Preface

'Crisis' has been one of the most-used words in the English language – if not the most used – in the five years from 2008 to the time of writing this book in 2013. Ever since the financial crash of 2008 – and of course the outbreak of the so-called 'euro crisis' in 2010 – 'the crisis' has been blamed for an almost endless variety of social and economic ills: unemployment, poverty, recession, public debt, political instability, social strife and in more recent years, austerity.

In this age of Tweet-like, lightning-fast, bite-sized information, phrases like '*the crisis* eases up' or '*the crisis* intensifies' – rather than, say, the more accurate but also more cumbersome '*policy makers* fail to develop adequate tools to restore the flow of credit to private businesses and boost employment' – have become commonplace. This is perhaps inevitable. In the months and years following the crash, though, this involuntary reification, or personification, of 'the crisis' ended up lending to it an almost god-like will of its own, and a *force majeure*-like sense of inevitability. The idea that the financial crisis of 2008 and subsequent First World recession, albeit triggered by the greediness of a few Wall Street bankers, actually reflected a deeper structural – economic, ecological, cultural, even spiritual – and thus *inevitable* – crisis, slowly sank into our collective consciousness.

There is certainly a lot of truth in this, and systemic, interdisciplinary critiques of our current socio-economic model are more needed now than ever. But the notion that the financial and economic crisis was the quasi-natural, end-of-history-style outcome of an unsustainable system – if not even the beginning of the 'final crisis' of capitalism – rather than a more mundane failure of policy making, overwhelmingly resulted in the opposite of radical critique: it resulted in complacency.

Like many (not all, of course) young radicals and environmentalists of my generation – I was 26 at the time of the subprime crisis – I too saw the crisis and subsequent recession as the necessary, albeit painful, slow-down and scale-down of Western consumerist turbo-capitalism that we had been advocating for so long. In a perversely naïve way, I believed that the system would self-correct itself, giving way to a better, fairer, greener world – not unlike what had happened in the United States after the Great Depression, and in Europe after the Second World War. As we all know, the exact opposite has happened, with Europe now facing its worst human, social and political crisis since the 1940s.

The left, I believe, bears a large responsibility. By contributing to the depoliticisation of 'the crisis', it has ingenuously helped the political-financial elites to transform it into a powerful ideology, in the Marxist sense of the word – a mystification of reality which ensures the continuous dominance of the ruling class, and one which came precisely at a time when the previous ideology of 'permanent war on terror' was starting to run out of steam – and to present the policy choices made since 2008 as neutral, structurally determined, inevitable ('there is no alternative') by-products of 'the crisis', rather than class-based, politically and ideologically motivated decisions.

I slowly and belatedly started to become aware of this after the outbreak of the so-called 'euro crisis', as I saw the blame for the crisis being shifted from the banks to the governments – and thus, more or less implicitly, to the ordinary citizens and workers – of Europe, who were accused of 'living beyond their means' for too long. 'The party is over', politicians and commentators almost unanimously declared. 'Europe simply can't afford to maintain the social and economic standards that its citizens have been accustomed to.' The continent (and especially the supposedly 'profligate' countries of the periphery), they said, needed a drastic austerity cure to atone for years of 'excesses'.

I – like many others, of course – sensed that something was deeply wrong, but found myself unable to articulate a critique much beyond a generic opposition to what I perceived as anti-social policies. More importantly, though, like many Europeans, especially those living in Mediterranean countries – I live in Rome – I felt myself vacillating under the weight of the post-2010 ideological onslaught, and to some extent even interiorising the blame for what was happening. 'Could it be that Europe is really running out of money? Have Italians, Spanish and Greeks – admittedly not the most frugal of people – had it too easy all these years?' I ashamedly asked myself. In more general terms, though, I failed to grasp what appeared to be a problem of overwhelming and daunting complexity, as rarely heard of terms started to appear on the news on a daily basis.

Thus, in early 2012, I went searching for answers: for a coherent explanation of what by then was known as the euro crisis. I hoped to find one that would offer a convincing rebuttal of the dominant narrative. Of course, I found a wealth of material – much of which confirmed my doubts about the official story. But all the works that I found seemed to take a compartmentalised, reductionist approach to the problem, focusing on individual issues – the financial crisis, public debt, the government bail-outs, the effects of austerity and so on – or specific countries. What was lacking, in my opinion, was a comprehensive, all-encompassing, critical, accessible explanation of what was happening, capable of linking together the various interconnected issues and crises.

This was also one of the main reasons, I concluded, that the policies imposed by the European political establishment, which would have been politically unthinkable just a few years earlier, were encountering relatively little resistance. Any attempt at resisting the 'austerity regime' would have to rest on solid theoretical grounds. Thus, I started slowly to put together the pieces of the puzzle. What I found as I went deeper and deeper down the rabbit hole exceeded even my wildest expectations. The yawning disconnect between the perception and the reality of the post-2010 'crisis management' policies pursued across Europe, and the root causes of the crisis, was beyond anything I had imagined.

This drove me to the disquieting conclusion that the European Union's insistence on pursuing austerity – despite the fact that it has proven to be a colossal failure of economic policy, not to mention a cause of immense human suffering – should not be viewed simply as a case of political and ideological short-sightedness. Rather, it represents as an attempt by the wealthy elite to do away with the last remnants of the welfare state and complete the neoliberal project. In other words, it is a classic case of economic shock doctrine – and the first instance in history where such 'therapy' has been applied to an entire continent.

Moreover, I came across ample evidence – presented in the book's final chapter – that the left's passive and defeatist attitude in the face of the current neoliberal onslaught, and its growing hostility towards the European Union and monetary union as such, are entirely unjustified. Not only is a radical, progressive overhaul of these institutions (in the direction of a genuine European supranational democracy and welfare state) technically feasible, it is arguably the best means to forward the interests of citizens and workers and tame the overwhelming powers of global financial and corporate leviathans.

Unfortunately, as far as the general public's understanding of the current crisis goes, things have hardly changed since I started writing this book. If anything, they have got worse. This is for a number of reasons: the deepening social and economic crisis, which is leading to nationalistic and populist backlashes; the power of the dominant ideology; the lack of convincing alternative narratives; the fact that 'the causes of the crisis are so complicated that they boggle the mind', as even George Soros, perhaps the world's most famous financier, admitted;[1] but perhaps most fundamentally, the assumption that these problems are beyond the comprehension of non-professionals, especially non-economists. This is not true – and is actually one of the pillars of the 'ideology of crisis'.

That is why most of the book is dedicated to an analysis of the true causes of the euro-crisis which is intended to be in depth but comprehensible to everyone. To be able to pursue a different path, after all, we first have to understand what went wrong. As financial specialist David Marsh recently stated, Europe needs nothing less than a Truth and Reconciliation Commission on the model of the one established in South Africa in the 1990s after the abolition of apartheid, to establish the 'crimes of negligence and incompetence' in the ongoing management of the euro crisis.[2] This book hopes to be a first step in that direction.

Acknowledgements

I would like to express my gratitude to the whole team at Pluto Press, and especially to David Castle, my commissioning editor, and Susan Curran, my ever-patient editor. A special thanks goes to Lulù, my canine friend who offered me around-the-clock company and encouragement during the writing of this book. As for everyone else, you know who you are. See you in the streets.

Thomas Fazi
July 2013

CHAPTER ONE

The Financial Crisis

The US Subprime Crisis

'It's not a crisis, it's a scam'—Occupy Wall Street

To understand the dramatic events unfolding in Europe today, we need to take a step back in time to the summer of 2008, when the so-called 'subprime mortgage crisis' exploded in the United States. To cut a long and fairly complicated story short, for years all the major American commercial banks had been handing out home mortgages to low-income and therefore highly risky borrowers (hence the term 'subprime'), and then reselling those loans to investors – investment banks, pension funds and so on – therefore cashing in on the loans and passing on the risk.

Imagine lending some money with interest to your friend Y and then getting your friend X to pay you the amount you loaned to Y, plus a little extra, so now Y has to pay the loan plus the interest back to X. As long as Y pays back, everyone is happy. This was done through sophisticated financial products known as collateralised debt obligations (CDOs), or mortgage-backed securities.

It's easy to see the gaping flaws in such a system: if the bank is not holding on to the loan, but instantly reselling it, it doesn't care whether the borrower actually has the means to repay the loan. It only cares about packaging as many loans as possible. That is how the US housing bubble was created.

Why would anyone buy a subprime (the lowest possible rating) loan, you might ask? Well, the investors didn't know that they were buying subprime loans, since the credit rating agencies – companies that assign credit ratings to certain types of debt obligations, supposedly helping investors in their decisions – were giving these CDOs a triple-A, the highest possible rating. Investors were led to believe that these subprime loans were as good as gold, and scrambled to buy them. The banks, on the other hand, were well aware of the value of what in internal communications they often referred to as 'crap'.[1] Take Goldman Sachs, which made billions of dollars betting on the insolvency of those same loans that it was selling on to unwitting investors.[2] This was done through yet another esoteric financial product known as derivatives. Derivatives – and in particular credit default swaps, or CDSs – allow financial institutions to take out insurance on assets they don't own. Hence, Goldman Sachs was able to take out insurance on – or to put it bluntly, bet against

– the bad loan it had just sold to a third party, and get paid from the insurance company when the loan defaulted – as Goldman expected it would. It would be as if you knowingly sold a faulty car to Y and then took out an insurance from X on that same car. As with securities, it's easy to see what's wrong with these financial products. Basically, both securities and derivatives encourage and facilitate fraud. And fraud happened, on a colossal scale.

As long as the value of the housing market kept rising, the system seemed to work. No market can keep growing indefinitely, though. Following a slight decrease in house prices, some loan borrowers started to default on their loans. This drove prices down even more, further amplifying the phenomenon, which soon exploded throughout the United States. This meant that a growing number of those subprime CDOs which investors worldwide had rushed to buy were becoming worthless, since thousands of borrowers stopped repaying their loans. Hence, they came to be know as 'toxic' or 'junk' assets.

Huge holes appeared in the balance sheets of banks and other financial institutions. At that point, the whole financial system was gripped by panic and ground to a halt. That's because banks daily borrow money from other banks on the interbank lending market. Because of the lack of transparency of the financial system, no one knew who held the toxic assets on their balance sheets, and what the losses amounted to. Mutual distrust ensued, and banks stopped lending money to each other – or anyone else. This is called a credit crunch. That's how the housing crisis turned into a financial crisis, and why the whole financial system risked going bust.

Faced with the very real prospect of a meltdown of the global economy, the US government decided to step in and inject huge amounts of public money into the financial system. In October 2008, following the collapse of Lehman Brothers, one of America's biggest investment banks, the US government approved a $700 billion plan to 'bail out' the big banks, deemed 'too big to fail' – despite many of them being directly responsible for the crisis. Although that's an enormous sum in itself, a 2011 audit by the US Government Accounting Office (GAO) revealed that over $16 trillion – more than the entire US gross domestic product (GDP) – was allocated to corporations and banks internationally, purportedly for 'financial assistance', during and after the 2007–08 crisis (see Table 1.1 on page 4).

In any case, the plan succeeded in averting the worst-case scenario: a global economic meltdown. But it wasn't long before the effects of the crisis were felt in the global economy, as they kick-started a global recession which by 2009 had already destroyed an estimated $50 trillion of wealth worldwide and made around 35 million more people unemployed.[3] As Andrew Haldane, executive director for financial stability at the Bank of England, declared in 2012, '[t]he banking crisis has been as bad for the economy as a world war.'[4]

The Crisis Comes to Europe

At the time, there was a widespread feeling in Europe that the crisis had been caused solely by those greedy Wall Street types, and that Europeans – who were starting to feel the effects of the recession – were innocent victims of an out-of-control US financial system. But things were not that simple. Even though the Wall Street bankers certainly played a major role in the crisis, Europeans – or rather, European banks – were no less guilty. As famed economist Nouriel Roubini and historian Stephen Mihm write in their best-selling *Crisis Economics*, '[m]any banks in Europe engaged in their own securitization party, slicing and dicing mortgages from homeowners in European countries'.[5] In 2007 alone, almost half a trillion euros worth of European loans became the basis of asset-backed securities, mortgage-backed securities and CDOs.

While US banks focused on subprime citizens, their European counterparts – especially those in Germany, the United Kingdom, the Netherlands, Spain, Austria, Belgium and Sweden – focused on 'subprime countries': particularly Latvia, Hungary, Ukraine and Bulgaria. When the crisis hit, many of these economies saw their currencies fall sharply, and thus borrowers, as in the United States, defaulted en masse on their loans, causing huge losses to the banks.[6]

Another problem facing European banks in the lead-up to the crisis was leverage. Basically leverage is debt, or rather the use of debt to acquire additional assets. A bank that purchases €20 million worth of mortgage-backed securities (CDOs) by putting up €1 million of its own capital and borrowing the remaining €19 million is said to be leveraged at a rate of 20 to 1 (20x). It's a highly profitable game (most of the time), but a risky one too: if the value of the purchased CDOs falls from €20 million to, say, €19 million – a drop of just 5 per cent – that is enough to wipe out the bank's capital. In this respect, European banks, on the eve of the crisis, were even more exposed than their American counterparts: Credit Suisse was leveraged at 33 to 1, ING at 49 to 1, Deutsche Bank at 53 to 1, and Barclays (the most leveraged of all) at a staggering 61 to 1. By comparison, Lehman Brothers – publicly vilified in the aftermath of the crisis as a paradigm of 'bad banking' – was leveraged at a relatively modest 31 to 1, and Bank of America was even lower, at 11 to 1.[7] This is why, when the housing market crashed, causing the value of CDOs to plummet and the interbank lending market to freeze, so many European financial institutions – most of which were extremely over-leveraged – found themselves in deep trouble.

In fact, cracks were forming on the European surface well before the crisis erupted in the United States. Indeed, many European institutions got into trouble in advance of their US counterparts: the French bank BNP, for example, suspended several of its hedge funds in the summer of 2007, a year before the collapse of Lehman Brothers. Interestingly, the first crisis-related bail-outs – although relatively small in magnitude – occurred in Europe, not in the United States. And

Table 1.1 US Federal Reserve loans to financial institutions, 2007–10 (in US$ billion)

Borrowing parent company	**TAF**	**PDCF**	**TSFL**
Citigroup Inc.	110	2,020	348
Morgan Stanley	–	1,913	115
Merrill Lynch & Co.	0	1,775	166
Bank of America Corporation	280	947	101
Barclays plc (UK)	232	410	187
Bear Stearns Companies, Inc.	–	851	2
Goldman Sachs Group Inc.	–	589	225
Royal Bank of Scotland Group plc (UK)	212	–	291
Deutsche Bank AG (Germany)	77	1	277
UBS AG (Switzerland)	56	35	122
JP Morgan Chase & Co.	99	112	68
Credit Suisse Group AG (Switzerland)	0	2	261
Lehman Brothers Holdings Inc.	–	83	99
Bank of Scotland plc (UK)	181	–	–
BNP Paribas SA (France)	64	66	41
Wells Fargo & Co.	159	–	–
Dexia SA (Belgium)	105	–	–
Wachovia Corporation	142	–	–
Dresdner Bank AG (Germany)	123	0	1
Société Générale SA (France)	124	–	–
All other borrowers	1,854	146	14
Total	**3,818**	**8,951**	**2,319**

Source: US Government Accountability Office.

surprisingly, they occurred in the continent's supposedly most virtuous country, Germany. In July 2007, IKB – a small bank that had gambled heavily on the subprime market – was bailed out by the government, and it was followed shortly afterwards by another German bank, Sachsen LB, for the same reason. Yet at the time the crisis seemed relatively contained.

When the subprime bubble eventually burst in the United States, all hell broke out in Europe as well. According to some estimates, the potential losses related to toxic or nonmarketable assets amounted on average to more than half the capital of European banks.[8] Certain institutions were in even worse shape: Credit Suisse had illiquid assets (that is, assets that are not readily saleable because of uncertainty about their value, such as subprime loans) which amounted to 125 per cent of its own capital. The figure was 200 per cent for Deutsche Bank and a staggering 600 per cent for the Franco-Belgian Dexia.[9] So much for the myth of the good European banks vs. bad US banks, although some banks – especially Italian ones – did indeed keep themselves out of the subprime frenzy.

CPFF	Subtotal	AMLF	TALF	Total loans
33	2,511	1	–	2,513
4	2,032	–	9	2,041
8	1,949	–	–	1,949
15	1,342	2	–	1,344
39	868	–	–	868
–	853	–	–	853
0	814	–	–	814
39	541	–	–	541
–	354	–	–	354
75	287	–	–	287
–	279	111	–	391
–	262	0	–	262
–	183	–	–	183
–	181	–	–	181
3	175	–	–	175
–	159	–	–	159
53	159	–	–	159
–	142	–	–	142
10	135	–	–	135
–	124	–	–	124
460	2,475	103	62	2,639
738	**15,826**	**217**	**71**	**16,115**

In the aftermath of the Lehman Brothers crisis, Angela Merkel declared that no other systemically important financial institution would be allowed to fail, but that each country was responsible for its own banks; in other words, there would be no EU-wide deposit-guarantee scheme or bail-out fund. Subsequently all major European governments declared their own heavily indebted and highly leveraged banks 'too big to fail' and announced massive bail-out plans. In 2008 alone, the United Kingdom, Germany, France, Austria and the Netherlands injected into the financial system a total of €1.7 trillion of public money (by country: United Kingdom, £500 billion; Germany, €500 billion; France, €360 billion; Austria, €100 billion; the Netherlands, €30 billion).[10] The United Kingdom went further than most governments, effectively nationalising two of its banks – Northern Rock and Bradford & Bingley – and part-nationalising another two, Royal Bank of Scotland and Lloyds Banking Group.

A little-known fact – which shows the extent to which the European financial elite was involved in the kind of 'casino capitalism' that caused the crisis – is that in 2008 Europe's biggest banks did not just get bailed out by their own governments. They were also bailed out by the US government, to the tune of billions of dollars. Of the Federal Reserve's bail-out cash, $354 billion went to Deutsche Bank, Germany's number one bank; $287 billion went to Swiss giant UBS; $262 billion to Credit Suisse; $175 billion to BNP Paribas, France's largest bank; $159 billion to Franco-Belgian Dexia (one of the most leveraged banks in the world at the time); $135 billion to another German bank, Dresdner Bank; and $124 billion to French heavyweight Société Générale (see Table 1.1).[11]

In many cases, these bail-outs were a by-product of the mother of all bail-outs, that of American insurance behemoth AIG. AIG had insured a massive amount of credit default swaps (CDSs) on subprime CDOs. That's the insurance that banks such as Goldman Sachs were taking out on the subprime, and soon to become 'toxic', loans that they were then reselling as triple-A CDOs. When thousands of borrowers in the United States started to default on their loans, that triggered the simultaneous payment of thousands of CDSs, which AIG did not have the money to pay. So the US government stepped in to guarantee the swaps. By bailing out AIG, though, the government was actually bailing out the banks to which AIG owed money. William Greider, an American journalist, matter-of-factly notes that '[b]ailing out AIG effectively meant rescuing Goldman Sachs, Morgan Stanley, Bank of America and Merrill Lynch (as well as a dozens of European banks) from huge losses'.[12] These banks won their gamble with AIG, and taxpayers got stuck with the bill – despite the fact that many banks were rigging the game by insuring loans that they knew to be toxic.

You might think that the injection of trillions of euros/dollars of European and American taxpayers' money into the European financial system – in 2008 alone – would stem the tide and pull the European economy out of the recession. Wrong. For a number of European countries, the worse was still to come.

Ireland: The 1995–2008 Boom and Bust

> '*The fundamentals are complete nonsense .... This is a classic bubble, it's going to end in tears, no question about it*'—Morgan Kelly, professor of economics at University College Dublin, 2007[13]

Throughout most of the 20th century, Ireland was a relatively poor country. As recently as the 1980s, a million Irish people – a third of the population – lived below the poverty line. What has occurred since then is without precedent in economic history. Between 1995 and 2000 the country's economy experienced an extraordinary growth, expanding at an average annual rate of 9.4 per cent – higher than China's growth rate over the same period.[14] By the start of the new millennium the Irish poverty rate was under 6 per cent, and by 2006 Ireland was one of the richest countries in the world, earning it the title of 'Celtic Tiger'.

There are many factors to which the 'Irish miracle' is attributed, such as the persistent lowering of the corporate tax rate, beginning in the 1980s, which turned Ireland into a tax haven for foreign corporations (a point we shall return to further on), but the main contributing factor was cheap credit, which in turn fuelled a colossal housing bubble – what the government's investigation into the banking crisis called 'a national speculative mania' – not unlike the US subprime bubble.[15] By 2007, Irish banks had loaned about €100 billion (basically the sum total of all Irish public bank deposits) to property developers and speculators, causing the Irish construction industry to balloon to nearly a quarter of the country's GDP – compared with less than 10 per cent in a normal economy – and housing prices to rise to unsustainable levels.[16] As Michael Lewis, contributing editor to *Vanity Fair*, wrote, 'all of Ireland had become subprime'.[17] By 2008, the whole country was basically a massive bubble waiting to burst. And if the real-estate market collapsed, the banks would be on the hook for the losses.

In September of that year, a huge bubble-bursting pin came in the form of Lehman Brothers' failure. Shares of Irish banks started to plummet, and big corporations started to withdraw their deposits from them. On 29 September the stock of Anglo Irish fell 46 per cent on a single day, and the stock of Allied Irish Bank (AIB) fell 17 per cent. A run on Irish deposits had started. That day the Irish government made a crucial decision which would end up having far-reaching and disastrous consequences for the country: it offered a blanket €440 billion government guarantee (corresponding to around 2.5 times the Irish GDP) to all shareholders and bondholders of the six main Irish banks. As Lewis explains:

> The Irish banks, like the big American banks, managed to persuade a lot of people that they were so intertwined with their economy that their failure would bring down a lot of other things, too. But they weren't, at least not all of them. Anglo Irish Bank [for example] was not, by nature, systemic. It became so only when its losses were made everyone's.[18]

As in the case of AIG, though, by bailing out the country's highly indebted banks, the Irish government was effectively bailing out the banks' foreign creditors, which included British, German, French and American banks (including the infamous Goldman Sachs).[19] Only a few months into the crisis, a disturbing pattern was already starting to appear. Not only were citizens everywhere being asked to pay for the recklessness of a corrupt banking system, they were being asked to pay the creditors under the pretext of bailing out the debtors. The reason given was one which would become a mantra in the coming years: 'There is no alternative.' But as Michael Lewis explains, that wasn't the case:

> These private bondholders didn't have any right to be made whole by the Irish government. The bondholders didn't even *expect* to be made whole by the Irish government .... People who had made a private bet that went bad, and didn't expect to be repaid in full, were handed their money back – from the Irish taxpayer.[20]

Precisely the same thing that had happened in the United States – and was happening all over Europe.

From that moment on, things started to spiral out of control. The Irish government had wildly underestimated the size of the banks' debts. The banks had borrowed money recklessly on the international markets for years (and then re-lent it to developers), and were bankrupt. By 2007, the country's foreign debt (the sum of all private and public debt) had reached 1,000 per cent of GDP – most of which was debt owed by the banks.[21] 'The Irish economy had become a giant Ponzi scheme and the country was effectively bankrupt', as Morgan Kelly, an Irish economist, put it.[22] The debts incurred by Irish banks were so huge that they could never realistically have been repaid, and yet the government pledged to repay them as if they were obligations of the state. In retrospect, Michael Lewis writes, 'the decision to cover them appears not merely odd but suicidal'.[23]

The government soon realised that the blanket guarantee would not suffice, and in January 2009 announced the nationalisation of Anglo Irish and its €34 billion (and mounting) losses – a staggering figure when you consider that its total loans amounted to €72 billion. A month later, the government carried out recapitalisation of the country's two largest banks, AIB and Bank of Ireland, with bail-outs of €3.5 billion confirmed for each one. Ireland thus became the first European country to witness the failure of its entire banking system. Over the course of the following two years – as the fate of the country became inextricably tied to that of its banks – Ireland's economic miracle would turn into a nightmare.

Ireland was not the only country that had experienced a housing bubble in Europe. Iceland, Estonia and Lithuania had all recently seen housing values appreciate at relentless rates. But the only country that could rival Ireland for the largest bubble was Spain.

Spain: The 1995–2008 Boom and Bust

> *'At the moment [the Spanish economy] is a monoculture based on bricks and mortar alone'*—Emilio Ontiveros, professor of business economics at the Universidad Autónoma de Madrid, 2006[24]

Spain's recent history resembles Ireland's in many ways. Spain too began its 'great leap forward' in 1995, with an average growth rate of 3 per cent until 2007, reaching an all-time high of 5.8 per cent in 2000. This period of unprecedented economic expansion is known as the 'Spanish fiesta'. In 2007 Spain, with a bigger

GDP than Canada – and by then the fourth-largest economy in the eurozone – had officially become an economic powerhouse. Unemployment was down to 8 per cent (the lowest figure since 1978) and the country was attracting a growing number of immigrants. And just like in Ireland, this economic 'miracle' was based on cheap credit provided by the banks.

Cheap money triggered a real-estate boom, as property developers borrowed heavily. In 2005 alone, 800,000 new apartments were constructed, more than were built in Germany, the United Kingdom and France combined that same year.[25] Entire new towns were built, such as Valdeluz, constructed for 30,000 people, plus a number of new airports, such as the €1.1 billion Ciudad Real Central Airport and the Castellón-Costa Azahar Airport. And since all those houses had to be sold, the banks started to flood Spanish families with cheap credit, causing them to take on a growing number of bigger and bigger mortgages. Construction and real-estate loans grew from 10 per cent of GDP in 1992 to 43 per cent in 2009, according to an International Monetary Fund (IMF) report.[26] At the end of 2006 average family indebtedness reached a record high of 115 per cent of disposable income, having grown at 25 per cent per year between 2001 and 2005, with 97 per cent of mortgages at variable interest rates.[27] The banks, meanwhile, thrived.

As a 2006 *Financial Times* article noted, though, 'economists have warned that growth based on a property bubble and a consumer spending spree – both fuelled by cheap credit – cannot last'.[28] And it didn't. The 'Spanish fiesta' came to an end on the same day that Ireland awakened from its dream: 17 September 2008, the day that Lehman Brothers collapsed on the other side of the Atlantic. The resulting credit crunch caused a great number of borrowers to default, and the value of the assets the loans were based on to plunge, leaving the banks saddled with around €300 billion in loans to house builders, equivalent to nearly one-third of the country's GDP.[29] At that point the banks turned off the tap and stopped lending money, bringing the economy to a halt.

When the speculative bubble popped, Spain became one of the worst affected countries: in the third quarter of 2008 the Spanish economy officially entered recession. Prices began to fall and housing demand halted, and unemployment jumped by 10 per cent, hitting 17.4 per cent at the end of March 2009. In less than a year the crisis caused 2 million people to lose their job, taking the total out of work to just over 4 million.

The Spanish banking system was considered one of the most solid and best-equipped of all Western economies. Just a few days before the collapse of Lehman Brothers, the Spanish prime minister José Luis Rodríguez Zapatero had boasted that Spain had 'perhaps the most solid financial system in the world'.[30] It's true that Spanish banks had not invested in the toxic products that sank banks elsewhere, thanks to the country's conservative banking rules and practices. Nevertheless, these rules were strongly relaxed during the housing bubble. The borrowing frenzy led banks to open more and more branches, making Spain one of the most 'over-banked' countries in the world.[31]

After the property bubble popped in 2008, banks began to acquire properties from developers before the loans that supported them went sour. As the economy entered recession, foreclosures mounted, landing the banks with a massive stock of empty homes. The situation was made worse by the fact that the Spanish banks – just like the Irish banks – had borrowed money on the international markets to lend to developers and home buyers, a much riskier strategy than using the deposits they got from savers. By 2009 they found themselves sitting on massive losses. And just like the Irish banks, they too owed large amounts of money to French and German banks (and to a lesser extent to British, American, Italian and Portuguese banks).[32]

As more and more borrowers defaulted on their loans, the banks found that their balance sheets were filled with non-performing loans and toxic assets: urban land, unfinished housing developments, unpaid real-estate loans to developers and so on. By 2009 the financial sector was sitting on €445 billion worth of property-related loans.[33] As it became clear that the banks were in worse shape than previously thought, the Bank of Spain decided to take over the Caja Castilla la Mancha – a mid-sized savings bank which had a capital shortfall and was heavily exposed to loans to the property sector – in the country's first bank rescue in recent years. In May it went further and created a bank bail-out fund, known as the Fondo de Reestructuración Ordenada Bancaria (FROB), with firepower of up to €99 billion, offering the banks the 'explicit, unconditional and irrevocable guarantee of the Kingdom of Spain'.[34] Once again the people were asked to step in and save the banks (and their creditors), while these proceeded to mercilessly evict thousands of insolvent borrowers.

Little did the Spanish people know that, as in Ireland, things were about to get unimaginably worse for them.

Iceland: Letting the Banks Go Bust

The events that occurred in 2008 and 2009 in Iceland are in a league of their own, in terms of their magnitude, but more importantly in terms of the government's response. Like their Irish and Spanish counterparts, the three main Icelandic banks – Glitnir, Kaupthing and Landsbanki – had over-leveraged themselves beyond all conceivable limits in the years leading up to the crisis, borrowing money from international lenders on a huge scale to finance asset purchases, both at home and abroad (thus fuelling an all-round economic bubble, like elsewhere). They purchased stakes in foreign companies and opened branches across northern Europe, most notably in the United Kingdom and the Netherlands.[35] At the outbreak of the financial crash, in 2008, with a balance sheet totalling €110 billion

– almost ten times the size of Iceland's gross domestic product (GDP) – the three banks found themselves landed with huge amounts of unserviceable foreign debt. In such a situation, a bank would normally ask for a loan from the central bank as a lender of last resort. However, in Iceland the banks were so much larger than the national economy that the Central Bank of Iceland (CBI) and the Icelandic government could not guarantee the payment of the banks' debts. In short, the banks were simply 'too big to bail' – rescuing them was not an option. Inevitably the banks defaulted, in the largest banking collapse (relative to the size of the economy) in economic history.

When the banks fell, the whole economy came crashing down. With the country on the verge of collapse, the government decided to assume far-reaching powers to secure the safety of the nation and its savers. It nationalised the three banks, injecting into them equity amounting to 30 per cent of the country's GDP, and imposed capital controls to prevent money fleeing the country. The stated aim of the emergency measures was to provide 'continued banking operations for Icelandic families and businesses'.[36] Take note: *Icelandic* families and businesses; no mention of foreign creditors or (mainly British and Dutch) depositors. 'We do not intend to pay the debts of the banks that have been a little heedless', stated the governor of Iceland's central bank, suggesting that foreign creditors would 'unfortunately only get 5–10–15 per cent of their claims'.[37]

Iceland's unorthodox handling of the crisis – letting the banks go bankrupt, nationalising them and safeguarding Icelandic citizens and depositors at the expense of foreign creditors and depositors – would turn the country into something of a hero in the eyes of many in the coming years, as the true cost of the bank bail-outs under way across the rest of Europe would become evident. As Nobel prize-winning economist Paul Krugman summarises the Icelandic experience, '[w]here everyone else bailed out the bankers and made the public pay the price, Iceland let the banks go bust and actually expanded its social safety net … [thus preserving] the basic decency of its society.'[38] Even the IMF noted that the decision 'not to make taxpayers liable for bank losses was right'.[39]

In short, by mid-2009, less than a year after it began, the financial crisis had caused widespread destruction and suffering across Europe and the United States – and to varying degrees, all around the world. By the end of the year, in Europe the financial crisis would take a unique (and particularly nasty) twist, morphing into the so-called euro crisis. Before we delve into the main subject of this book, and the one that readers are probably most anxious to get their hands on, though, let me ask you to bear with me a little longer, as we take a deeper look at the historical and ideological roots of the financial crisis – a necessary step for understanding the events currently unfolding in Europe.

Even though the mainstream narrative of the euro crisis has encouraged the myth (one of many) that the financial crisis and the euro crisis are two fundamentally unconnected events (in the simplest possible terms: the first was caused by banks, while the second was caused by governments), they are in fact part of the same systemic (ideological, political and economic) crisis. The latter is in many ways a direct consequence of the former. In a deeper sense, though, they both share the same ideological-historical roots.

The first and foremost of these was the dismantling of the post-Great Depression framework of financial regulation (in which Europe played a crucial role), resulting in the deregulation and liberalisation of the entire financial system. Others were the cancerous growth of financial institutions, itself part of the wider financialisation of the economy, resulting in the growth of speculative boom–bust cycles; the belief in the ability of the market to self-regulate and self-manage itself, and a fundamental distrust of democratically elected institutions, resulting in a steady curtailing of democracy; the systematic attack on the post-war system of social welfare, workers' bargaining rights and progressive taxation, resulting in historically high concentrations of wealth and rates of inequality, and booming public debt levels; and the rise of an increasingly leverage-based financial economy and private-debt-based real economy.

The euro crisis, of course, has a number of specific causes that do not apply to the financial crisis, but relate to the rather unique political and economic architecture of the European Monetary Union (EMU). But these share a single, underlying origin with the other issues just mentioned: the 30-year-long (and ultimately successful) takeover of society and the economy by financial markets, which was itself part of the wider rise of neoliberalism as the dominant economic paradigm. Understanding the financial crisis (and its ideological and historical roots) is thus essential for understanding the euro crisis, so it is where we shall begin this investigation. More specifically, we shall start by looking at the way modern banking and finance functions, and especially its reliance on debt, or leverage. This is a crucial point for understanding how the financial crisis subsequently morphed into a 'sovereign debt crisis'.

Banking 101: How Finance Rules the World

> *'Banks are dangerous institutions'*—Mervyn King, governor of the Bank of England (2003–13)[40]

As we have seen, the various national financial crises that exploded in 2008–09 in the United States and Europe all followed a very similar pattern, with the US subprime crisis acting as a mere catalyst. They involved reckless borrowing and lending by the banks (facilitated by complex financial products such as securities and derivatives), which fuelled an excessive accumulation of household and bank debt, which in turn fuelled a series of huge housing bubbles (and/or other credit-driven booms), which caused asset prices and private (household and bank) debt levels to rise to unsustainable levels. When the supply of the overpriced asset exceeded demand, the bubbles burst, causing banks to cut off the supply of credit, or even worse, to collapse under the weight of their own debts (only to be subsequently 'bailed out' by governments). This drove the economy into recession, causing widespread destruction and suffering, and as we shall see, sowing the seeds of the ensuing euro crisis.

These events are known as boom–bust cycles, and the key word to understand them (and in particular the 2008 global boom-gone-bust) is debt, or leverage in the banks' case. In order to understand debt/leverage, it is crucial to understand how our modern banking and financial systems function.

Banks create debt or credit (in the form of loans and mortgages), and also take on debt themselves. First we shall look at the role of banks in debt creation. We all know that banks 'create' debt by handing out loans and mortgages to households and businesses; this is perfectly normal, of course, and is the whole purpose of banking. What is less known (and arguably less 'normal') is how banks do this. Most people think that banks collect deposits from savers and lend these deposits to borrowers. But that is not how today's 'fractional reserve banking system' works.

In reality, when a bank makes a new loan, it simply taps some numbers into a computer and creates brand new money which it then deposits into the borrower's account. The bank's pre-existing deposits are not even touched; the money is effectively created out of thin air. Instead of deposits leading to loans, it actually works the opposite way: it's the loans that lead to newly created deposits.[41] Basically, the banks lend money that they don't own, at a rate of interest. This is not something new. In fact it has been a central aspect of banking since the 17th century, when bankers, upon taking deposits in gold coins, started to issue paper receipts promising repayment on demand – which merchants could then use to buy goods and services. This allowed banks to dramatically enlarge their business as moneylenders, because from then on, when the public came to borrow money, the bankers could lend them freshly printed paper receipts.

With the invention of computers, of course, the ability of banks to 'create money' hugely expanded. Today, when we talk about the ability of banks to create money, we are in fact talking of 'digital money' (the ones and zeroes that make up the money in our bank accounts), not cash – which only central banks are allowed to create. Given that today over 99 per cent of payments (by value) are made electronically, the overwhelming majority of the money in circulation (an estimated 97 per cent) is in fact privately created digital money, not cash printed/minted by the central banks.[42] This means that to a large degree, private banks – not central banks – control the supply of money in the economy. Every time they expand their lending, they increase the supply of money (often leading to speculative booms), and every time they contract lending, they reduce it (exacerbating the post-boom recession). In short, the creation of money – one of the most crucial aspects of a country's monetary and economic policy – has effectively been privatised.

This creates a number of problems. First and foremost, digital money is always accompanied by a debt (which is not true where the actual money represents the amount of wealth). Today, the world's total public and private debt is far higher the world's GDP. What this means is that there is simply not enough money in circulation to pay back all outstanding debt. Basically, the entire global economy is not only trapped in a 'web of debt': it is a boom waiting to go bust. This is especially apparent if we take into account the fact that the banks can cut off the flow of cash just as easily as they encouraged it – which is precisely what they did when their credit-induced bubbles burst in 2008.

Furthermore, banks don't simply control how much money (and thus debt) is created; they also control where this money goes. By their very nature, financial markets pursue short-term profit, which is why, in the years leading up the financial crisis, banks pumped huge amounts of money into the most profitable sector of all, the housing market. This fuelled its boom and pushed prices up year after year, at the expense of all the other sectors of the economy.

As Adair Turner, a member of the UK Financial Policy Committee and former chair of the Financial Services Authority, says, '[b]anks which can create credit and money to finance asset price booms are thus inherently dangerous institutions'. In fact, Turner believes that the failure of governments to constrain the private financial system's creation of private credit and money was one of the root causes of the financial crisis.[43] Moreover, by having commercial banking and investment under the same roof (the so-called 'universal bank' concept, to which we shall return further on), the money-creation process inherent in commercial banking enables the development of investment banking, as the newly created money can then be used to feed speculative banking activities.

To be fair, governments have created some rules to limit the amount of money (and thus debt) that commercial banks can create in the form of loans. These are known as reserve requirements, and they set the minimum reserves each commercial bank must hold, rather than lend out, of customer deposits and notes. Through the process of mortgage securitisation, though, commercial banks – the ones issuing the (often subprime) mortgages and then selling them on to investment banks and other institutions – were easily able to circumvent these requirements. If a bank issues a loan and then sells it on to a third party, the loan is cleared from its balance sheet and therefore the bank is free to issue a new loan without exceeding its minimum reserve requirement. This gives the banks the power to create a potentially infinite supply of money, fuelling massive credit bubbles. This is partly what led to the housing bubbles in the United States and

Europe. Before it burst, the US mortgage-backed securities market was worth more than $11 trillion, almost as much as the entire US GDP.[44]

As the late Hyman P. Minsky, one of the 20th century's most prescient economists, wrote, '[s]ecuritization implies that there is no limit to bank initiative in creating credits.'[45] Moreover, most countries have deposit-guarantee schemes in which the country's central bank commits itself to act as lender of last resort should a bank not be able to honour its deposits. Such measures, although designed to limit the impact of banking crises and protect customers (me, you and everyone else), also create what in economic theory is known as a 'moral hazard': a situation where a party will have a tendency to take risks because the costs that could be incurred will not be felt by the party taking the risk. This is exactly what happened in 2008, and it would later play a crucial role in the euro crisis. As Mervyn King, former governor of the Bank of England, explains, '[b]anks and their creditors knew that if they were sufficiently important to the economy or the rest of the financial system, and things went wrong, the government would always stand behind them. And they were right.'[46]

Given the ability of banks to externalise the consequences of their reckless habits, with little to lose when things take a turn for the worst, it's hardly surprising that they encourage booms so enthusiastically. A good example is the practice of 'predatory lending', which the *Investor Dictionary* describes as 'the practice of a lender deceptively convincing borrowers to agree to unfair and abusive loan terms, or systematically violating those terms in ways that make it difficult for the borrower to defend against'. This was a practice common to many US banks during the subprime lending boom, and to a lesser extent also to European (especially Spanish) banks.[47]

It is important to understand that when a boom goes bust, things don't simply return to pre-boom conditions. The bursting of the bubble can cause catastrophic meltdowns whose effects reverberate long afterwards, causing plenty of collateral damage and leading to recessions and/or depressions (or worse, as the euro crisis would show). The costs of these far outweigh the benefits enjoyed (by some more than others) during the boom. 'The damage done in these boom-and-bust cycles is greater than politicians and the media usually acknowledge', Nouriel Roubini says.[48] 'When handled carelessly, crises inflict staggering losses, wiping out entire industries, destroying wealth, causing massive job losses, and burdening governments with enormous fiscal costs' – as the euro crisis would dramatically demonstrate.[49]

More importantly, the costs and benefits – and the responsibilities – of these boom–bust cycles are far from being equally distributed across society. It would be very misleading to view these cycles as drunken parties where everyone has an equally good time – banks, borrowers and so on – and an equally severe hangover. During the recent boom, banks and other financial institutions worldwide reaped enormous profits (banks worldwide saw their profits soar from $372 to $788 billion between 2000 and 2006)[50] – and they were bailed out when things imploded, despite their being the main culprits. Homeowners who defaulted on their mortgages, on the other hand, didn't just lose their homes (which is arguably worse than never having owned one in the first place, given the trauma involved); on top of bearing the cost of the bail-outs, they – and society as a whole – also had to suffer the consequences of the crisis-induced recession. Moreover, during the bust, wealth and assets are acquired at fire-sale prices by the people with access to cash. In this sense, boom–bust cycles actually facilitate the transfer of wealth from the working and middle classes to the wealthy at each market correction. In other words, the rich get richer and the middle class and poor get poorer. The financial institutions and the wealthy elite stand to gain from every stage of the boom–bust cycle, at the expense of all other sectors in society.

This would be made painfully evident in Europe, where the 2008 booms-gone-bust took a particularly vicious turn, as in the immediate aftermath of the financial crash a number of countries across the continent (especially those in the EMU periphery) stepped in and injected huge amounts of public money into the financial system to keep their hyper-leveraged banks afloat, transferring liabilities from European banks to European taxpayers and sending government debt levels through the roof (since governments had to borrow the money on the financial markets). This would have far-reaching consequences, as we shall see: it exacerbated the core–periphery imbalances created by the neoliberal and hyper-financialised architecture of the EMU, transformed the financial crisis in a sovereign debt crisis and gave Europe's financial-political elites the perfect excuse to impose devastating austerity policies on the weaker countries of the union.

But banks don't just create debt, in the form of loans and mortgages. They also take on debt themselves to make investments and acquire additional assets. This is known as leverage, and it is the speciality of investment banks. Rules limiting the banks' leverage ratio differ from reserve requirements, and usually take the form of capital requirements and leverage caps (which set the minimum percentage of capital that a bank must hold relative to its investments, or assets). These rules were significantly relaxed in the years leading up to the financial crisis, allowing banks to buy huge quantities of mortgage-backed securities, inflating the housing bubble and creating 'countless towers of leverage and debt'.[51] Moreover, banks started increasingly to resort to the so-called 'shadow banking system' – consisting of financial institutions that look like banks, act like banks but importantly *are not regulated like banks* – to conduct many of their transaction in ways that didn't show up on their conventional balance sheet (hence the term 'off-balance-sheet transactions'). This allowed them to take on even more debt than the already very flexible rules in place allowed.

By lifting the restrictions on leverage and permitting the development of shadow banking, governments paved the way for the pathological growth of banks – some of which today have balance sheets that rival the budget of many states – and of the financial system as a whole. By 2007, Europe – unsurprisingly, considering that European regulators had always taken a more lax attitude to leverage than their US counterparts – was leading the way. Of the 20 largest financial groups in the world, only three were American, while 14 were European (with total assets exceeding those of the US banks).[52] Globally, in 2007, financial assets were worth 4.4 times more than the world's entire GDP.[53]

An important thing to understand about assets is that their value can quickly diminish in the aftermath of a crisis. When that happens, huge assets can turn into huge debts (which then get transferred to the rest of the economy). This is what happened in 2008, and is the reason why renowned Italian sociologist Luciano Gallino describes the modern financial system as 'the greatest generator of socio-economic insecurity the world has ever known'.[54] By mid-2006, the financial system, with its extraordinary reliance on leverage – and its blind faith that asset prices would continue to rise indefinitely – was primed for a breakdown of colossal proportions. The 'official' financial system – titanic in itself – was dwarfed by the derivatives market, which by the end of 2007 amounted to a staggering $670 trillion, about 14 times the size of the world's GDP, which in 2007 amounted to $47 trillion.[55] Derivatives – which we have already seen at play in the subprime crisis in the form of CDSs – can be used for speculation or for insurance (although in this context the latter can be a form of speculation in itself). The most common form of derivatives is foreign exchange transactions, which consist of the buying and selling of international currencies for a profit. In 2007 the volume of foreign exchange transactions was about $3.3 trillion per day. One day's exports or imports of all goods and services in the world amount to about 2 per cent of that figure – which means that 98 per cent of transactions on these markets are purely speculative.[56]

Unlike what most people think, many of these transactions are not made by slick-looking traders screaming 'Buy, sell!' into a phone. Roughly half of them are done using a tool called 'high-frequency trading', in which lightning-fast computers are pre-programmed to execute transactions in milliseconds and even microseconds (millionths of a second). The whole thing is largely beyond the control of human beings. As American economist David C. Korten observes:

> The most sinister aspect of modern capitalism is not its concentration of wealth in the hands of a tiny, greedy elite. It is about an institutional system of autonomous rule by money and for money that functions on autopilot beyond the control of any human actor and is unresponsive to any human sensibility.[57]

In simple terms, 'speculation' is the practice of engaging in risky financial transactions in an attempt to profit from short- or medium-term fluctuations in the market value of a tradable good such as a financial instrument, rather than attempting to profit from the underlying financial attributes embodied in the instrument, such as capital gains, interest or dividends. In other words, speculation can be understood as the practice of 'making money from money' (commonly known as gambling), rather than from investments in the real economy which benefit society as a whole. Banks speculate on pretty much anything: real estate, food, fine art, collectibles, company stocks and, more importantly insofar as this study is concerned, government bonds – as the euro crisis would make frighteningly clear. The financial system – whose original purpose was, quite simply, to allocate money to businesses and families and aid the growth of the economy – has thus forgone its basic function of money lending to concentrate on trading and speculation, becoming a leviathan which benefits only a tiny portion of society, at the expense of everyone else.

In light of this, some high-profile commentators are starting to question the very existence of the financial system – in its present form at least. Adair Turner of the UK Financial Policy Committee describes much of what happens on Wall Street and in other financial centres as 'socially useless activity'.[58] Paul Woolley of the London School of Economics depicts finance as 'a cancer that is growing to infinite size, until it takes over the entire body'.[59] George Soros simply describes the market-dominated times that we live in as 'evil'.[60]

How did we allow the markets to gain so much power over our lives? It hasn't always been this way, after all. Our current system, and the crisis it produced, are not the consequence of single, isolated actions – such as the lifting of the restrictions on leveraging or the development of the shadow banking system, although these were important catalysts. Rather, they should be viewed as the final stage of a 30-year-long (and ultimately successful) takeover of society and the economy by the financial markets, which was itself part of the wider rise of neoliberalism as the dominant economic paradigm.

After the Great Depression: The State Strikes Back Against Financial Markets

> *'Crises aren't a function of something as banal as the opening of new markets or shifts in investor psychology .... Capitalism* is *crisis'*—Nouriel Roubini and Stephen Mihm, *Crisis Economics*[61]

The financial crisis of 2008 was not unprecedented, or even unpredictable. The forces that gave rise to the various subprime crises and the subsequent Great Recession – not to mention the euro crisis – were eerily similar to the ones that led to the crash of 1929, and subsequent Great Depression. Then as now, radical free-market capitalism, minimal financial regulation, little-understood financial products and over-indebted households and banks all conspired to create a huge speculative bubble which, when it burst, brought the financial system crashing down – and with it, the entire global economy.

If 19th- and early 20th-century economics had a consensus, 'it was the idea that markets are fundamentally self-regulating, always moving toward some magical equilibrium'.[62] Faith in the fundamental stability of markets gave rise to an important corollary: if markets are fundamentally self-regulating, and their collective wisdom is always right, then the prices of assets bought and sold in the market (no matter how high) are accurate and justified. Moreover, if left to its own devices, the economy will inevitably generate stability and full employment. This idea harked back to Adam Smith, the father of modern economics, and to his theory of the 'invisible hand' of the market, which would miraculously guide the economy to equilibrium. This was known as *laissez-faire* ('let it be') capitalism.

By 1933, when Franklin D. Roosevelt was elected president, the crisis had wrought havoc and destruction across the United States. Roosevelt, unlike his predecessor Herbert Hoover – whose apathy and inaction had earned him the nickname of 'do-nothing president' – understood the need to act swiftly and decisively. More importantly, he understood the root cause of the Great Depression: out-of-control, unfettered capitalism, which called for radical reforms of the US financial system. In a legislative flurry known as 'the 100 days', Roosevelt forced through more radical reforms in three months that Hoover had done in four years, with some of the laws being proposed, discussed and voted on in a single day.[63] As the French economist Pierre Larrouturou writes, Roosevelt's 'aim was not to "reassure the markets", but to *rein them in*' (my italics).[64]

The laws and regulative agencies created by Roosevelt to 'rein in the markets' included the Glass–Steagall Act of 1933, which separated commercial and investment banking; the Securities Act of 1933, which regulated the securities market; and the setting-up of the Securities and Exchange Commission (SEC). Many of today's institutions and mechanisms, from the welfare state to financial regulation, are a direct consequence of the Great Depression in the 1930s, following which the state took on the role of 'macro-stabilisation' to curb the excesses of *laissez-faire* capitalism.[65] Bankers and investors, understandably, vigorously opposed these measures, threatening that they would lead to a financial catastrophe. As it turned out, these rules – and in particular the Glass–Steagall Act, which prevented commercial banks from speculating with depositors' money – gave the United States three decades of relative social and economic stability, from the 1940s until the 1970s, during which inequality fell sharply, median incomes grew rapidly, and the working and middle classes experienced a rise in their living standards. Bankers had no choice but to acquiesce. In the 1930s, following a regulatory crackdown, compensation in the financial sector plummeted.[66] The United States' answer to the crisis, in short, was 'more democracy'. Europe, as we know, took a very different road.

It is often forgotten that although the 1929 crash on Wall Street marked the beginning of the crisis, it was actually the sudden implosion of a European bank that triggered the Great Depression. In 1929 Credit-Anstalt, Austria's largest bank, became burdened with hundreds of millions of dollars of bad assets and had to be bailed out by a government that was itself on the brink of insolvency. In May 1931, following a run on its deposits, the bank went bust. Since many of Europe's most powerful and important banks had lent money to it, its failure triggered a European banking crisis. As the crisis worsened, Danatbank, at the time the second biggest bank in Germany, went bust some two months later. On 13 July it failed to open for business, triggering yet another wave of massive bank runs across Germany.

The fall of Credit-Anstalt – and the dominoes it helped topple across continental Europe – did not just represent the failure of a bank. It was in many ways 'a failure of civilization', as Peter Coy, economics editor for *Bloomberg Businessweek*, puts it.[67] Nearly all sovereign borrowers subsequently defaulted on all or part of their external debts, beginning with Germany. Unemployment in Europe reached an agonising peak in 1932: in July of that year, 49 per cent of German trade union members were out of work. The political consequences are well known, although they were conveniently forgotten over the course of the euro crisis. 'Anti-system' parties gained strength all across the continent, most notably in Germany. While 24 European regimes had been democratic in 1920, the number was down to 11 in 1939.[68] We all know what happened next.

Following the Second World War, Europe and many countries elsewhere in the world (Canada and Japan, for example) abandoned *laissez-faire* capitalism, which had helped set the stage for the war, in favour of strongly state-regulated economies, known also as mixed economies. A mixed economy is a system in which both the state and the private sector direct the economy. It can be described as a market economy with strong regulatory oversight, in which the government yields considerable influence through fiscal and monetary policies designed to counteract economic downturns and capitalism's tendency towards financial crises and unemployment, as well as through the promotion of social welfare.

In Europe governance mostly took the form of social democracy. Social democracy argues that all citizens should legally be entitled to certain social rights, such as education, health care, workers' compensation, and other services including child care and care for the elderly. Throughout the West, from the 1940s until the 1970s, real wages and economic conditions steadily improved.[69] Looking back, Adam Przeworski and Michael Wallerstein conclude that 'by most criteria of economic progress the [post-war] era was a success'.[70] Importantly, these measures did not just improve living conditions, they also boosted economic growth. Even more interestingly, Roubini argues that such progress was not achieved despite the existence of a strongly regulated welfare state, but precisely *because of it*:

> The rise of the middle class and the rising living standards of the working class were … not mechanical results of economic growth but the active outcome of many economic policies – such as universal publicly provided education financed by progressive taxation, to give just one example. These policies improved the skills, knowledge, and economic opportunities even of individuals born in disadvantaged circumstanced. Social mobility in any society was never the result of market forces but rather the outcome of progressive economic, fiscal, taxation, and other social policies.[71]

During that period, progress and stability was achieved not just within countries, but between countries as well. In 1944, economists and policy makers from the Allied nations met in Bretton Woods, New Hampshire, to lay the foundations of a new international economic order. Their deliberations gave rise to the IMF, as well as the forerunner of the World Bank, and to a new system of currency exchange rates known as the 'Bretton Woods system', or 'dollar exchange standard'. For about 25 years, during which the United States reigned supreme, the dollar exchange standard worked flawlessly, fuelling a period of unprecedented growth for the global economy and especially for those countries most hit by the war – Germany, Italy and Japan – which greatly benefited from the stability afforded by the system.

That same year, the International Labour Organization (ILO) – founded in 1919 upon the principle that 'universal and lasting peace can be established only if it is based upon social justice' – adopted the Declaration of Philadelphia, outlining rules on salary, working time and the fair and equitable sharing of salaries and dividends to be respected in each country and in global trade. Roosevelt praised it as a declaration as historically significant as the US Declaration of Independence.[72] As Roubini and Mihm write, this new system of global governance

> began a remarkable – and extraordinarily anomalous, given the previous centuries' crises – era of financial stability, a *pax moneta* that depended on the dollar and on the military and economic power of the newly ascendant United States.[73]

That stability, though, also rested on a strong financial regulatory framework: on the widespread provision of deposit insurance to stop bank runs; strict regulation of the financial system, including the separation of US commercial banking from investment banking; and extensive capital controls to reduce currency volatility. All these domestic and international restrictions kept financial excesses and bubbles under control for over a quarter of a century.

The Neoliberal Counter-Revolution

Sounds great, doesn't it? Unfortunately, all good things come to an end. In the 1970s, the world economy entered a 'structural crisis'. Its main aspects were diminished growth rates, growing unemployment, cumulative inflation and – most importantly, in terms of its political consequences – a dramatic decline in the profitability of capital, or business. There were a number of reasons, but two factors were crucial: overproduction (as a growing number of people in the West had satisfied their basic consumerist needs, more goods were being produced than people were willing to buy) and collective bargaining rights for workers, which ensured that profits were equally shared between employees and stockholders. Gérard Duménil and Dominique Lévy, directors of research at the Centre National de la Recherche Scientifique in Paris, write:

> It is easy to understand that, under such conditions, the income and wealth of ruling classes was strongly affected. Seen from this angle, this could be read as a dramatic decline in inequality. Neoliberalism can be interpreted as an attempt by the wealthiest fraction of the population to stem this comparative decline.[74]

Neoliberalism was a term coined in the 1930s to describe a market economy under the guidance and rules of a strong state, a model which came to be known as 'social market economy'. Throughout the 1970s and 1980s, though, the term came to signify something radically different, and not all that 'neo' – namely, old-school *laissez-faire* market fundamentalism. It was seized on by die-hard free-market economists who held fast to the idea that the 1929 crisis had not been caused by excessive deregulation, but by excessive regulation and government intervention. After the Great Depression and the Second World War, these economists had retreated to their academic departments of economics and finance (most famously, at the University of Chicago), from where they started to wage a fierce intellectual battle against the post-war dominant economic paradigm.

Neoliberalism aimed at proving, once again, that markets are utterly rational and efficient, and that if governments stop providing public services and regulating markets, the economy will correct itself. In effect, it breathed new life into the old fallacy of the self-regulating market. This was coupled with innovations in trade and technology, which started to erode the effectiveness of post-war financial regulation, leading to a rise of financial-sector power. There were also changes in public opinion, and an elite and corporate backlash against diminishing profits. Together, these factors slowly caused a shift in government policy towards an ever greater freedom of the market and a rolling-back of the state's role in the economy.

Shunned for decades, by the 1970s the 'efficient-market hypothesis' had once again become conventional wisdom. In 1979 Margaret Thatcher was elected prime minister of the United Kingdom. Just over a year later Ronald Reagan was elected president of the United States. Both the United Kingdom and the United States were now ruled by free-market fundamentalists.[75] This marked the beginning of what Gérard Duménil and Dominique Lévy call the 'neoliberal counter-revolution' – during which the lessons of the Great Depression (first and foremost, the need for strict regulation of the financial system to limit the excesses of unregulated *laissez-faire* markets and their effects on inequality) were all but forgotten, and the post-war regulatory framework was systematically phased out or eliminated.

Reagan and Thatcher paved the way to a new era of unfettered and unregulated market capitalism known as the Anglo-Saxon model – a new social order that first took hold in the countries of the centre, and then was gradually exported to the periphery, according to the diktats of the so-called 'Washington consensus'. This was the reform package prescribed to developing countries by Washington-based institutions such as the IMF and the World Bank, based upon privatisation of state enterprises, trade liberalisation and deregulation of the financial sector. The underlying ideology is well summed up by Reagan's now-famous phrase: 'Government is not the solution to our problem; government *is* the problem.'[76]

The 'Paris Consensus'

> *'The French did not merely acquiesce to ... the new reality of globalization .... Several French policymakers led the charge'*—Rawi E. Abdelal, professor of business administration at Harvard Business School[77]

Over the next 30 years, neoliberalism became the dominant ideology in university faculties, management schools, financial institutions, central banks, and all international bodies, from the World Bank to the IMF to the European Commission. One by one, all the firewalls and regulations created to prevent a Great Depression-style crisis were systematically dismantled. Europe was often at the forefront of these regressive changes. In fact, in the 1980s and 1990s, European governments often anticipated the United States in deregulating the financial system.

The first restrictions to go, in the 1980s, were the ones limiting movement of capital. Capital controls are mechanisms or instruments to limit the amount of capital that is flowing into and/or out of a country. These were an integral part of the post-war Bretton Woods system, and at the time were endorsed by most mainstream economists and international institutions (including the IMF), since unfettered cross-border capital flows were considered inherently volatile and destabilising.[78] As renowned economists Carmen Reinhart and Kenneth Rogoff explain, the relative calm that characterised the period between the late 1940s and early 1970s 'may be partly explained by booming world growth, but perhaps more so by the repression of the domestic financial markets (in varying degrees) and the heavy-handed use of capital controls that followed for many years after World War II'.[79]

Throughout the 1970s, though, as neoliberalism gained strength worldwide, the United States, other Western governments, and the international financial institutions (such as the IMF and the World Bank) began to take an increasingly critical view of capital controls. This was despite the fact that, as Reinhart and Rogoff note, they had contributed to all but eliminating financial crises of the kind that had rocked the world in the 1920s and 1930s. The idea was that capital account liberalisation would allow for more efficient global allocation of capital, from capital-rich industrial countries to capital-poor developing economies. Surprisingly, the decisive push towards a full freedom of movement for capital came from the most unlikely of places: the French left.

Throughout most of the 1980s, capital flows had remained tightly regulated in the European Community (a precursor to the European Union). When the Socialist Party won the French elections in 1981, it adhered to the common wisdom regarding capital flows: namely, that they were inherently destabilising and needed to be regulated. As a reaction to the Socialists' ambitious plan of economic reform and social redistribution, though, capital started to flee France. Despite the imposition of 'draconian capital controls', the government was unable to halt the flight.[80] Finally in 1983, following renewed speculative attacks against the franc, the Socialists reversed course, admitting their defeat in the battle (both practical and ideological) against capital, and in 1985 began a process of broad deregulation, which included the liberalisation of virtually all capital transactions.[81]

That same year Jacques Delors, who had served as economics and finance minister under French President Mitterrand, became president of the European Commission. In that position he proceeded to export France's new views on capital movements to the rest of Europe. From the mid-1980s to mid-1990s, he succeeded in radically changing Europe's approach to capital controls. EU member countries were persuaded to introduce full capital mobility by 1990, effectively making the free movement of capital a central tenet of the emerging European single market. This was a binding obligation not only among EU members but also between EU members and third countries. Delors also got Europe to fully embrace the neoliberal counter-revolution, or what some call the 'Paris consensus', the European equivalent of the Washington consensus. The consequence of this was a European financial system 'that was in principle the most liberal the world had ever known', according to Rawi E. Abdelal, professor of business administration at Harvard Business School.[82] The global implications of this counter-revolution are well explained by Abdelal: 'This new definition of the European [was] itself the engine of free capital's spread on the world stage .... Global financial markets are *global* primarily because the processes of European financial integration became open and uniformly liberal.'[83]

These trends were to profoundly influence the construction of the monetary union in the coming years. In France's defence, it is probably fair to say that it was up against a formidable enemy. That the Socialists were all but forced by market pressure to abandon their programme of progressive economic reforms is a telling demonstration of the extent to which the growth of private financial institutions had seriously curtailed the ability of national governments to exercise democratic control over economic policy.

Among the numerous promoters of the Paris consensus, two more are worth mentioning: Michel Camdessus, the über-liberal governor of the Bank of France (1984–7) who subsequently became head of the IMF (1987–2000), and Henri Chavranski, who chaired the Organisation for Economic Co-operation and Development's (OECD's) Committee on Capital Movement and Invisible Transactions from 1982 to 1994. Europe's decision to lift all restrictions on capital movements is seen by many as one of the root causes of the cancerous growth of the financial system in subsequent years, which paved the way for the 2008 financial crisis. As Jacques de Larosière, managing director of the IMF for nearly a decade between 1978 and 1987 and then governor of the Bank of France until 1993, says: 'Without the right institutions and the right surveillance procedures in place, capital movements could create havoc. And they have.'[84]

From the 1980s onwards, as capital restrictions were gradually lifted, financial crises started to re-explode with increased frequency. Unregulated capital flows played a crucial role in most of them, especially in the euro crisis. According to the IMF, between 1970 and 2007 there were 124 banking crises, 208 monetary crashes and 63 sovereign debt crises – a staggering total of 395 systemic crises, an average of more than 10 per year.[85] As Stephany Griffith-Jones, José Antonio Ocampo and Joseph E. Stiglitz write, '[f]inancial crises are not new, and the growing financial market liberalisation since the 1970s has led to a good number of them'.[86] As the great 20th-century economist John Maynard Keynes more eloquently put it, '[w]hen the capital development of a country becomes a by-product of the activities of a casino, the job is likely to be ill-done.'[87]

The Deregulation Years: From the 1980s to the 2000s

> *'I think the deregulation [of Wall Street] was probably helpful to the growth of our economy'*—John McCain, US senator, 2008[88]

If the 1980s was the decade of capital flow deregulation, the 1990s and the first half of the 2000s were the decades of banking deregulation, during which all the vestiges of the Great Depression-era legislation were systematically eradicated. This process mostly concerned the United States; European countries – which were busy plotting their mutual destruction while Roosevelt was regulating finance on the other side of the Atlantic, in the mid-1930s – had a rather weak regulatory framework to begin with. Although deregulation had slowly been under way in the United States since the 1980s, by far the most crucial deregulatory act was the Clinton administration's Gramm–Leach–Bliley Act (GLBA) of 1999, also known as the Financial Services Modernization Act. This repealed the Glass–Steagall Act of 1933, which separated commercial and investment banking, and is widely credited with giving the United States 50 crisis-free years of financial stability. With the passage of the Financial Services Modernization Act, commercial banks, investment banks, securities firms and insurance companies were once again allowed to consolidate.

Today, many consider the repeal an important cause of the late-2000s financial crisis. By allowing financial institutions to consolidate and to take on ever-bigger risks and debts (through securities and other financial products), the GLBA paved the way to the rise of the so-called too-big-to-fail banks, and to the kinds of structural conflicts of interest that were endemic in the 1920s. As Harvard Law School professor Elizabeth Warren notes, the whole purpose of Glass–Steagall was to prevent banks from doing 'crazy things'.[89] Interestingly, although the US banking sector had been seeking a repeal of the Glass–Steagall Act since the 1980s, some commentators argue that the decisive push came from Europe. The European banking model had always been that of the so-called 'universal bank': one that participates in many kinds of banking activities and is both a commercial and an investment bank (precisely what Glass–Steagall prohibited). This meant that the major European banks had over the years become significantly larger and more concentrated than their US counterparts. They had bought up many smaller banks across the continent, giving rise to the European megabanks.

By the 1990s, these now-internationalised universal megabanks had turned their attention to their smaller American counterparts. In those years Credit Suisse acquired First Boston, SBC acquired Dillon Read, and Deutsche Bank acquired Banker Trust.[90] The US banks blamed Glass–Steagall for preventing them from competing fairly with their European counterparts – and technically they were right. The European banks, in short, provided them with the ideal excuse to demand, and obtain, a repeal of Glass–Steagall. GLBA was followed in 2004 by the lifting of the leverage cap on US investment banks, and away went the last remaining bricks of the post-Great Depression wall erected to keep banks fenced in. Now they were once again free to go 'crazy', as governments and regulators – reassured by their blind faith in the market – looked the other way.

As the report of the commission of investigation into the Irish banking crisis states, '[f]or several years before the banking crisis, the authorities operated under the assumption that financial markets generally were efficient and self-regulating; this was generally considered as the modern and reasonable approach both in Ireland and abroad.'[91] To make things worse, as well as scrapping the existing laws and regulations, governments allowed the financial services industry to create a whole array of new esoteric products (such as securities and derivatives) which led the banks to reap enormous profits and gain unprecedented power at the expense of the rest of society. In 1980, financial assets were more or less equal to the world's GDP; by 2007 they had grown to be around 4.4 times larger.[92] In ten years the value of the derivatives market jumped from $92 trillion to $670 trillion in 2007, about 14 times the size of the world's GDP.[93] Most tellingly perhaps, between 1980 and 2007 the world's GDP grew at an average rate of 3 per cent, while the value of financial assets grew at more than 8 per cent – a gap which can only be explained in one way, as Italian sociologist Luciano Gallino observes: '[M]oney creates itself instead of creating use value.'[94]

Thirty years of neoliberalism and deregulation, though, did not just make the financial sector richer and more powerful – and more dangerous – than ever before. They also made (almost) everyone else relatively poorer.

Divided We Stand: The Rise of Inequality in the West, and its Role in the Financial Crisis

> *'We may have democracy, or we may have wealth concentrated in the hands of a few, but we can't have both'*—Louis D. Brandeis, associate justice of the US Supreme Court (1916–39)[95]

The deregulation and subsequent growth of the financial sector was just one of the consequences of the neoliberal takeover of the world. In reality, neoliberalism deeply transformed the functioning of capitalism and society, at every level. One of its most perverse effects has been a staggering increase in the rates of social and economic inequality. Although this process hugely benefited private capital at the expense of the public domain, it would not have been possible without the active contribution of politicians and governments worldwide. Mario Pianta, professor of economic policy at the University of Urbino, writes:

> The official story is that politics took a 'step back', confiding in the efficiency and transparency of the markets and financial system, and in their ability to generate the best results when unhindered by the complications of democracy. The truth is that politics actively worked to accrue the power of the markets and the financial sector, at the expense of everyone else – small manufacturers, workers, citizens.[96]

Governments resorted to a wide array of tools to attain this: the liberalisation of all goods and capital markets; the privatisation of resources and social services; the deregulation of business, and financial markets in particular; the reduction of workers' rights (first and foremost, the right to collective bargaining); the lowering of taxes on wealth and capital, at the expense of the middle and working classes; the slashing of social programmes, and so on. These policies were systemically pursued throughout the West with unprecedented determination, and with the support of all the major international institutions and political parties.[97]

Luciano Gallino comments that 'politics relinquished its historical mission of governing and civilising the economy and human relations ... instead of regulating the economy to adapt it to society's needs, politics laboured to adapt society to the needs of the economy'.[98] As mentioned already, the profitability of business had plunged in the 1960s and 1970s, mainly because of overproduction and workers' struggles for better salaries. Beginning in the 1970s, though, the bargaining power of workers started to decline dramatically as a result of the process that we now call globalisation. As new and cheaper labour markets started to open up across the developing world, transnational corporations were able to 'delocalise' jobs to countries with lower labour costs. Also, as cheaper goods from those countries started to flood Western markets, Western companies found themselves under growing pressure to drive down prices to remain competitive. Under the threat of delocalisation, workers in the West were forced to accept a dramatic decline in rights and salaries which continues to this day. This – coupled with an aggressive attack on organised labour, the deregulation of business and the privatisation of state-owned enterprises – caused a huge shift in power from employees to employers, or from workers to capital.

Another response to the declining profitability of business was the financialisation of corporations, itself part of the wider financialisation of the entire economy. Financialisation can be described as a 'pattern of accumulation in which profit-making occurs increasingly through financial channels rather than through trade and commodity production'.[99] The financialisation of companies is linked with the ascendancy of the modern corporation's so-called 'shareholder value model'. In the 1980s, with the growth of capital markets allowed by the deregulation of capital flows, and the rise of powerful institutional investors such as pension funds, corporations become increasingly dependent on the stock market – and ultimately on shareholders – for finance. 'Shareholder value' thus became the guiding principle of corporate governance and corporate strategy, meaning that the primary goal for a company became to increase the wealth of its shareholders, at the expense of everyone and everything else – employees, consumers, the environment, society. Investors expect ridiculously high levels of return on equity (ROE) from corporations, as much as 15 or even 25 per cent, and corporations have no choice but to comply. After all, unsatisfied investors can go elsewhere in no time. This system does not simply exert a powerful downward pressure on wages, salaries and workers' rights (leading to an increase in unemployment and inequality), as businesses increasingly find themselves at the mercy of the whims of investors. It also hampers growth, first by reducing the purchasing power of workers, and second by favouring the short-terms profits offered by financial investments rather than the long-term ones offered by investments designed to enhance productivity and employment.

At the same time, as a result of the growing mechanisation of work, workers were becoming more and more productive. From the 1980s onwards, productivity has continued to increase steadily, while low- and medium-level wages have plummeted. This has effectively shifted an increasing proportion of surplus value from labour (and in particular from low-wage workers) towards capital (and top earners).[100] This shift was particularly extreme in the United States, where chief executive officer (CEO) salaries increased by an average of 400 per cent during the 1990s, while workers' wages increased by less than 5 per cent, and the federal minimum wage actually *decreased* by more than 9 per cent.[101]

This was not just an American phenomenon. During the past three decades, the share of national income represented by wages, salaries and benefits – the labour share – has been declining, and that of capital increasing, in nearly all OECD countries. Between the early 1990s and late 2000s, the median labour share in advanced countries dropped from 66 to 61.5 per cent of GDP.[102] After having peaked in the late 1970s and early 1980s (at around 70 per cent of GDP), the labour income share started to decline in most EU member states – despite the fact that labour productivity was skyrocketing – and now the continent-wide average stands at a meagre 58 per cent of GDP, very close to its pre-crisis historical low (see Figure 1.1).[103]

As the French economist Pierre Larrouturou writes: '[W]e are experiencing a revolution without precedent in human history. It took 140 years, from 1820 to 1960, for productivity to double; since then it's grown *five-fold*. Wages, on the other hand, have been stagnant for decades.'[104] In other words, workers have become more productive, but also more exploited. As mentioned, though, not

Figure 1.1 The widening wages–productivity gap in the European Union from 1970 onwards

* EU-15 data (indexed, 1970=100).

Sources:
Labour productivity data: European Environment Agency.
Wage share data: AMECO (own calculations; 1970–94 data refers to EU-15).

all workers have fared the same: the compensation of top earners has increased dramatically (with the wage income share of the top 1 per cent, in both private companies and government-controlled enterprises, increasing by an average of 20 per cent between the mid-1970s and mid-2000s).[105]

The shrinking of the wage share was only one of the effects of the neoliberal transformation of society and financialisation of the economy. Central to the neoliberal ideology was the belief in supply-side, or trickle-down, economics, which can be summed up as the idea that economic growth can be created most effectively by improving productivity through the lowering of high-income taxes, capital gains taxes and corporate taxes, the deregulation of business and the lowering of trade barriers. This in turn will benefit society as a whole, since the increased gains of the wealthy will then 'trickle down' to the poorer members of society. (That didn't happen, as we shall see.) The famed 20th-century economist John Kenneth Galbraith jokingly called it the horse-and-sparrow theory: that '[i]f you feed the horse enough oats, some will pass through to the road for the sparrows'.[106] These ideas were first put into practice by Reagan, who led the way by slashing the top marginal tax rate from 70 to 28 per cent, and reducing the maximum capital gains tax to 20 per cent, the lowest rate since the Great Depression – while *raising* payroll taxes on the working class.[107] Similar policies were pursued by Thatcher in the United Kingdom, where capital–income tax rates fell by more than half from the 1950s to the 1980s.[108] The same happened in all major OECD countries, where rates of high-income tax fell from 60–70 per cent in the 1980s to around 40 per cent on average by the late 2000s (see Figure 1.2).[109]

At the same time, the deregulation of capital flows also allowed the wealthy to hide their income and wealth in tax havens, to some extent forcing governments to increase fiscal pressure on the working classes and increasingly resort to public debt for their financing needs. For the past 30 years corporate taxes have been declining throughout the West as well. Today the European average is an all-time low of 23 per cent, almost half the US average of 40 per cent, mainly because of the lack of common fiscal policy, which means that member countries compete with each other in a bid to attract capital (Figure 1.3).

These policies have driven up social inequality in all high-income countries at an unprecedented rate. Even though in most advanced countries GDP grew by 60–70 per cent between the early 1990s and the second decade of the 2000s, three-quarters of that growth went to 5 per cent or less of the population.[110] As confirmed by various OECD studies, the latest trends show a widening gap between rich and poor not only in some of the already high-inequality countries like the United States and Italy, but also – for the first time – in traditionally low-inequality countries such as Germany, Denmark, Sweden, Norway and Finland, where inequality grew more than anywhere else in the 2000s.[111] Poverty levels have also been rising steadily in all advanced countries since the mid-1980s.[112]

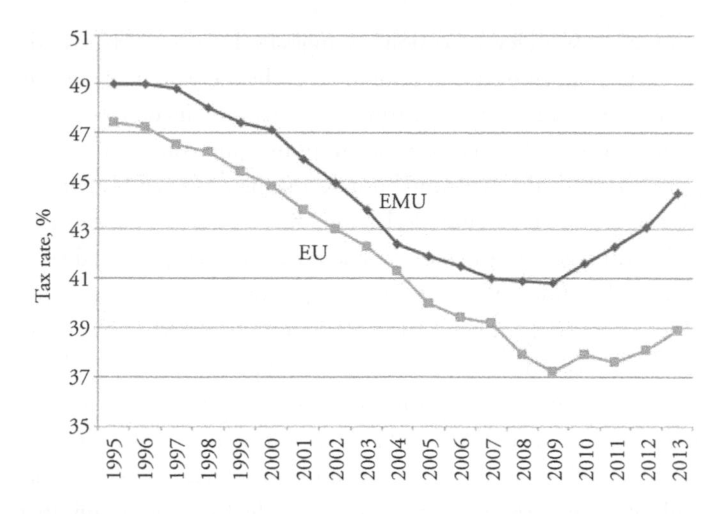

Figure 1.2 Top income tax rates in the European Union and European Monetary Union, 1995–2013

Source: Eurostat.

The OECD attributes this rise in poverty and inequality largely to 'changes in the distribution of wages and salaries', as well as the tax cuts introduced in the 1980s, which caused the wage share of those at the top to grow at the expense of those at the bottom.[113] In all countries, the share of national income going to the highest earners has increased between 1980 and 2010.[114] Today, the average income of the richest 10 per cent of the population in OECD countries is about nine times that of

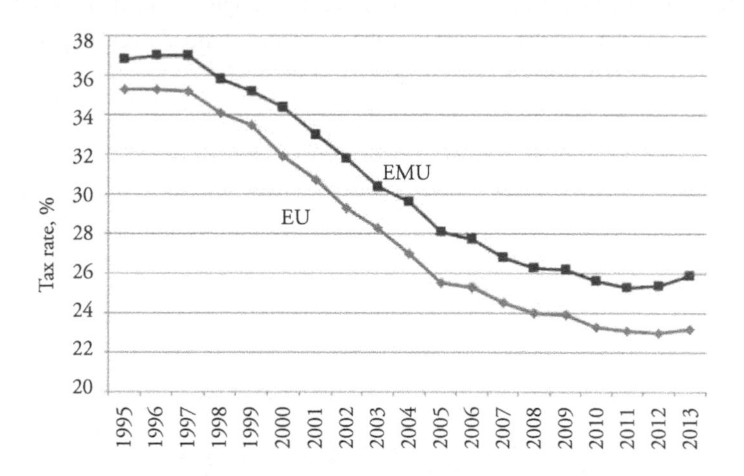

Figure 1.3 Top corporate tax rates in the European Union and European Monetary Union, 1995–2013

Source: Eurostat.

the poorest 10 per cent.[115] With few exceptions, changes in the income share of the richest 1 per cent of the population account for most of the increase in the income share of the top decile (one-tenth) of the distribution – with the income of the top 1 per cent showing increases of 70 per cent or more in some countries (such as Ireland) (see Figure 1.4).[116] As the American business magnate Warren Buffett, one of the world's wealthiest people, recently declared: 'There's class warfare, all right, but it's my class, the rich class, that's making war, *and we're winning*' (my italics).[117]

So much for the trickle-down effect. As Cambridge economist Ha-Joon Chang puts it, 'making rich people richer doesn't make the rest of us richer'.[118] Neoliberal policies have instead succeeded in concentrating obscene amounts of wealth in the hands of a very small minority, creating huge global imbalances. In 2007 the official number of 'high net worth' individuals (with wealth of at least $1 million) climbed to 10 million for the first time in history. These individuals had a combined wealth of around $41 trillion – and, as we shall see further on, their share has kept growing ever since.[119] That means that on the eve of the financial crisis, 1/600 (0.15 per cent) of the world population possessed one-sixth (almost 17 per cent) of all wealth.

This process was particularly marked in Europe, where the ratio of private wealth to national income jumped from two-and-a-half times in 1950 to more than five times by the early 2000s – an even higher ratio than in the United States.[120] The Tax Justice Network (TJN), a British non-profit organisation, believes that the situation is even worse than official statistics show, because of the unrecorded assets hoarded in tax havens around the world. According to their estimates, the bottom half of the world's population possesses barely 1 per cent of global wealth, while the top 10 per cent own 84 per cent. Even more shockingly, fewer than 100,000 people – 0.001 per cent of the world's population – now control over 30 per cent

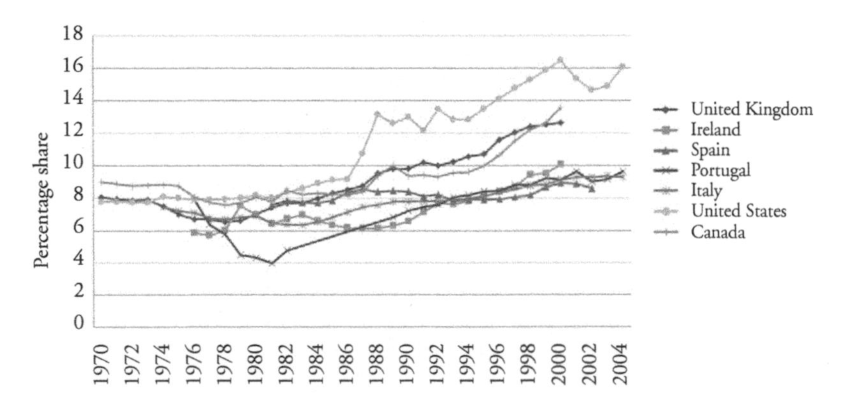

Figure 1.4 Share of pre-tax income of the richest 1 per cent of the population in selected OECD countries, 1970–early 2000s

Sources: OECD and Top World Incomes Database.

of the world's financial wealth.[121] As John Christensen of the TJN comments: 'These estimates reveal a staggering failure. Inequality is much, much worse than official statistics show, but politicians are still relying on trickle-down to transfer wealth to poorer people.'[122]

Italian sociologist Luciano Gallino describes the shift that has occurred over the course of the past 30 years as 'the largest transfer of income and wealth from the lower to the higher strata of society – also known as exploitation – in history':

> The neoliberal mythology has succeeded in lending an appearance of rational inevitability to what was in effect a counter-revolution ... aimed at re-establishing the power and wealth of the dominant classes in the wake of ... the social conquests of the working classes in the thirty years following the Second World War.[123]

The OECD agrees with Gallino on this point. These changes were not inevitable, a recent report states, but were the outcome of 'policy choices, regulations, and institutions' – such as the decision to slash top income and corporate tax rates – which have the power to 'shape how globalisation and technological changes affect the distribution of income'.[124]

The reason that even traditionally neoliberal-minded institutions such as the IMF and the OECD have begun to speak out against some of the most pernicious consequences of neoliberalism is that the growing disparities in wealth and income have evolved to the point where it is no longer a simple matter of equality. A number of studies (including reports by the OECD and the IMF) show that more unequal societies tend to experience higher political instability and a wide range of negative health and social outcomes.[125] More surprisingly perhaps, a 2011 UNICEF study found that for 141 countries where inequality could be measured, those with rising inequality tended to grow more slowly over the period studied (1990–2008).[126] Also the IMF and the OECD have begun to acknowledge this.[127]

In short, supply-side economics does not even stimulate growth, which is its sole justification. In fact quite the opposite is true: since the onset of neoliberalism, the industrialised world has seen average per capita growth rates fall from 3.2 to 2.1 per cent.[128] If there was a period of extraordinary growth, it was the strongly regulated one that followed the Second World War, during which living standards more or less doubled. As Jason Hickel, professor of anthropology at the London School of Economics, writes, 'neoliberalism has completely failed as a tool for economic development, but it has worked brilliantly as a tool for restoring power to the wealthy elite.'[129]

There is also growing evidence that inequality was a crucial factor behind the global economic and financial crisis since 2007/8 and the subsequent euro crisis. In a very basic sense, extreme concentration of wealth in the hands of a tiny minority leads the wealthiest members of society to wield disproportionate influence and power, and skew the priorities of society as a whole, by feeding a demand for financial products at the expense of investments in goods and services, for example. In this sense, it is worth remembering that someone's debt (or everyone's debt, in the case of public debt) always corresponds to someone else's credit. But there is an even more direct causal link between inequality and the recent financial crisis, many commentators argue. As we have seen, from the 1980s to mid-2000s the economy of advanced countries continued to grow but the share of national income going to salaries registered a steep decline. As well as leading to an increase in inequality, this also posed a risk for the wider economy and the profitability of capital, because it caused the purchasing power of labour to decline. Profits, after all, can only be made if there is a sufficient demand for goods and services.

The response, as Nouriel Roubini writes, was a 'democratization of credit'. Basically, households borrowed more and more to make up the difference between spending and income, leading to a colossal rise in private debt, particularly in the United States, but also in the United Kingdom, Ireland and some continental European countries like the Netherlands, Denmark, Spain and Greece, and in Eastern Europe. This helped fuel the asset and credit bubbles that exploded in 2008.[130] In other words, for years the economy continued to grow primarily because banks were distributing the purchasing power – through debt – that businesses were not providing in salaries.'[F]inancial innovations seemed to have offered a short-term solution to the crisis of neoliberalism in the 1990s: debt-led consumption growth', writes Özlem Onaran, professor of workforce and economic development policy at the University of Greenwich.[131] In a way, we could say that finance lent back to workers and citizens, with due interest, the money it had extracted from salaries and investments throughout the years. When the amount of money subtracted reached unsustainable levels and income levels became too polarised, the mountain of debt came crashing to the ground.

In short, while this crisis was precipitated by the collapse of the housing bubble in the United States and propagated by reckless financial speculation, the underlying causes lie in the fundamental economic imbalances that have resulted from three decades of neoliberal economic policies. In this sense, unemployment is not just a consequence of the crisis but is actually one of its main causes. This was recently acknowledged also by none other than Andrew Haldane, executive director for financial stability at the Bank of England. He said that the Occupy movement is right to focus on inequality as the chief reason for the 2008 crash, following studies that showed that the accumulation of huge wealth funded by debt was directly responsible for the domino-like collapse of the banking sector in 2008: '[T]he hard-headed facts suggest that, at the heart of the global financial crisis, were – and are – problems of deep and rising inequality.'[132]

This is not the first time in history that extreme inequality has generated a societal collapse. It is not a coincidence that the last time the United States witnessed such extreme concentrations of wealth, high rates of inequality and private debt levels was – 1928. Data show that the percentage of income going to, and wealth held by, the richest US citizens – as well as the gap between the top 1 per cent and bottom 90 per cent – peaked in 1928 and 2007, *right before each crash* (Figure 1.5).[133]

It looks as if this is another crucial lesson from the Great Depression that was lost sight of – or was wilfully suppressed – during the neoliberal frenzy of the past 30 years. Robert Reich, professor of public policy at the University of California at Berkeley and former secretary of labor under the Clinton administration, draws some striking parallels between the period leading up to the Great Depression and that leading up to the 2008 crash. In both periods, the share of national income going to wages reached rock-bottom levels, leading to a colossal increase in private debt. At the same time, the wealthy accumulated more and more wealth, fuelling speculative investments and creating huge stock and real-estate bubbles – which, as they always do, eventually burst.[134]

In other words, the facts seem to indicate that, beyond a certain threshold, excessive inequality and concentration of wealth necessarily throw societies into a systemic crisis. Roosevelt probably understood this. As soon as he was elected president he raised the top marginal tax rate from 25 to 63 per cent, and then to 79 per cent.[135] Top marginal income tax rates in the United States and the United Kingdom remained above 70 per cent until the 1980s.[136] Almost everyone, regardless of their political leaning, would balk at the idea of a 70 per cent tax rate for the rich today, in the United States as well as in Europe. This is a good example of the extent to which neoliberalism has profoundly colonised our worldview.

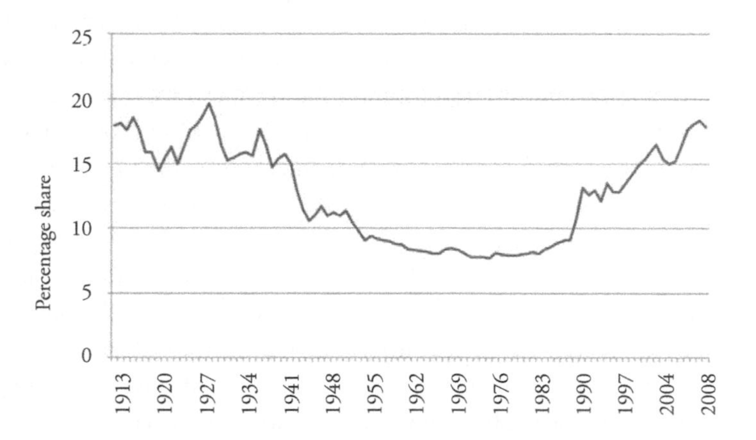

Figure 1.5 Share of pre-tax income of the richest 1 per cent of individuals in the United States, 1913–2008

Source: Top World Incomes Database.

The Aftermath of the Crisis: New Deal or 'Business as Usual'?

Following this theoretical and historical digression, which was necessary to gain a deeper understanding of the unfolding drama, we can now get back to the main focus of this study. As we saw, by the beginning of 2009 the financial crisis had caused widespread damage, triggering a global recession and destroying jobs and livelihoods worldwide. The United States and Europe, the epicentres of the crisis, were the worst hit. The Irish and Icelandic banking systems had all but failed; the Spanish one was on the brink of failure; all the major financial institutions on both sides of the Atlantic, in the wake of the bursting of the US (and to a lesser extent, European) subprime bubble, had suddenly registered huge losses on their balance sheets, rendering many of them effectively insolvent. To avoid a meltdown of the global economy, in 2008 alone trillions of euros/dollars of European and US taxpayers' money were injected into the European financial system to save those banks deemed 'too big to fail'.

What caused the crisis? Although it was indeed precipitated by the collapse of the housing bubble in the United States, the underlying causes, as we have seen, lie in the fundamental economic imbalances that have resulted from three decades of neoliberal economic policies, and in particular, in the deregulation and liberalisation of the entire financial system. The analyses proposed from various quarters, in the immediate aftermath of the crisis were diverse, contradictory and generally lacking the depth and scope of the ones that would be elaborated in the coming years. But everyone (bar a few free-market fundamentalists) agreed on one simple point: the crisis had been caused by the banks, and the severity of the situation called for a radical reform of the financial sector.

Although a number of commentators had been warning for years about the dangers of a coming crash and about the need to take regulatory action before it was too late – Nouriel Roubini was probably the most vocal – their voices were regularly drowned out by the cacophony of neoliberal cheerleading. These reformist commentators – whose ranks experienced a sudden surge in the months following the crash – saw the crisis as an opportunity to fix the financial system once again. In early 2009, with the global financial system on the verge of collapse, a G20 summit was called for April. Many hoped that this would be the occasion to introduce major reforms of the financial sector, which in its recklessness had almost led to a meltdown of the global economy. By April 2009, though, the momentum for radical change had passed, as policy makers argued that the post-crisis measures (such as the huge bail-outs of failing banks) had been effective in averting a catastrophic scenario. The implication was that the worst was over.

Some mild reforms of the financial industry – including a watered-down version of the Glass–Steagall Act – were introduced in the United States in the form of the Dodd–Frank Wall Street Reform and Consumer Protection Act, proposed by the Obama administration in June 2009 (and signed into law on July 2010). The changes proposed in the European Union were even weaker, consisting essentially of appeals for greater self-regulation by the industry, with minimal government intervention.[137] Despite the European politicians' reluctance to implement any serious New Deal-style reform of the financial system and the over-optimistic 'worst is over' attitude of all major continental and global institutions, throughout 2009 EU governments kept throwing money at the banks – with no strings attached.

By mid-2009, the European Commission reported that European governments had committed a total of €3 trillion in 'guarantee umbrellas, risk shields and recapitalisation measures' to bail out banks.[138] Although governments were forking out billions of euros of taxpayers' money to drag the banks out of the ditch they had dug by gambling in the global financial casino, they did not feel obligated to enforce any significant change in the way banks conducted their business. Instead, they kept relying on the same failed paradigm that had produced the crisis in the first place: self-regulation. As the EU competition commissioner Neelie Kroes commented regarding the bail-outs, '[t]he responsibility now lies with the financial sector to clean up their balance sheets and restructure to ensure a viable future.'[139] In short, despite ample demonstration of the financial system's inability to self-regulate itself, governments were once again relying on the banks to put themselves back on the right path.

In reality, the bail-outs would end up having the exact opposite effect. As Mervyn King commented, '[t]he massive support extended to the banking sector around the world, while necessary to avert economic disaster, has created possibly *the biggest moral hazard in history*' (my italics) – a fact that the euro crisis would make very clear, with the bailed-out banks turning against those very governments that had rescued them.[140]

Despite the governments' attempts at playing down the crisis and the need for reform, the heat on the banks remained high throughout 2009. The effects of the global recession were starting to be felt, and there was no doubt among citizens and workers where the blame laid. On May Day, banks were the target of (often violent) protests all around the world – from Istanbul to Athens, from Paris to Rome, from Madrid to Hong Kong. With neoliberal policies and the financial system widely discredited, it was becoming increasingly difficult for governments in Europe (and elsewhere) to ignore the calls for change coming from social and workers' movements across the continent.

Then something happened that changed everything.

CHAPTER TWO

The Coup

'If history shows anything, it is that there's no better way to justify relations founded on violence, to make such relations seem moral, than by reframing them in the language of debt – above all, because it immediately makes it seem that it's the victim who's doing something wrong.'—David Graeber, *Debt: The First 5,000 Years*

Greece: The First Bail-Out

In October 2009 the newly elected Greek government of George Papandreou revealed a black hole in the national accounts. It declared that the budget deficit was double the previous government's estimate and would hit 12.7 per cent of GDP.

The deficit, in simple terms, is the excess that a government spends every year over the revenues that it generates, mainly through taxes. It also takes account of interest payments on the national debt. The Maastricht Treaty, which sets the economic criteria for eurozone states, allows for a maximum annual deficit-to-GDP ratio of 3 per cent. At the time of Greece's announcement, official data from Eurostat, the European Union's statistical agency, gave the average deficit of the EMU as 2 per cent (although as we shall see, the real number was much higher). Greece had already been estimated to have the highest deficit in the EMU, but this announcement put the country in a league of its own. (The second-worst country that year, Ireland, had a deficit of 7 per cent.)

Two months later, in December, the Greek government made an even more startling announcement: the country's debt stood at €300 billion, the highest level in its modern history. Governments, like households, finance their budget deficits through borrowing, so the national debt reflects (again, in simple terms) the accumulation of yearly deficits. Maastricht sets the maximum ratio of government debt to GDP at 60 per cent; Greece's debt amounted to 113 per cent of GDP, so by this criterion too the country was seriously out of line with its EU obligations. The government's announcement put Greece at the top of this unenviable chart as well (with Italy in second place), but in the debt department the country was in good company: in 2009 as many as nine member states exceeded the 60 per cent limit.

Greece's public debt had been stable at roughly 100 per cent of GDP in the 1990s, but it started to rise markedly following the adoption of the euro in 2000 (see Figure 2.1). Later we shall explore the complexities of this situation, but in broad terms this happened because Greece had been on a massive spending spree,

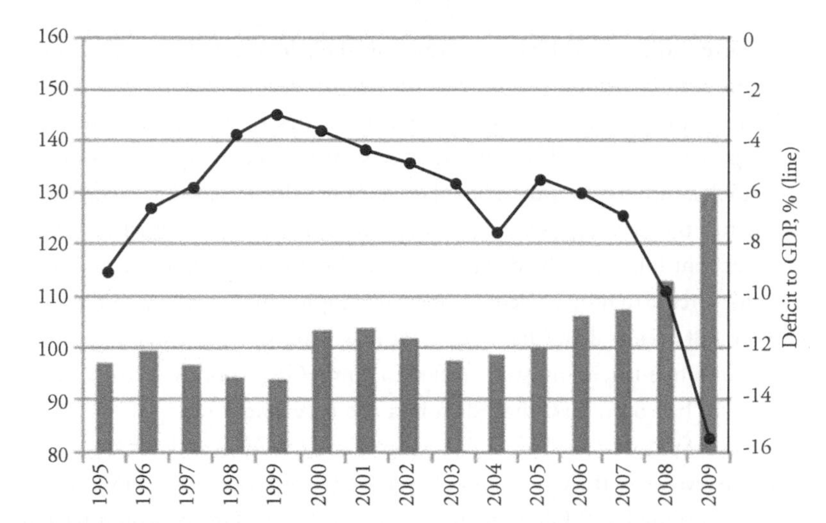

Figure 2.1 Greece's deficit-to-GDP and debt-to-GDP ratios, 1995–2009

Sources: ECB and Eurostat.

fuelled by cheap loans from international banks, while concealing the true extent of its debt from its European partners.

Anger over Greece's book-cooking, and fear that new surprises might lurk behind its leaders' statements, led most of its European partners to react unsympathetically. The country came under intense pressure from international banks and the European Union to improve its public finances and comply with EU deficit limits. As a result the government announced a draconian austerity programme, intended to reduce the public debt and bring the budget deficit below the EMU 3 per cent requirement by the end of 2013. Unimpressed by these budget-slashing efforts, the three main US credit-rating agencies – Standard & Poor's, Moody's and Fitch – all in rapid succession downgraded Greece's rating – which supposedly assesses a country's ability to pay back its debt – to the lowest level in the eurozone. This was the first time in ten years that a leading rating agency had given Greece a credit rating below A.

As fear mounted over Greece's deteriorating public finances and its ability to repay its debt, investors started to dump Greek stocks and bonds, further worsening the country's position. As borrowing costs for Greece began to climb, a term that had till then featured rarely in the mass media came to prominence across Europe. The *spread* is the difference between the interest rates that countries (or businesses, or individuals) have to pay. Those whose credit risk (that is, the risk of their defaulting on loans) is considered high normally have to borrow at higher rates of interest than those with a perceived low credit risk. Germany usually acts as the European benchmark: it typically pays less than the rest of the EMU countries for its borrowing. In short, as investing in Greece came to be seen as riskier, investors started to demand higher interests on their loans, widening the spread between European countries.

At the beginning of 2010 Greece unveiled a series of drastic new austerity measures, sparking strikes and riots in the streets. At the end of April the country's debt crisis took a turn for the worse: Standard & Poor's downgraded its credit rating to 'junk' status, the lowest possible grade. Bond yields started to skyrocket – rising above 11 per cent following the downgrade – to the point where it was no longer an option for Greece to fund its debt from private capital markets. The country lost the ability to roll over its debt (that is, to agree new loans to replace maturing ones) and it went into free-fall, as investors rushed to dump Greek bonds. In the space of months Greece had been downgraded from a top investment rating to junk. The prospect of a default started to seem dangerously real. A few days later, on 2 May, in a complete reversal of their previous policy, the EU countries and the IMF agreed on a record-breaking €110 billion loan package. In return Greece would have to submit to an 'economic adjustment programme' (also known as a memorandum of understanding, or MoU) involving more major austerity cuts.

That day also marked the appearance on the European stage of a tripartite committee – with representatives of the European Commission, the European Central Bank (ECB) and the IMF – charged with 'overseeing' the implementation of the austerity programme. This 'troika' was soon to be infamous. The Greek government submitted an unprecedentedly tough bill – a Deutsche Bank analyst described it as 'Herculean' in scope – to parliament on 4 May.[1] It was met with a nationwide general strike and massive protests the following day, in which three people were killed (when a bank was firebombed) and dozens injured. On 6 May, amid widespread social unrest, the austerity package was approved.

Many commentators have subsequently argued that the Greek 'rescue' – as the EU-IMF loan was widely but ill-advisedly viewed at the time, and is still viewed by many to this day – came too late. The much-feared 'contagion' was already under way.

Enter the PIIGS

In the weeks leading up to the Greek bail-out, amid growing unrest and speculation about a possible Greek default, a subtle but sinister trend started to emerge throughout Europe. Spokespersons for dominant European countries, led by Germany, and a number of other commentators (many of them American), started to raise concerns about the debt levels of other European countries. They hinted that the measures imposed on Greece were just the beginning. For instance, a spokesperson for German chancellor Angela Merkel's parliamentary grouping said at the end of 2009 that 'Greece is the current problem child, but it's not an isolated case, it's just the tip of the iceberg.' The message was that Italy, Spain and other countries had similar deficit- and debt-related problems.[2] Harvard professor and former IMF chief economist Kenneth Rogoff ominously announced that '[t]he specter of sovereign default … has returned to the rich world'.[3]

The notion of 'sovereign default' rests on rather shaky and ideologically biased theoretical pillars (as we shall see), but it became a fixture of the debate over the evolving Greek 'debt crisis', and contributed to the self-fulfilling panic which would subsequently engulf the entire eurozone. Most politicians and commentators blamed what they regarded as the excessive debt of some countries on reckless spending habits. This reflected the idea, common in certain European circles, that some countries had been 'living beyond their means' for too long, and that it was time for a reckoning.

Around this time another phrase became common currency in Europe. The rather unpleasant acronym PIIGS was coined in the mid-1990s, and used by financial markets and Brussels clerks to refer to the more heavily indebted and/or 'weaker' countries of Europe – Portugal, Italy, Ireland, Greece and Spain. In a classic example of self-fulfilling prophecy, or at best of positive feedback loop, borrowing costs did indeed start to rise for some of these countries – in particular Ireland and Portugal – at the beginning of 2010. This prompted the Spanish and Portuguese governments to announce a wave of austerity measures, which fuelled speculation about the 'Greecification' of these countries. In response borrowing costs rose even more, and so did the government responses, in a vicious downward spiral.

Shortly after the Greek bail-out, in a clumsy attempt to stop the contagion spreading to other countries, the ECB activated the Securities Markets Programme (SMP), under which it pledged to intervene in the government bond markets of weaker countries by buying on the secondary market (that is, from banks and at market prices) the bonds that it would normally have accepted as collateral. The markets were unimpressed, and after a brief dip the interest rates on the government bonds of periphery countries started to rise rapidly once more.

The Irish Bail-Out

Throughout 2010 Ireland and Portugal witnessed the steepest rises in bond yields, and in November of that year Ireland came into the European spotlight again. After long insisting that it would not need a bail-out, the government had to request financial support from the European Union and the IMF. This move was 'welcomed' by the EU finance ministers and the ECB.[4] At the end of the month the European Commission, the ECB, the IMF and the Irish state agreed on a massive €85 billion bail-out package, to be repaid by the Irish government at an average (and rather onerous) interest rate of 5.83 per cent. To understand how a country like Ireland – which on the eve of the financial crisis had had a budget surplus and a low and declining public debt (around 25 per cent of GDP in 2007)

– found itself on the verge of bankruptcy just two years into the crisis, we have to take a step back in time.

Chapter 1 outlined the Irish banking crisis in 2008–9 and the government's controversial decision in early 2009 to offer a blanket guarantee to the country's highly indebted banks. This effectively nationalised (that is, shifted onto taxpayers' shoulders) the bank's debts, transferring obligations directly from the private sector to the state. At the same time the Irish economy crashed, with GDP falling by 3 per cent in 2008 and 7 per cent in 2009. This drastically reduced government tax revenues. Meanwhile unemployment jumped from 5 to 12 per cent, increasing the need for government spending on welfare payments. This led the deficit to soar to a staggering 31 per cent of GPD – widely regarded as the highest peacetime deficit ever recorded in a developed country – and the country's public debt to increase fourfold to almost 100 per cent of GDP by 2010 (see Figure 2.2).

By March 2010 it had become clear that the government was unable to meet its mounting obligations to provide cash to the banks – in particular the Anglo Irish Bank, which had been nationalised in 2009. Thus, in consultation with the ECB, Dublin drafted a new deal with the bank, 'promising' to pay Anglo Irish the bail-out cash through regular instalments (known as 'promissory notes') of €3.1 billion a year. The bank in turn would be able to use that 'sovereign promise' to keep borrowing money to remain afloat.[5] By September 2010 government support for the six guaranteed banks had risen markedly to 32 per cent of GDP, but the banks were still unable to raise finance on the markets. The yields on

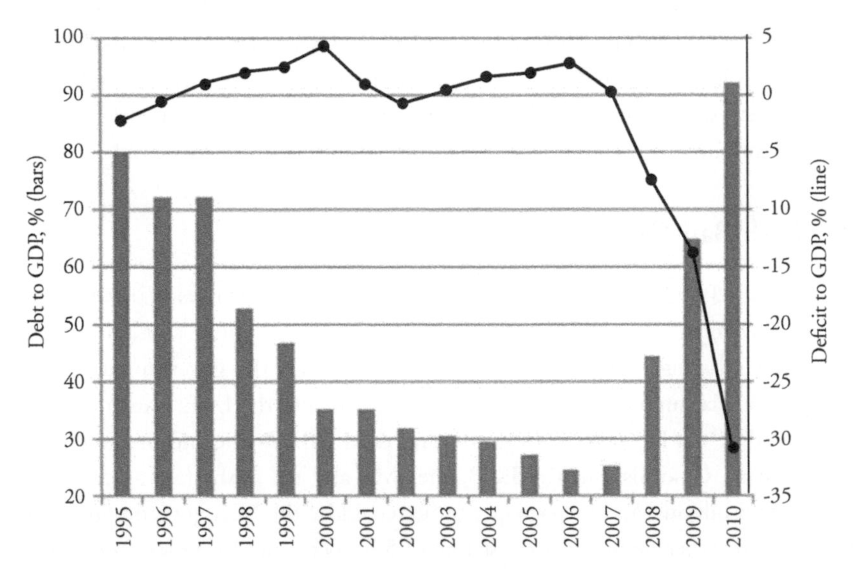

Figure 2.2 Ireland's deficit-to-GDP and debt-to-GDP ratios, 1995–2010

Source: Eurostat.

government bonds began to rise, in a telling demonstration of how the guarantee had inextricably tied the country's fate to that of its banks. Fatally, later that month the government decided to partly renew the annual guarantee covering the six main banks. By October yields were above 7 per cent, making further market borrowing unrealistic. Moreover, to remain afloat, Ireland's biggest banks had borrowed €86 billion from the ECB to pay back private creditors.[6]

Once the last bondholders had been repaid, in September 2010, a window of opportunity closed for the Irish government. As Michael Lewis put it, '[a] default of the banks now would be a default not to private investors but a bill presented directly to European governments.'[7] In mid-November Brian Lenihan, Ireland's minister for finance, received a letter from Jean-Claude Trichet, then president of the ECB. The full contents have never been disclosed, but the gist was that Ireland was advised to enter an EU-IMF bail-out programme.[8] An advisor to Lenihan said:

> The ECB were getting very hostile about the amount of money that it was having to lend to Ireland's banks. The ECB demanded something be done about it and it mentioned Ireland going into the bailout. They were keen to get Ireland into the programme.[9]

Soon afterwards the government started negotiations with the ECB and the IMF.

The bail-out deal comprised €35 billion for propping up the Irish banking system and €50 billion to help with the government's day-to-day spending. Even though the crisis in Ireland had been caused by private – not public – debt, and despite the fact that the bail-out money was to go either directly to the banks or to help the Irish state cope with its own bank bail-out and with the effects of the recession (caused again by bank actions), the EU-ECB-IMF troika prescribed the same treatment as it had imposed on Greece. Greece had undeniably had a government spending problem before the crisis; Ireland had not. But it was to get its funding, the ECB ominously announced, 'under strong policy conditionality': it would have to undertake a cuts programme negotiated by the Commission and the IMF, in liaison with the ECB.[10]

A narrative which saw the main cause of the unfolding crisis to be excessive public spending, rather than the recklessness of financial markets, had come to dominate European political discourse over the course of the previous year, courtesy of the Greek debt crisis; this was now showing its dramatic effects. The Irish Republic soon passed the toughest budget in the country's history, involving deep cuts in spending and public-sector jobs, a lower minimum wage and higher taxes, with the aim of reducing its excessive deficit by 2015. The government's announcement sparked massive anti-austerity demonstrations in Dublin. '[People are] furious because they feel like the government has handed over the keys to the country', a local journalist told CNN.[11] 'That [was] the strangest consequence of the Irish bubble: to throw a nation which had finally clawed its way out of centuries of indentured servitude back into it', said Michael Lewis.[12]

The Irish government, like the Greek one, was effectively relinquishing control of the country's finances to the non-elected authority of the troika. More, this authority was a faceless one. The European Commission, IMF and ECB refused to reveal the identities of the team that landed in Dublin to oversee the austerity programme. A spokeswoman for the ECB said: 'People do not need to know who these inspectors are.'[13] From that moment on, they would simply be known, in Ireland and elsewhere, as 'the men in black'. To add insult to injury, the former Irish Green Party leader later claimed that in the aftermath of the Irish banking collapse, the ECB had supported the government's decision to offer a blanket guarantee to the banks.[14] In fact, although there was initial public criticism of the guarantee, within a month the ECB was advocating that other member states in similar situations should also give such guarantees. (This is attested by an October 2008 ECB paper.[15]) In short, the ECB had backed up the government's disastrous decision, but was now not only punishing the Irish people for it, but taking a hand in doling out the medicine to them.

Even more worryingly, it became increasingly clear around that time that the Irish bail-out would provide the blueprint for all future 'rescue programmes'. So regardless of the underlying causes of a country's economic troubles, they would be treated as if the problem was government overspending. The bail-out-*cum*-austerity recipe was fast becoming standard policy in recession- and crisis-stricken Europe.

Rewriting History: Wolfgang Schäuble and the Financial Crisis

At the end of 2010, Europe's new post-crisis paradigm was clearly expressed by Wolfgang Schäuble, Germany's minister of finance, in a widely distributed article.[16] Schäuble first acknowledged that the financial markets had caused 'the most serious financial and economic crisis in 80 years' and that an all-out global depression had only been averted by 'unprecedented worldwide deficit spending'. But he then took his argument in a radically different direction: 'And yet the financial crisis and the ensuing recession only go so far towards explaining these high levels of indebtedness. The truth is that a number of European and G20 countries have over the past decades *lived well beyond their means*' (my italics). In a few lines, Schäuble had summed up the radical shift in narrative that had taken place in Europe in the two years following the 2008 crash. After paying lip service to the responsibilities of the banks, Schäuble's article barely mentioned the financial sector. In this too he mirrored the quasi-Freudian suppression that had come to characterise European political debate. The rest of the piece was entirely dedicated to the new spectre haunting the continent (thanks in no small part to articles such as this one): government spending. As the German minister went on to explain:

> The additional debt burden of recent years was just the last straw to break the camel's back – albeit a rather heavy one. Even in good times, governments have for too long been spending more than they earned .... The profligacy of governments has led to levels of debt that will become unsustainable if we do not at once begin to reduce them.

Surprisingly Schäuble included his own country, Germany, among the spendthrifts in need of an austerity cure. In explaining his proposed austerity plan for Germany, he implicitly sketched out a blueprint for other countries as well. He explained that the best way to reduce the debt was to 'cut ... welfare spending'. 'All the eurozone governments need to demonstrate convincingly their own commitment to fiscal consolidation *so as to restore the confidence of markets*' (my italics) – a phrase to keep in mind, since it would become a common refrain in the subsequent months and years. Spurring growth through government spending rather than private investment was not an option, said Schäuble, since 'more debt will stunt not stimulate economic growth'. (In saying this he cut short in eight words a debate, as yet unresolved, that has divided economists for centuries.) Schäuble admitted in his piece that the unfolding euro crisis was partly a consequence of the EMU's 'current rules', but only insofar as they 'are insufficient to impose enough fiscal discipline on eurozone members'. He hinted that this should be the priority as far as reform of the monetary union was concerned. 'It is worth remembering', Schäuble wrote, 'that monetary union was not intended to be a panacea for eurozone members ... nor was it meant to be a system of redistribution from richer to poorer countries.' These must learn 'to live within their means and strengthen their competiveness'. In conclusion, indebted governments were ultimately solely responsible for their condition, since 'less competitive members of the eurozone allowed wages to rise and the public sector to become bloated and then looked the other way as easy credit fuelled both debt and asset bubbles'.

The German minister of finance's reading of the crisis can be summed up as follows:

- The recklessness of the financial system was not the real cause of the crisis. It was merely a trigger ('the last straw').
- The real cause was excessive government debt.
- This was caused by excessive government spending by countries that have 'lived well beyond their means'.
- The deficit/debt needs to be reduced 'at once' before it is 'too late'.
- Spurring growth through government investment is not an option.
- The only way to reduce the deficit/debt is by reducing welfare spending

(through austerity), since 'cutting expenditure offers much better prospects for growth than raising revenues'.

- Eurozone reform should be focused on imposing 'fiscal discipline' on member states.
- Countries must learn 'to live within their means and strengthen their competiveness'.

By the end of 2010 this extremely partisan and ideological reading of the crisis had become conventional wisdom among most European politicians, commentators and bureaucrats – influencing policy responses all throughout Europe. As Paul Krugman put it, 'deficit scaremongering took over the debate'.[17] By mid-2011, even relatively rich and healthy European countries such as the United Kingdom and France had followed all the PIIGS minus Italy (Portugal, Ireland, Greece, Spain), as well as various Eastern European countries, in drinking the austerity Kool-Aid. The trademarks of the post-war European social model – wealth redistribution through taxes and welfare programmes, social rights, collective bargaining and the rest – started to be called openly into question.

To varying degrees, the same form of economic shock therapy was being prescribed all over Europe, even though the original test country, Greece, was reacting very badly to the cure, even in purely economic terms. The EU authorities had originally forecast that Greek GDP would shrink by 4 per cent in 2010 and 2.5 per cent in 2011. Instead it fell by 4.5 per cent in 2010, with unemployment rising from 9 per cent in mid-2009 to over 15 per cent in early 2011 (see Figure 2.3).[18]

Not only had the austerity programme deepened the recession in Greece, it was not even serving its stated aim of 'reassuring the markets'. Ten-year government bond yields climbed to almost 13 per cent by mid-2011, following another downgrade by the credit rating agencies. And while austerity was failing in economic terms, in social terms it was proving nothing less than disastrous. There had been cuts of 15 per cent in public-sector workers' pay, reductions of more than 10 per cent in pensions, and painful increases in VAT and other taxes. Such a retrenchment, the *Economist* wrote, 'was on an unprecedented scale in recent European history'.[19] As many commentators and foreign correspondents noted, the austerity programme was starting to tear apart the fabric of Greek society, with the proportion of the population living at 'risk of poverty or social exclusion' rising to almost 30 per cent.[20]

What is worse is that as early as 2010, a number of non-mainstream economists had warned about the dangers of austerity, in both economic and social terms. Paul Krugman was one of the most vocal, writing in mid-2011 that the 'savage austerity programs' would prove self-defeating. But such objections were waved away by the ECB, which embraced austerity as a 'universal economic elixir'. 'The ECB is acting

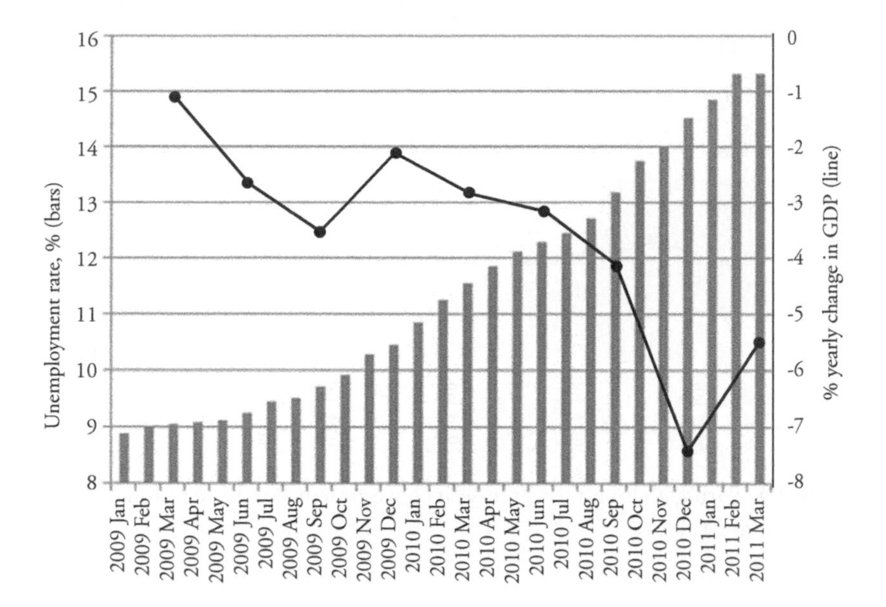

Figure 2.3 Greece's unemployment and GDP growth rates, 2009–11

Source: ECB.

as if it is determined to provoke a financial crisis', was Krugman's rather prophetic conclusion.[21] The EU authorities were of a different opinion. They believed that Greece needed to step up 'without further delay' its programme of structural adjustment, as Jean-Paul Juncker, then president of the Eurogroup, the informal gathering of the finance ministers of the eurozone, declared in mid-May.[22]

The Portuguese Bail-Out

In May 2011, as the politicians and the media had been anticipating, warning and/or threatening for months, Portugal became the third country, after Greece and Ireland, to have to ask for an EU-IMF bail-out, to the tune of €78 billion. Since Portugal is widely considered a marginal country, the news did not raise many eyebrows on the continent. It should have: the Portuguese bail-out marked the beginning of a new – and even more ominous – phase in the euro crisis.

This request for a bail-out came, like the Greek and Irish ones, after a sudden increase in the interest rate on ten-year government bonds (the famous 'spread'). It had gone in just a year and a half from 4 per cent to 10 per cent, making it increasingly difficult for Portugal to roll over its debt (see Figure 2.4).

The new post-crisis conventional wisdom, which was repeated frequently in articles and news pieces on the bail-out, was that this was because investors had 'lost faith' in the country's ability to manage its debts. As one of the PIIGS, Portugal was

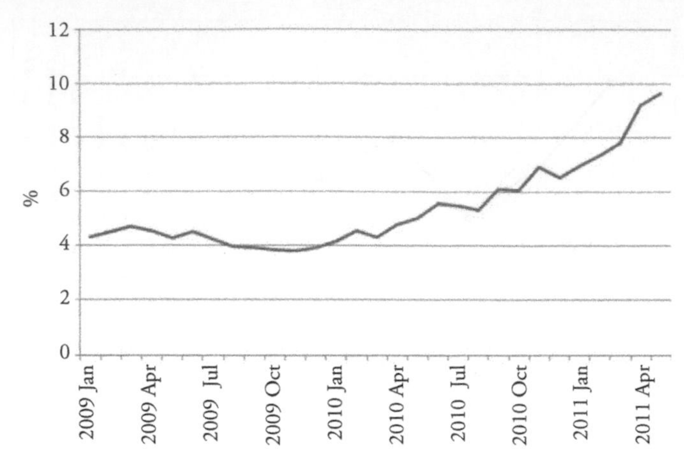

Figure 2.4 Portugal's long-term (ten-year) government bond interest rate, 2009 to mid-2011
Source: ECB.

(and is) considered by many to have an inherently dysfunctional economy. In fact Portugal had performed rather well throughout the 1990s, and was managing its recovery from the global recession better than several other European countries. In 2010 its public debt was just above Germany's level at 77 per cent of GDP, while its budget deficit was lower than that of several other European countries, and falling rapidly. But from 2010 onwards Portugal had come under pressure from bond traders, speculators and credit-rating analysts. This had led its borrowing costs to rise to unsustainable levels, and it was this factor that forced it to seek a bail-out.

Greece and Ireland both presented undeniable structural problems, respectively in the public and private sector; Portugal did not. In this sense, it could be argued that the country's sovereign crisis was largely engineered by financial markets, and then exploited by the European Commission-ECB-IMF troika to impose on the country its trademark austerity cure.

Robert M. Fishman, professor of sociology at the University of Notre Dame, commented at the time that this was a disturbing (yet largely under-appreciated) development in the eurozone crisis. Portugal's plea for help from the EU-IMF 'should be a warning to democracies everywhere', he wrote:

> If left unregulated ... market forces threaten to eclipse the capacity of democratic governments ... to make their own choices about taxes and spending .... By distorting market perceptions of Portugal's stability, the rating agencies – whose role in fostering the subprime mortgage crisis in the United States has been amply documented – have undermined both its economic recovery and its political freedom.[23]

We shall take a more in-depth look later at how sovereign debt speculation works, and the role that it played in the outbreak and worsening of the eurozone crisis, further on. But it should be apparent even from this brief summary that the Portuguese bail-out was a telling demonstration of the power of financial markets (banks and credit rating agencies) to influence government policies through speculation – and of their readiness to use that power mercilessly. That Portugal's economy had fared surprisingly well in the face of the 2008 financial crisis did not prevent the troika from requiring its complete overhaul. The implication behind this was that if the approach was failing in Greece and Ireland, it was not because austerity programmes were self-defeating, but because the previous programmes had not gone far enough.

A Portuguese economist noted at the time that the EU policies were 'beginning to seem like the West's version of China's Great Leap Forward: impossible targets based on but pure ideology'.[24] As if to confirm this, two months after Portugal's bail-out, the European Union agreed on a second €109 billion bail-out for Greece, which was again on the verge of collapse. Just a month before, Standard & Poor's had downgraded Greece to the lowest credit rating in the world, from B to CCC. In a classic domino effect the second Greek bail-out caused borrowing costs to increase for Italy and Spain.

Italy: A Soft 'Regime Change'

In August 2011 it was Italy's turn to come under the spotlight. On 5 August there was a stir over the news that Italian government bond yields had risen above Spain's for the first time in more than a year. This it was widely interpreted as a sign of the markets' doubts about Rome's ability to meet its debt obligations. (In other words, the commentary followed the now-conventional wisdom about the eurozone crisis: that it was all about legitimate market concerns over excessive government debt.) That same day, ECB president Jean-Claude Trichet and his anointed successor Mario Draghi sent a letter to the Italian government which was intended to remain secret, although it was subsequently leaked.[25]

The letter claimed that Italy's post-crisis deficit-cutting plan was 'not sufficient', and set out detailed demands aimed at 'a major overhaul of the public administration'. This included 'the full liberalisation of local public services'; 'large scale privatizations' (even though citizens had recently overturned through a referendum the government's attempts to privatise the country's water services); 'reducing the cost of public employees, by strengthening turnover rules and, if necessary, by reducing wages'; 'reform [of] the collective wage bargaining system'; 'more stringent … criteria for seniority pensions'; and even 'constitutional reform tightening fiscal rules'. All this, of course, was needed 'to restore the confidence of investors'.[26]

Giulio Tremonti, Italy's then minister of economy and finance, later privately told a group of European finance ministers that his government had received two threatening letters in August: one from a terrorist group, the other from the ECB. 'The one from the ECB was worse', he quipped.[27] Nonetheless the government gave in: on 7 August Tremonti faxed a letter to the ECB pledging far-reaching reforms and deeper budget cuts. The ECB responded positively by agreeing to intervene to buy Italian bonds to keep borrowing costs down. The following month, Italy stepped in line with the other PIIGS (as well as other, more 'respectable' countries) and passed a €50 billion austerity budget, with the aim of balancing the budget by 2013. But a few days later Standard & Poor's downgraded its debt rating from A+ to A, with the implication that the austerity programme did not go far enough.

On Saturday 12 November Italy, Europe and most of the world were shocked (and relieved) to hear that after the Italian parliament had passed an austerity act on the lines dictated by the ECB, the prime minister Silvio Berlusconi had resigned. Berlusconi had lost his parliamentary majority on the previous Tuesday, and had promised to resign once the austerity measures had been passed by both houses of parliament. On the Wednesday the interest rate on ten-year Italian government bonds had touched 7 per cent, the rate at which Greece, Ireland and Portugal had been forced to seek bail-outs from the European Union. That same day, president Giorgio Napolitano appointed Mario Monti to form a new government.

Monti was a technocrat, not a politician. He had been a European commissioner and an international advisor to Goldman Sachs since 2005 (a position he resigned from just a few days before being sworn in). The government he headed was intended to be a technocratic one (in Italian, a *governo tecnico*).[28] This marked the beginning of yet another chapter in the eurozone crisis: the rise of the technocrats.

Monti was sworn in as prime minister on 16 November, just a week after having been appointed a senator for life. A number of commentators argued that Angela Merkel and especially the ECB had played a pivotal role in Berlusconi's resignation. This was borne out by the sequence of events. Italy's bond yields had risen to dangerously high levels in August 2011. The ECB had intervened by buying Italian bonds, but had also intervened politically by demanding budget cuts and far-reaching reforms. Then, when Berlusconi failed to act with sufficient haste, the ECB had eased off on its bond purchases, prompting financial markets to push interest rates up even higher; and it was this that effectively forced Berlusconi to quit.[29] So it could be said that the ECB worked with the bond markets to get a government that would do as it wished in Italy.

Such an event was unprecedented in modern European history, for a number of reasons. Stephen Foley, former associate business editor of the *Independent*, wrote:

> The ascension of Mario Monti to the Italian prime ministership is remarkable for more reasons than it is possible to count. By replacing the scandal-surfing Silvio Berlusconi, Italy has dislodged the undislodgeable. By imposing rule by unelected

> technocrats, it has suspended the normal rules of democracy, and maybe democracy itself. And by putting a senior adviser at Goldman Sachs in charge of a Western nation, it has taken to new heights the political power of an investment bank that you might have thought was prohibitively politically toxic.[30]

However Italy was not the only country in which 'the normal rules of democracy' were being increasingly called into question.

Greece: The Second Bail-Out

In October 2011, the troika brought the second bail-out loan for Greece, which had been on the table since July, up to €130 billion, conditional on the implementation of another austerity package. The bail-out also included an agreement with banks to accept a 50 per cent write-off of (a part of) the Greek debt. (This is also known as a 'haircut'.) In other words, Greece's creditors were forced to pay a price, although the bulk of the pain was still being borne by Greek citizens.

The country had already been swept by waves of anti-austerity strikes and demonstrations, and was all but certain to resist any further measures. Papandreou announced that he intended to call a referendum on the new EU-IMF rescue plan. This news was met by markets and other EMU leaders with indignation. Merkel and France's president Nicolas Sarkozy issued an ultimatum that unless the new measures were approved, they would withhold an overdue €6 billion loan payment to Athens.[31] The message was clear: the terms of the bail-out were not negotiable. A few days later Papandreou abandoned his plans to hold a referendum. This dramatic about-face was welcomed by European leaders and financial markets.

This subversion of democracy by the European elites and international financial markets would have been deeply troubling even if the austerity measures undertaken by Greece had proven to be working – which they were not. In 2011 Greek GDP dropped by 7.1 percentage points and industrial output ended 28.4 per cent lower than in 2005. The unemployment rate reached a record high of 19.9 per cent that November, and youth unemployment rose from 22 per cent to 48.1 per cent. Greece's citizens might have been thought justified in questioning whether the policies being followed were self-evidently correct ones.

On 10 November Papandreou resigned as prime minister. He had agreed with a majority in parliament that a new prime minister should be appointed with the brief of implementing the measures the ECB was demanding. The person chosen for this task was Lucas Papademos, a former governor of the Bank of Greece and former vice-president of the ECB. In other words, just as in Italy, a technocrat replaced an elected politician, for the specific purpose of doing as the financial markets wanted.

Political and media circles broadly accepted the rise to power of this new class of unelected technocrats. Most commentators agreed that it was justified by the gravity of the crisis. The technocrats were seen as 'experts' supposedly untainted by politics, with the implication that the policies they carried out were not a political choice but something entirely rational and necessary. If there were no material interests or political-ideological inclinations involved, how could the policies be criticised?

This implies, though, that the technocrats were ideologically neutral. Even if it is accepted that ideological neutrality is possible, it is questionable whether either Monti or Papademos displayed it. Papademos was a banker, and Monti had been an adviser to the world's number one investment bank. An observer might perhaps have been forgiven for concluding that these individuals were not neutral with regard to the relative claims of the financial sector, and the rest of the economy and population.

Greece held new elections in May 2012. Most voters opted for parties that rejected the bail-out agreement. Attempts to form a coalition government failed. In mid-May, the Greek political impasse led to strong speculation that Greece would have to leave the eurozone, a possibility that became known as 'Grexit'. As always, the international markets responded. New elections were set for June. In the weeks preceding the elections, several EU officials reminded Greeks that the choice facing them was stark. They could either agree to follow the agreed 'rescue plan', with all the austerity conditions that had been attached to it, or the loan offer would immediately be cancelled, which would lead to an uncontrolled default and exclusion from the EMU.[32] On 17 June the Greeks voted in a pro-austerity party, New Democracy (as well as the neo-Nazi party Golden Dawn, for the first time in Greek history). Sighs of relief could be heard all over Europe.

The Fiscal Compact: Austerity Forever, for Everyone

It should be borne in mind in regard to what follows that European commissioners, ECB officials and IMF officials are none of them democratically elected. However it was these individuals who effectively dictated EU policy over the euro crisis, supported by certain dominant European countries (above all, by Germany). And it was largely spokespeople for these unelected institutions who promoted the view that government overspending, and not financial deregulation, was the root cause of the crisis, and that the only possible way to resolve it was to impose an even more radically neoliberal framework on the EMU.

This line was broadly accepted by both politicians and the media. It resulted in the signing by all EU member states (with the notable exceptions of the United Kingdom and the Czech Republic) of the so-called Fiscal Compact (formally, the Treaty on Stability, Coordination and Governance in the Economic and Monetary Union; or more plainly the Fiscal Stability Treaty). Its aim was to enforce an even stricter budget discipline on member countries.[33]

The new treaty brought the post-crisis European obsession with fiscal tightening to a whole new level. Member states were required for the first time to take legal steps to impose a 'balanced budget rule', 'through binding and permanent provisions, preferably constitutional', and to provide for a self-correcting mechanism to prevent their breach.

In many ways, the Fiscal Compact can be seen as the indefinite institutionalisation and crystallisation on a European scale of austerity. It took no account of the fact that by early 2012 it was clear that the austerity programmes imposed on states that had needed bail-outs were failing to deliver even in purely economic, let alone social, terms. The public interest groups Corporate Europe Observatory and the Transnational Institute issued a joint statement after the signing of the treaty: 'Far from presenting us with a solution to the crisis, the new EU rules on economic policy show clear signs of a neoliberal regime change – a *civic coup*' (my italics).[34]

As if to confirm critics' worst fears, Mario Draghi, president of the ECB, gave an interview to the *Wall Street Journal* a few weeks later. Asked about the Fiscal Compact, he cut short any debate: 'There was no alternative to fiscal consolidation', he said. 'The European social model has already gone.'[35] A few days later, the ECB announced that it had loaned more than €1 trillion to European banks at a record-low rate of 1 per cent, and reiterated the commitment it had previously given to provide unlimited loans to solvent banks.[36]

The loans that the ECB was offering to states were all at interest rates between 5.5 and 6 per cent, although these were subsequently reduced to 3.5 and 4 per cent. And there were, as we have seen, extremely harsh conditions attached. But at the same time it was making huge loans to the very banks responsible for the crisis, at record-low rates and with no conditions attached.

It is worth remembering that the 2008 financial crisis was caused by excessive leveraging by banks, not by excessive government spending. Nonetheless, following the crisis governments and central banks kept pumping money into the financial system – €4.6 trillion (equivalent to 36.7 per cent of the continent's GDP) in the European Union alone between 2008 and 2011.[37] In short, banks were allowed to keep on merrily accumulating debt for speculative purposes, while governments were permanently banned from borrowing in order to fund infrastructural projects, social services, research – in a broad sense, from investing in the future.

The minimal post-crisis financial 'reforms' allowed banks to keep on leveraging themselves up to their eyeballs, a privilege they were more than willing to use. In mid-2011 the IMF reported that German banks were leveraged at 32 to 1, Belgian banks at 30 to 1, French ones at 26 to 1. On average, in 2011, European banks were still operating with a leverage of 26 to 1 – double the ratio in the United States[38] – safe in the knowledge that they would be bailed out with taxpayers' money if they went belly up. To put things in perspective, a leverage of 30 to 1 means a debt-to-capital ratio of 3,000 per cent, compared with the 60 per cent debt-to-GDP ratio allowed to states by the Maastricht Treaty (which was further tightened by the Fiscal Compact). Most countries proceeded to ratify the Fiscal Compact with little or no public or parliamentary debate. Ireland was the only country to hold a referendum on the treaty. After much debate it was approved in May.

The Spanish Bail-Out

On 9 June 2012 Spain became the fourth country – after Greece, Ireland and Portugal – to require a bail-out, and the first country to make a request to the new European permanent bail-out fund, the European Stability Mechanism (ESM, formerly the European Financial Stability Facility, or EFSF).

Chapter 1 outlined how Spain responded to the 2008 financial crisis by giving massive support to its banking system. By mid-2012 the government had injected €34 billion into it.[39] That May the government nationalised Bankia, Spain's fourth-largest bank, which required an additional €19 billion. Then, in June, faced with mounting losses in the banking sector, a crippling recession (deepened by a series of extremely harsh austerity measures) and record-high (in Spain's modern history) debt and borrowing costs, the country's conservative prime minister Mariano Rajoy was forced to request €100 billion of financial aid from the EU. As recently as 28 May Rajoy had said that there would 'be no rescue of the Spanish banking sector'.[40]

The Spanish government was keen to stress that the bail-out money was going to its banks, rather than to the central government, but in practice the Spanish bail-out closely resembled previous bail-outs. First and foremost, the money did not go directly to the banks, but was channelled through the government's bank restructuring agency, the FROB. So although the banks got it, it also added to state debt (to be repaid by the Spanish people).

The rescue loan did not come with explicit conditions attached, but Rajoy pushed through his own spending cuts in order to avoid having them imposed from abroad, so the results were very much the same. Germany also stressed that the Spanish bank rescue would be 'overseen' by the troika.[41] The austerity measures announced between May and September 2012 were so harsh that they prompted the United Nations Committee on Economic, Social and Cultural Rights to call on the Spanish government to 'revise' them, because they were causing 'disproportionate' harm and violating the human rights of the most vulnerable sectors of society.[42]

The fact that such pain was inflicted on the Spanish people is particularly hard to digest when you take into account the fact that, just as in Ireland, the crisis had absolutely nothing to do with reckless government spending. Before 2008 the Spanish government was one of the least spendthrift in the eurozone, unlike Greece, or even Germany. In 2007 the country's debt-to-GDP ratio was an incredibly low (and declining) 36 per cent, compared with Germany's 65 per cent. Moreover, in the years leading to the financial crisis, it had run an average balanced budget, even registering a 2 per cent surplus in 2007. There was indeed a build-up of debt in Spain prior to 2008, but it was comprised largely of private debt (which in 2008 amounted to 100 per cent of GDP, compared with a public debt-to-GDP ratio of 40 per cent) (see Figures 2.5 and 2.6).

When the house of cards came crashing down, in 2008, the government, as usual, was landed with the clean-up bill: the collapse of the housing bubble created a hole in the Spanish economy equivalent to 10 per cent of the country's GDP, causing the country's budget to go from a surplus to a massive deficit, as a result of the collapse in revenues.[43] Spain had had the lowest public expenditure per capita among the early members of the European Union (the EU-15),[44] but in the aftermath of the financial crisis the government was forced to borrow heavily to deal with the effects of the housing crash and the resulting recession – not to mention the bank bail-outs. As a consequence, between 2007 and 2011, Spain's budget collapsed from a 2 per cent surplus to a 9.4 per cent deficit (a dramatic 11-point drop), while its public debt soared from 36 per cent of GDP to almost 70 per cent (see Figure 2.6).

By mid-2012, speculation that Spain might be forced to request financial assistance from the European Union left the country no choice but to do just that. As experts realised that a €100 billion bail-out loan would send Spain's government debt shooting up from 70 to 80 per cent, interest rates on government bonds started to rise steadily. In May, interest rates on 10-year Spanish bonds were well above 6 per cent – not far short of the 7–8 per cent level that had prompted Greece, Ireland and Portugal to go cap-in-hand to Brussels for a bail-out (and had resulted in Berlusconi's ousting). Indeed, this looks like another case of self-fulfilling market prophecy.

A month later came the bail-out – handed to the banks, billed to the taxpayer. Following the EU loan, Spain's public debt rose to a higher than expected 85 per cent of GDP. As elsewhere, this was accompanied by a further tightening of

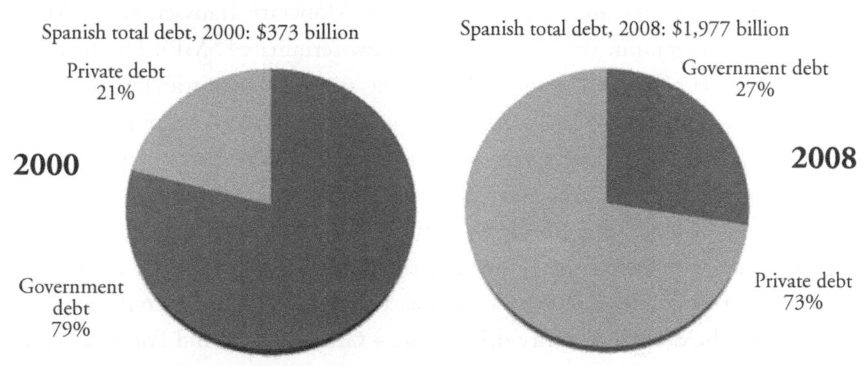

Figure 2.5 Private and government debt in Spain as a percentage of total debt, 2000 and 2008

Source: Bank for International Settlements.

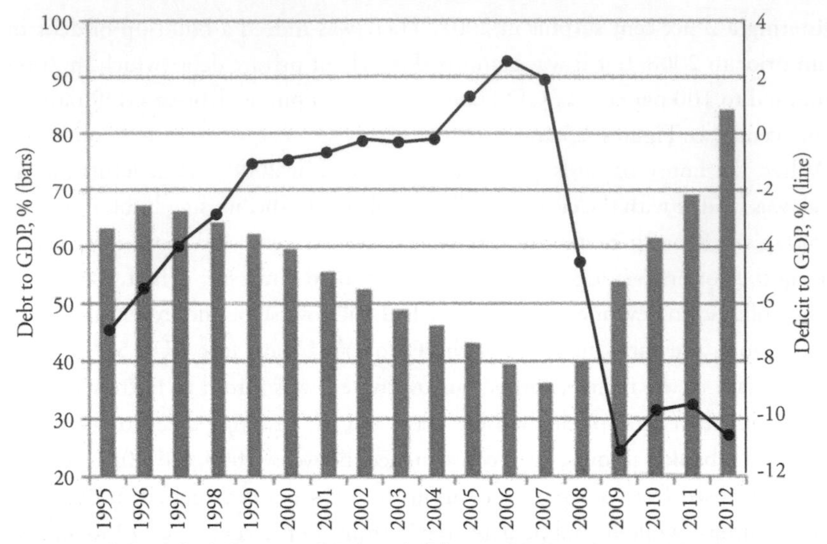

Figure 2.6 Spain's deficit- to-GDP and debt-to-GDP ratios, 1995–2012

Source: Eurostat.

austerity measures, despite the fact that by March 2012 unemployment had risen to 24.1 per cent, Spain's highest for nearly 20 years, with more than half of all workers under the age of 25 without a job. Once again, citizens were being made to pay – first, through the effects of the crisis-induced recession, second through a rise in the country's collective debt, and third through savage welfare cuts – for a crisis that had been caused entirely by the recklessness of the banks, and to endure an 'austerity cure' that, where previously tested, had proven disastrous not only socially but also in economic terms.

Shortly thereafter, as increasingly aggressive speculative attacks caused borrowing rates for certain countries of the periphery, primarily Italy, to reach unsustainable levels, posing a serious threat to the survival of the eurozone, the European Central Bank announced its 'Outright Monetary Transactions' (OMT) bond-buying programme (which replaced the now-terminated SMP). This had the immediate effect of lowering bond yields in Italy and other countries by providing a lender of last resort-style backstop. The plan's temporary success prompted the EU establishment to self-righteously announce that the euro crisis was 'over'.[45]

This was not true: the economic crisis was rapidly turning into a major social crisis. By the end of 2012 unemployment in the EMU had risen to a record 11.7 per cent, with youth unemployment rising to 24 per cent in the EMU and 23.4 per cent across the European Union as a whole. In the three countries that had suffered the deepest austerity-driven cuts – Greece, Spain and Portugal – the situation was now verging on a social and humanitarian crisis, according to a number of sources.[46] As well as generating devastating social consequences, the austerity regime was not delivering even in purely economic terms. By mid-2012 Europe had been in recession for more than six months, and the eurozone's debt-to-GDP ratio was at an all-time high. In the meantime, the financial sector – in Europe even more than in the United States – had emerged from the crisis virtually unscathed. The five biggest banks in Europe reaped profits of €34 billion in 2011.[47] On 14 November 2012 millions of people participated in the first-ever European general strike, with bloody street battles ensuing in Italy, Spain, Portugal and Greece.

The Cypriot Bail-Out

The EU establishment's self-congratulatory optimism was brutally shattered in early 2013, when the small island of Cyprus became the latest in the rapidly growing list of countries to be almost sunk by their over-indebted banks. When it had become clear that the Irish banking system was imploding, corporations and wealthy individuals had put a large chunk of the money they withdrew from Irish banks into Cyprus, whose banks offered higher interest rates than average and by some accounts were not too picky about the provenance of the money they accepted. According to German intelligence, approaching a third of the bank deposits were coming from Russia. This led to accusations that the country was turning into a tax haven for Russian companies wanting to evade taxes in their home country, or worse, Russian tycoons wanting to launder dirty money.[48]

In 2008, according to a study by the McKinsey Global Institute, $40.7 billion was funnelled into Cyprus through loans and bank deposits.[49] In the context of global capital flows this was a tiny amount, but relative to the size of the Cypriot economy it was huge, amounting to 161 per cent of the Cypriot GDP that year.[50] In just a few years the Cypriot banking system inflated beyond all reasonable limits, with the total assets of all banks growing to around nine times the country's GDP by the end of 2011. This was more than twice the EMU's (already high) average bank assets-to-GDP ratio of 3.5.[51]

The country's two main banks, Cyprus Popular Bank and the Bank of Cyprus, then invested huge chunks of that money in Greek debt, both public and private. When the Greek government imposed a haircut on creditors as part of its 2011 bail-out deal, the two banks lost €2.5 billion and €1 billion respectively. Fearing the worst, and following the failed precedents set in previous banking crises, the Cypriot government nationalised Popular Bank and heavily recapitalised the Bank of Cyprus. As a result Cypriot public debt started to rise rapidly (going from 61 per cent of GDP in 2010 to 86 per cent in 2012) and its government bond interest rates reached the dreaded 7 per cent threshold.

Cyprus requested financial assistance from the European Union in early 2013. Given the sheer size of Cyprus's banking sector, rescuing the country's banks was not an option. The banks were not only too big to fail, they were too big to bail – a situation similar to the one faced by Iceland in 2009. At the end of March 2013, the European Union and the Cypriot government reached an agreement on the conditions required for Cyprus to receive the requested €10 billion loan. Cyprus Popular Bank would be closed, with all insured deposits up to €100,000 and, more controversially, the entire amount of deposits belonging to financial institutions being transferred to the Bank of Cyprus. The Bank of Cyprus would face a massive restructuring, with deposits over €100,000 being cut by 37.5 per cent (with an additional 22.5 per cent held as a buffer).

In reality the depositors' money was not obliterated, but converted into 'class A' shares of the banks – a procedure known as 'bail-in'. To avoid a massive outflow of euros when its banks reopened, and the total collapse of its banking system, Cyprus became the first eurozone country ever to be authorised by the European Commission to impose a set of radical temporary capital controls. Limits were imposed on credit card transactions, daily withdrawals, money transfers abroad and the cashing of cheques.

The Cypriot case hailed the beginning of yet another phase in the euro crisis. One feature of this was the use of hitherto taboo crisis-response tools such as the bail-in and capital controls, but perhaps more important is what it shows about EU policy overall. Ever since the 2008 crash, the EU elite had refused to address the structural flaws of Europe's financial system: out-of-control capital flows, over-leveraged banks, unregulated tax havens and so on. As a result, the crisis was still not over.

The End of Austerity?

At the end of May 2013 the European Commission presented its annual economic policy recommendations to EU member states.[52] In its country-specific recommendations, the Commission decided to allow seven countries (France, Poland, Slovenia, Spain, Belgium, the Netherlands and Portugal) to ease the pace of austerity. They were granted more time to 'put their fiscal house in order' and reach the deficit target of 3 per cent of GDP. A further recommendation was to end the 'excessive deficit procedure' opened against Italy in 2009, which gives the Commission heightened powers to impose 'corrective' fiscal and budgetary policies on countries that exceed the allowed deficit-to-GDP ratio.

Various commentators interpreted this extra breathing space granted by the Commission as an important 'change of track', if not 'the end of austerity'. But in reality there was little to indicate the 'end' of anything – let alone of austerity. The Commission's recommendations did not indicate that it had changed its mind about austerity. They merely acknowledged that countries were failing to implement the necessary reforms fast enough, and thus needed more time to reach their deficit targets. To clear any doubts about their unwavering commitment to austerity, Commission officials insisted that they were not abandoning 'fiscal discipline' altogether, noting that many countries, while receiving extensions to their deadlines, would still have to take stringent measures to reduce their deficits.[53] Indeed, by mid-2013, austerity had effectively become institutionalised through the Fiscal Compact, and there were plans under way which would make it even more so, through a further deepening and strengthening of Europe's new austerity-driven system of economic governance by way of a more tightly integrated banking, economic and fiscal union (as we shall see further on).

In the five years since the onset of the worst financial crisis since the Great Depression, Europe's political, economic and social landscape has been radically transformed – more than any other continent in the world. What has not been transformed to remotely the same extent is its financial system.

We saw in Chapter 1 how the roots of the crisis lay in the recklessness of an out-of-control financial system, just as in 1929. And we saw how this was a product of the neoliberal deregulatory frenzy of the 1980s and 1990s, which itself brought more inequality, insecurity and instability, seriously eroding social welfare and labour rights. But in Europe the blame for the crisis was subtly shifted from the banks to their victims – the European states and their citizens. The remedies that were proposed were entirely unrelated to reining in the financial sector. Instead the universal remedy was to cut public services and wages to public servants – measures which hit not the rich, but the least well off. This shift of blame from the private sector to the public sphere has been described as nothing less than a 'civic coup'.

As a consequence, the financial sector – in Europe even more than in the United States – has emerged from the crisis virtually unscathed, and in some ways strengthened. By unconditionally bailing out and offering unlimited lines of credit to the banks, without imposing on them any real reform, governments and central banks have created what Mervyn King has called 'the biggest moral hazard in history'.

European governments, and in particular the weaker economies of the periphery, assumed huge debts in order to save the financial sector (and, it was argued, the wider economy) in the two years following the crash of 2008. But by 2010 they were being seen not as victims of the crisis, but as its cause. The accusation of 'living beyond their means' is (in most cases) not borne out by the state of their finances prior to the crash, but even so it has become widely accepted. Meanwhile, the weaker countries of Europe came under attack from the very banks they had rescued.

The draconian austerity measures demanded by the EU-ECB-IMF troika in return for financial assistance have been described by many as the most violent attack on the European welfare state in history. They also provided a template for other nations. To varying degrees, all European countries – including those outside the EMU such as the United Kingdom – have committed themselves to 'fiscal consolidation'.

Another result of these measures is that democracy on the continent has been dangerously curtailed. Unelected institutions (in particular the ECB, the European Commission and the IMF) have assumed growing powers at the expense of national parliaments. This represents the rise of technocracy over democracy.

To add insult to injury, in spite of its devastating cost to individuals, the European-wide austerity regime is not delivering even in economic terms. Since the end of 2011 Europe has been in recession. There was a very timid recovery in mid-2013, largely as a result of improved conditions in core countries, but at the expense of periphery states. Meanwhile countries have registered record-high, and growing, unemployment and debt-to-GDP rates.

Austerity is creating a widening social and economic core–periphery gap, as parts of Europe begin to drift away from each other. The result of all this is the reawakening of long-dormant nationalistic, populist and anti-European sentiments, on both the right and the left. As European institutions work towards a greater economic and political (albeit technocratic and austerity-oriented) integration between member states (the much talked-about 'United States of Europe'), hostility towards those very institutions is at a historic high. They are, with much justice, perceived as anti-democratic and anti-social. The public hostility poses a serious threat to the very survival of the European project.

Is an alternative to the current austerity regime and European political-economic framework possible? Can Europe be made to work in the interests of the people, rather than those of powerful banks and corporations? Can the European dream – of a continent built through economic and social progress, the extension of democracy and welfare rights – be reignited, before it turns into a nightmare?

Before we try to answer these fundamental questions, it is necessary to debunk some myths about Europe, the euro and the current crisis.

CHAPTER THREE

The Real Causes of the Euro Crisis

The Pauperisation of Europe

'The main cause of the euro crisis is excessive government debt, caused by excessive social welfare spending.' This is arguably the founding myth of the austerity regime. We have in part addressed the question in relation to single countries, especially Ireland and Spain. Let us now take a more comprehensive approach to the issue.

As we saw, by the end of 2010 a consensus was already setting in that the main problem afflicting Europe was not the continent's overly leveraged financial institutions or its societies' increasing inequality, but excessive government debt, caused by countries 'liv[ing] well beyond their means', as Germany's minister of finance put it. A number of economists, though, have dismissed the popular belief that the debt crisis was caused by excessive social welfare spending. According to their analysis, the increased debt levels were mostly caused by the large bail-out packages provided to the financial sector during the late 2000s financial crisis, and the global economic slowdown thereafter. The data seem to confirm this. The average public deficit in the eurozone was only 0.7 per cent of GDP in 2007; by 2010 it had jumped to 6 per cent. At the same time, the eurozone's overall public debt increased from 66 to 85 per cent of GDP. In short, prior to the crisis, both the fiscal deficit and the public debt of the EMU were in line with, or very close to, the parameters of the Maastricht Treaty (which sets the maximum deficit-to-GDP ratio at 3 per cent and debt-to-GDP ratio at 60 per cent). Overall, between the mid-1990s and 2007 fiscal deficits and government debts in the eurozone actually shrank (see Figure 3.1).

Nor was it the case that the 'virtuous' countries of northern Europe were compensating for the spendthrift countries of the south, the so-called PIIGS. Portugal's debt-to-GDP ratio, which was 63 per cent in 2007, had jumped to 108 per cent by 2011. Spain's ratio, below 40 per cent in 2007, had risen to 69 per cent by 2011. Ireland went from a debt level as low as 25 per cent in 2007 to a staggering 106 per cent in 2011. (A 2011 audit of Ireland's public debt revealed that 75 per cent of the country's debt was ascribable to the government's bail-out of the banks.[1]) Italy's public debt has been relatively high since its entrance in the EMU, a legacy of the admittedly irresponsible public policies pursued in the 1970s and 1980s, but had

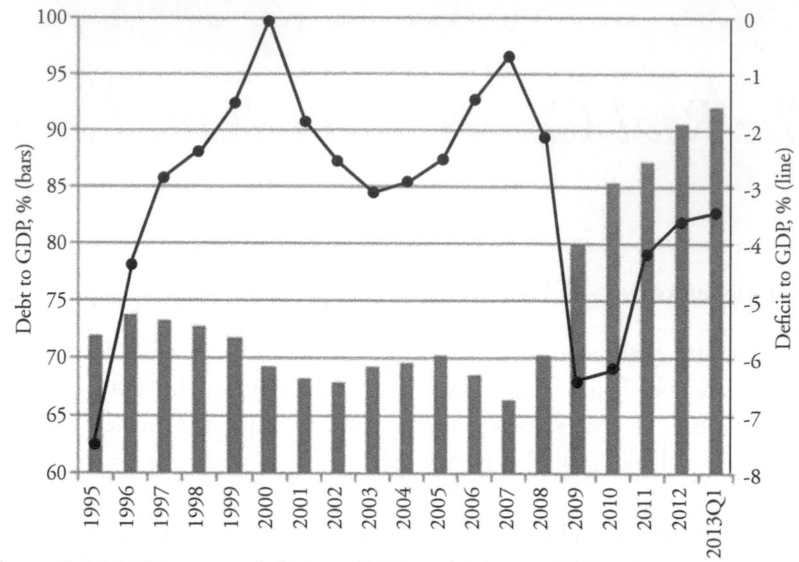

Figure 3.1 EMU average deficit-to-GDP and debt-to-GDP ratios, 1995–2013

Source: Eurostat.

been hovering stably around 105 per cent in the years leading up to the financial crisis. More importantly, up to 2007 the debt-to-GDP ratio of the PIIGS as a whole (minus Greece) had been steadily declining. That is, far from looking as if they were being profligate, the PIIGS as a group seemed to be improving their fiscal position over time (see Figure 3.2). There was indeed a build-up of debt, in the countries of the periphery as well as those of the core, in the run-up to the crisis, but (with the notable exception of Greece) this was mostly private – not public – debt. It was only with the crisis that public debt soared, especially in the periphery, as banks stepped in to save their over-leveraged banks.

As Paul Krugman and others have argued, Greece is the only country where fiscal irresponsibility contributed to the crisis (but still was not solely responsible for it).[2] Moreover, an overview of the average budget deficits of EMU countries between 1999 (the introduction of the euro) and 2007 shows that there is no direct correlation between excessive deficits and the trouble incurred by some member states in the aftermath of the financial crisis. Greece and Italy were the only two countries to make the 'top five' list of deficit spenders, alongside France, Germany and the Slovak Republic.[3]

The post-crisis increase in public debt was not just a European trend. OECD data shows that the world's advanced countries as a whole went from an average deficit of 1.4 per cent in 2007 to 6.6 per cent in 2011 ('the largest peacetime government deficits in history', according to the IMF)[4] and from an average public debt of 73.5 per cent in 2007 to 102 per cent in 2011.[5] In short, public

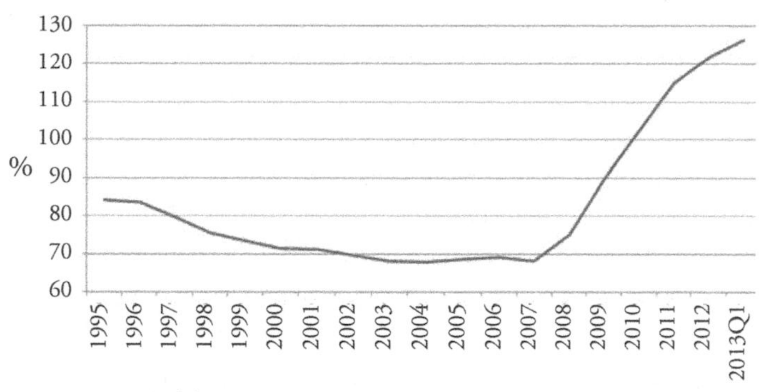

Figure 3.2 PIIGS debt-to-GDP ratio, 1995–2013

Source: Eurostat (own calculations).

debt skyrocketed everywhere as a consequence of the financial crisis. This is hardly surprising, considering that in the three years following the crisis the world's governments injected into the financial system between $12 and $15 trillion of taxpayers' money – of which €4.6 trillion was contributed in the European Union alone.[6] These countries did not have the money to hand, though; they had to borrow it. In other words, states got themselves into debt because they had to borrow from financial markets the money necessary to save the financial markets, thus transferring a mountain of debt directly from the financial system to governments – and sowing the seeds of the euro crisis in Europe. The crisis was not resolved, but simply postponed, with the liabilities transferred from one sector of society to another. In this sense, increased public indebtedness is the direct result of the 2008 financial crisis. As Paul Krugman and Richard Layard write, 'the large government deficits we see today are a consequence of the crisis, not its cause'.[7]

This is only part of the story, though. If there is little doubt that the dramatic increase in public debt over the course of the past six years, not only in Europe but in the entire developed world, is the direct result of the 2008 financial crisis, there is also little reason to deny that government debt ratios, after a steep decline between the mid-1940s and mid-1970s, have been steadily on the rise in advanced countries for the past 30 years, especially in Europe and the United States (see Figure 3.3).[8]

Does this mean that the pro-austerity camp is right after all, and that 'the additional debt burden of recent years was just the last straw to break the camel's back', weighted down as it was by years of excessive social welfare spending, as Wolfgang Schäuble so eloquently put it? While public expenditure did indeed increase in advanced countries throughout the 1980s, many experts attribute the rising primary deficits registered in a number of countries over the same period to weak economic growth, to the steady decline in the share of GDP going to salaries (as a result of neoliberal labour policies), and to a large degree, to the fiscal counter-revolution of the 1980s, which reduced the fiscal burden on high income-earners and

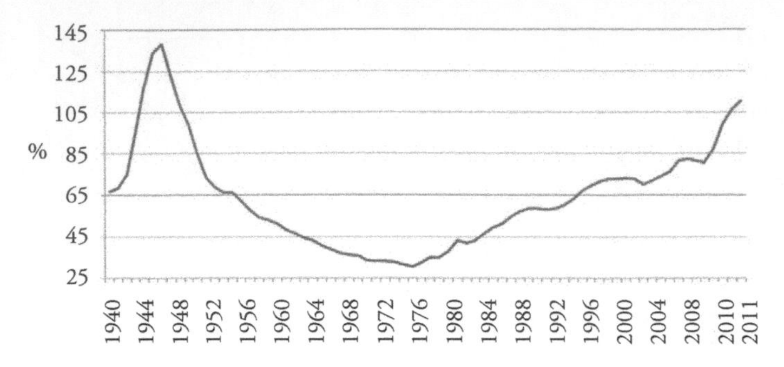

Figure 3.3 Debt-to-GDP ratio of G20 advanced countries, 1940–2011

Source: IMF.

corporations, at the expense of the working and middle classes – and of governments, which in various cases saw their revenues decrease or stagnate.[9] This in turn led to an increase in public debt levels, as governments were forced to borrow from well-off households and financial markets to make up for the loss in tax revenues.[10]

In fact, despite the fact that public spending has been stable or declining in most developed countries since the early 1990s, public debt levels have continued to grow (also as a result of the interest payments on the accumulated debt).[11] Moreover, even in those countries that registered a primary balance or surplus (meaning that their governments collected in revenues as much as or more than they spent) – and advanced countries on average had an almost continuous primary balance/surplus from the post-war period up to the financial crisis – revenues were not sufficient to keep up with skyrocketing debt-servicing costs, resulting in overall budget deficits. The rise of borrowing costs was another by-product of financial liberalisation (among other reasons), as the IMF notes: under the Bretton Woods regime, strict capital controls and tight financial regulation forced banks to invest nationally rather than internationally, which led to low borrowing costs and allowed governments to spend extensively on infrastructural development and welfare programs. By contrast, the turn towards neoliberalism – marked by the liberalisation of capital movements and the deregulation of finance – caused governments to increasingly lose control over interest rates, leading to increased borrowing costs.[12]

This has further exacerbated social inequality, in what the French *collectif* of Appalled Economists calls the 'jackpot effect': tax cuts for the wealthy increase the disposable income of those who need it the least, who as a result can invest their increased capital in government bonds, and the interest on these is paid by the state from the tax revenues paid by all taxpayers.[13] 'On the whole, a mechanism of upwards redistribution has been set up, from the lower to the upper classes, via public debt', they write.[14] In this sense, the increase in public debt in Europe and the United States is the result not of expensive social policies, but rather of a policy in favour of the lucky few – what today we call the 1 per cent – and of course the banks. In short, neoliberal policies and financial liberalisation have not just made the rich richer and everyone else relatively poorer, increasing social inequalities and household debt and thus paving the way to the financial crisis of 2008, as we saw in Chapter 1. They have also made states poorer and more indebted – which is one of the main reasons that so many European countries registered relatively high levels of public debt even before the financial crisis sent those levels through the roof.

In Europe, to make things worse, since the introduction of the euro member states have engaged in tax competition with each other, lowering corporate taxes, as well as taxes on high incomes and assets, in a bid to attract capital. This is called 'fiscal dumping', and is one of the reasons that today the average corporate tax in Europe is at an all-time low of 23 per cent, almost half the US average of 40 per cent. Fiscal dumping enables some of the largest corporations operating in Europe to get away with paying even less than the (already low) European average, by resorting to increasingly sophisticated, elaborate (and totally legal) book-keeping tricks to game the system and avoid billions in taxes. They do this mostly by channelling their earnings through low-tax countries like Ireland, Switzerland and Luxembourg. Some of the worst offenders include global behemoths like Apple (which in 2012 ended up paying a ridiculously low tax rate of 1.9 per cent on its foreign earnings by running its foreign operations through Irish and Dutch subsidiaries), Amazon, Google, Ebay, Starbucks and Cisco Systems.[15] Estimating the revenue loss from tax avoidance is extremely complicated, but Richard Murphy, director of Tax Research UK, concluded in one of the most comprehensive studies to date that it could be as high as €150 billion per year.[16]

Neoliberal fiscal policies and the related issue of tax avoidance – that is, the utilisation by companies and top income-earners of legal measures to pay less taxes – are only part of the problem, though. When it comes to the question of 'tax justice' (or lack thereof) and its repercussions on inequality and public debt, these are only the tip of the iceberg. The deregulation of capital flows in the 1980s and 1990s offered the world's wealthiest individuals and corporations an even better tool for paying less (or no) taxes: tax havens.

There is disagreement over what exactly constitutes a tax haven. According to the UK-based Tax Justice Network (TJN) 'blacklist', there are 73 tax havens – or 'secrecy jurisdictions', as the organisation prefers to call them – in the world, defined as jurisdictions whose laws and other measures are designed first and foremost to attract illicit flows by enabling individuals or corporations to evade the taxes or regulations of other jurisdictions, and comprising some of the world's biggest and wealthiest countries.[17] Shockingly, eight of the world's 20 largest and most secretive tax havens – Switzerland, Luxembourg, Jersey, Germany ('the home for large volumes of tax-evading and other illicit flows and assets from around the globe'), the United Kingdom, Belgium, Austria and Cyprus – are located in Europe (and with the exception of Switzerland and Jersey, are part of the European Union).

Another three – the Cayman Islands, the British Virgin Islands and Bermuda – are overseas territories of EU countries. The list also includes a host of other European countries, dependencies or overseas territories: Ireland, the Netherlands, Italy, Denmark, Portugal (Madeira), Spain, Malta, Hungary, Liechtenstein, Latvia, Monaco, San Marino, Gibraltar, Andorra, Guernsey, the Isle of Man, the Turks and Caicos Islands, the Netherlands Antilles, Montserrat and Anguilla.

Because of the innate shadiness and secrecy of tax havens, the precise amount of money that is held in these 'treasure countries' is unknown, as is the proportion that is illicit. While incomplete, the available statistics nonetheless indicate that offshore banking is a very sizeable activity. In the most thorough study to date, James S. Henry, former chief economist at consulting firm McKinsey & Company and senior advisor for TJN, places the estimate between \$21 trillion and \$32 trillion. That is equivalent to 24–32 per cent of total global investments, and is as much as the US and Japanese GDPs put together. Of this, \$9.8 trillion is owned by the top tier of fewer than 100,000 people who each have financial assets of \$30 million or more.[18]

Contrary to long-held popular views, the biggest users of tax havens are not terrorists and drug traffickers, but big corporations and wealthy individuals. This system of tax evasion is 'basically designed and operated' by a group of highly paid specialists from the world's largest private banks, led by UBS, Credit Suisse and Goldman Sachs (and including various financial institutions that received generous government bail-outs in the aftermath of the crisis), law offices and accounting firms. This activity is tolerated by international organisations such as the Bank for International Settlements, the IMF, the World Bank, the OECD and the G20 – unsurprisingly, given that rich countries are the main recipients of these illicit flows.[19]

The sheer size of the wealth hidden offshore by this global super-rich elite is so great that it suggests that inequality, both globally and within countries – which has reached unprecedented proportions even according to official estimates – is actually radically underestimated. According to TJN estimates, at least a third of all private financial wealth, and nearly half of all offshore wealth, is now owned by world's richest 91,000 people – just 0.001 per cent of the world's population. The next 51 per cent of all wealth is owned by the next 8.4 million, another trivial 0.14 per cent of the world's population.[20]

Henry says:

> This 'offshore economy' is large enough to have a major impact on estimates of inequality of wealth and income; on estimates of national income and debt ratios; and – most importantly – to have very significant negative impacts on the domestic tax bases of 'source' countries.[21]

The report indicates that this hidden money results in a huge loss in tax revenues for countries – a black hole in their economies. TJN has estimated, conservatively, that between $190 billion and $280 billion – assuming a 3 per cent capital gains rate and a 30 per cent capital gains tax rate – are lost in taxes every year by governments worldwide solely as a result of wealthy individuals holding their assets offshore.[22] When the losses from corporate tax evasion are factored in as well, the results are simply astonishing – and enraging. Murphy's comprehensive study estimated the revenue losses from tax evasion in the European Union to be €860 billion a year.[23] In other words, it is likely that tax evasion and tax avoidance together cost EU member states €1 trillion a year.

In his ground-breaking report, Murphy also estimated the size of the shadow economy in relation to each member state's economy. The results are again shocking. On an unweighted average basis, according to the study, European shadow economies amount to 22.1 per cent of total economic activity, equivalent to 17.6 per cent of the total government spending of EU countries, and 105.8 per cent of total health-care spending. In other words, the money governments lose from tax evasion is more than they spend on health care. Murphy then goes on to compare the revenue losses from tax evasion with government deficits and total government borrowing in the European Union: see Table 3.1 (overleaf).

In 16 of the EU member states – and in the EU as a whole – the estimated taxes lost because of the shadow economy are greater than the annual deficit. So tackling tax evasion could, in theory, entirely clear the EU annual deficit in just a few years. If only part of the lost tax was collected it would still contribute significantly, and 'debt would cease to be an issue threatening the well being of hundreds of millions of people in Europe as a result', as Murphy writes.[24] In conclusion, Murphy's report shows that while not all EU countries are equally affected by tax evasion – Italy is estimated to lose the most, more than €180 billion a year, equivalent to 253 per cent of its annual deficit – this is not an individual country problem.

Murphy spells out a clear message: '[T]ax evasion and tax avoidance undermine the viability of the economies of Europe and have without doubt helped create the current debt crisis that threatens the well being of hundreds of millions of people across Europe for years to come'.[25] This puts to shame the argument that the crisis was caused by workers toiling too little, governments spending too much and citizens enjoying too 'generous' welfare systems – and that 'there is no alternative' to austerity. It shows that the main culprits of Europe's debt crisis are the continent's wealthy, corporations and banks – precisely those that the European elites have been aiding and abetting for decades through tax cuts, hand-outs, bail-outs, privatisations, neoliberal attacks on labour and welfare systems, and now austerity. It shows that tax havens have played a crucial role in the systematic plunder of Europe's wealth and pauperisation of its governments, and that putting an end to tax evasion could solve most of Europe's debt problems.

And yet the core European public discourse is still dominated by the claim that Europe cannot afford to maintain the social and economic standards to which

Table 3.1 Tax evasion and public finances

Country	GDP (2009, € billion)	Size of the shadow economy (€ billion)	Taxes lost as result of the shadow economy (€ billion)
Austria	284	27.5	11.8
Belgium	353	77.3	33.6
Bulgaria	36	12.7	3.7
Cyprus	17	4.8	1.7
Czech Republic	145	26.7	9.2
Denmark	234	41.4	19.9
Estonia	15	4.7	1.7
Finland	180	31.9	13.7
France	1,933	290.0	120.6
Germany	2,499	399.8	158.7
Greece	230	63.3	19.2
Hungary	98	23.9	9.4
Ireland	156	24.6	7.0
Italy	1,549	418.2	180.3
Latvia	18	5.3	1.4
Lithuania	27	8.6	2.5
Luxembourg	42	4.1	1.5
Malta	6.2	1.7	0.6
Netherlands	591	78.0	29.8
Poland	354	96.3	30.6
Portugal	173	39.8	12.3
Romania	122	39.8	10.7
Slovakia	66	11.9	3.44
Slovenia	36	9.4	3.5
Spain	1,063	239.2	72.7
Sweden	347	65.2	30.6
United Kingdom	1,697	212.1	74.0
Total or unweighted average	12,271	2,258.2	864.3

Source: Richard Murphy, *Closing the European Tax Gap.*

its citizens have been accustomed. This widespread and powerful assumption has slowly percolated into the public consciousness, which is probably one reason that in some countries austerity measures have not sparked the kind of resistance that might have been expected. Many of those who oppose austerity in principle have nonetheless internalised the idea that 'we're running of out of money', and have thus been more willing to accept the post-crisis 'brave new Europe'. All this is perfectly understandable, considering that 'crisis' has been one of the most-used words in the English language over the last five years.

But the evidence of these studies is that Europe (as a whole) is far from broke. It is still the largest economy in the world. With a GDP of more than €15.5 trillion,

Annual deficit (2010, € billion)	Taxes lost as a percentage of annual deficit	Government borrowing (2010, € billion)	Years it would take lost taxes to repay debt
13.2	89.3	205.2	17.4
14.4	234.3	341.0	10.1
2.3	161.9	11.4	3.1
0.9	180.4	10.6	6.4
6.8	135.1	55.8	6.1
6.3	315.3	102.0	5.1
-0.02	0.0	1.0	0.6
4.4	310.2	87.2	6.4
136.5	88.3	1,519.2	13.2
81.6	194.5	2,079.6	13.1
24.2	79.2	328.6	17.1
4.1	229.5	78.6	8.3
49.9	13.9	148.1	21.3
71.2	253.1	1,843.0	10.2
1.4	100.9	6.9	4.9
1.9	132.1	10.3	4.1
0.7	212.9	7.7	5.1
0.2	255.2	4.2	7.4
32.0	93.2	371.0	12.5
28.0	109.5	194.7	6.4
15.8	78.2	160.5	13.0
7.8	137.5	37.6	3.5
5.2	66.1	27.0	7.8
2.0	175.0	13.7	3.9
98.2	74.0	638.8	8.8
0.0	0.0	138.1	4.5
176.5	41.9	1,357	18.3
785.6	139.3	9,778.8	8.8

the EU economy is larger than that of the United States. With 20 per cent of world trade, the European Union is also the world's second-largest exporter (after China) and importer (after the United States).[26] The European Union is, quite simply, the world's leading commercial power. Europe, alongside the United States, is also the region with the highest total wealth in the world, as well as the one with the highest ratio of private wealth to national income.[27] That's not all, though: Europe is also the region that is home to the second highest percentage of the richest 10 per cent in the world (after the United States).[28] The majority of the richest 1 per cent in the world are found in the United States (with Europe in second place), but surprisingly many are concentrated in European countries whose area and population are much smaller: France (7 per cent), the United Kingdom (5 per cent), Germany (5 per cent), Italy (5 per cent) and Switzerland (2 per cent).[29] Although the European Union's millionaires (70 per cent of whom live in those five countries) make up only 1.8 per cent of the population, their wealth is equivalent to two-thirds of the European Union's total GDP – €7.6 trillion in 2012.[30]

In other words, it is not Europe that is poor, but its governments (and a growing percentage of its citizens). And this is largely a consequence of the neoliberal fiscal policies and capital flow liberalisations introduced in the 1980s and 1990s, which allowed the continent's wealthiest individuals and corporations to avoid paying their fair share of taxes. It is also one of the main reasons that some of the wealthiest countries in the world, especially in Europe, are also among the most indebted. As Gabriel Zucman of the Paris School of Economics writes matter-of-factly in his study *The Missing Wealth of Nations*, 'rich countries taken as a whole are rich, but some of their wealthiest residents hide part of their assets in tax havens, which contributes to making governments poor'.[31]

The 'Enronisation' of Europe's Sovereign Debt

If the neoliberal answer to the widening gap between income and spending (itself a consequence of neoliberalism) was, as we saw in Chapter 1, debt-led consumption through a 'democratisation of credit' – a perfect example of the problem being offered as the solution – finance's answer to the rise in public debt levels in Europe from the 1980s onwards (itself a consequence of neoliberal anti-redistributive tax policies, tax havens and financial deregulation) was – window-dressing.[32]

In 1992, the members of the European Union signed the Maastricht Treaty, under which they pledged to limit their deficit spending to 3 per cent of GDP and their debt levels to 60 per cent of GDP. However, a number of EU member states were able to circumvent these rules through the use of complex currency and credit derivative structures. These financial products helped countries lower their deficit-to-GDP and debt-to-GDP ratios by many tenths of a percentage point for individual years – helping governments obey the rules for EMU membership – while increasing their long-term liabilities. Such structures were designed and pitched to governments by prominent US investment banks, which received substantial fees in return for their services. In very simple terms, the banks provided cash upfront for governments, in return for (very hefty) repayments in the future, while allowing countries to keep the loans off their balance sheets and hide their mounting debts. This was a Wall Street tactic akin to the one that fostered the subprime crisis in the United States.

According to Nicholas Dunbar, one of the first journalists to break the story of the 'Maastricht derivative structures' in 2003, this was a direct consequence of the unrealistic limits imposed by the Maastricht Treaty: 'For some time, economists have argued that the combination of strict external targets with considerable local autonomy in sovereign debt management almost inevitably leads high-deficit countries towards derivatives', he wrote.[33] The most notable example is Greece. As we saw, the spark that ignited the euro crisis was the announcement by the newly elected Greek government, in autumn 2009, that the country's budget deficit was almost double the previous government's estimate (12 per cent instead of 7 per cent). How had the Greek government managed to conceal such a black hole in its accounts? The answer came in early 2010, when it was revealed that Greece had paid Goldman Sachs and other banks hundreds of millions of dollars in fees since 2001 for arranging transactions that hid the government's actual level of borrowing, allowing the country to artificially comply with the monetary union guidelines. Most notable was a €2.8 billion 'cross currency swap', signed in 2000 and 2001 – the largest sovereign derivative deal ever reported – where billions worth of Greek debts and loans were converted into yen and dollars at a fictitious exchange rate by Goldman Sachs, thus hiding the true extent of the Greek loans. The swap reduced the country's euro-denominated debt by €2.37 billion and lowered its debt as a proportion of GDP to 103.7 per cent from 105.3 per cent, according to a statement by Goldman Sachs.[34] As Nicholas Dunbar explains:

> The effect of this was to create an upfront payment by Goldman to Greece at inception, and an increased stream of interest payments to Greece during the lifetime of the swap. Goldman would recoup these non-standard cashflows at maturity, receiving a large 'balloon' cash payment from Greece.[35]

Dunbar estimates that Greece ended up paying Goldman Sachs 'a crazy borrowing rate' of about 16 per cent a year, earning the US investment bank hundreds of millions of dollars.[36] Interestingly, just as it was standard practice for Goldman Sachs, in the lead-up to the US subprime crisis, to bet on the insolvency (through the use of credit default swaps) of those same loans that it was selling on to investors – a move that earned Goldman billions of dollars when the subprime bubble eventually burst – the American investment bank also chose to hedge its exposure to Greece by buying a credit default swap on the Greek deal from the Frankfurt-based Deutsche Pfandbriefbank. While such contracts are a win-win deals for banks like Goldman Sachs, over time they can prove disastrous for the countries involved – and even more so for their citizens. Surprisingly, such deals were perfectly legal under European regulation (until the rules on swaps were eventually tightened in March 2008).[37]

According to Reuters, most deals were known to Eurostat, the European Union's statistics agency, at the time they were conducted.[38] Following the disclosure of the Greek swap deal, the EU authorities went out of their way to keep the details of the deal secret. In December 2010 the US news company Bloomberg took legal action to try to force the ECB to provide the documents about the Greece–Goldman Sachs swap deal under EU freedom of information rules, but the ECB has consistently refused to disclose any documents related to the case. Such lack of transparency is worrying, especially since Greece was not alone in resorting to such financial wizardry. Experts believe that in the 1990s and early 2000s to varying degrees all EU countries resorted to highly structured financial products to 'clean up' their accounts. The most notable was Italy, which earned itself the title of 'Enron of the European Union' for the great number of alleged derivative deals signed in the late 1990s while Mario Draghi, current president of the ECB, was director-general of the Italian Treasury. He went on to join Goldman Sachs International in 2002.[39]

Although the full extent of the exposure of EU countries to the derivatives market is unknown, not least because of the implicitly shady nature of these deals, Bloomberg recently revealed that Italy – one of the most exposed countries in the European Union, if not on the planet – holds derivatives contracts on about €160 billion of debt. This is equivalent to almost 10 per cent of all government securities in circulation. Italy is estimated to have lost more than $31 billion on the deals at current market values.[40]

In early 2011 one of the first measures undertaken by the newly appointed technocratic government of former Goldman Sachs advisor Mario Monti was to pay US financial giant Morgan Stanley €2.57 billion – equal to half the amount the government planned to raise with a controversial sales tax increase that year, or 0.15 per cent of Italy's GDP – to terminate an interest rate swap struck with the bank more than 20 years earlier.[41] According to a source within the Italian Treasury quoted by Bloomberg, Italy 'paid the money to unwind derivative contracts from the 1990s that had backfired'.[42] This dramatically underscores the danger of resorting to derivatives. Citizens are now paying huge interests on decades-old derivative deals peddled by big banks to government officials who often 'lack the technical expertise to fulfill their duties optimally' and have 'no understanding of the nature' and implications of these contracts, says Italian academic Gustavo Piga, who first exposed the Italian derivatives scandal in 2001.[43]

Although it is hard to believe, even national parliaments are often kept in the dark about such deals. According to the Italian weekly magazine *l'Espresso*, no government in the past 20 years has informed the Italian parliament about the full derivative exposure of the Treasury, or its relative losses and gains.[44] Such a state of affairs is unacceptable in a democracy. As stated by a manifesto signed by dozens of European unions and social movements, it calls 'for an audit of public debt under citizens' control, to assess the part of the debt which is illegitimate and whose burden and reimbursement should not fall on the shoulders of the citizens'.[45]

In short, neoliberalism did not simply lead to a colossal rise in private debt, as households borrowed more and more to make up the difference between spending and income. It also led to a dramatic rise in public debt, as governments borrowed more and more (from their wealthiest citizens and from the financial markets) to make up for the fall in tax revenues because of lowered tax rates on high incomes and corporate profits, and industrial-scale tax evasion. Then (in Europe at least) they covered up the holes through complex derivative schemes, which were also provided by the financial industry, to comply with the unrealistic limits imposed by the Maastricht Treaty.

In this sense the crisis really was 'the last straw to break the camel's back', but the previous burden on the camel had been imposed not by excessive welfare spending, but by neoliberal economic policies. If anything, it was the biggest welfare states in Europe – the Nordic countries that resisted blindly applying the neoliberal welfare-slashing, tax-cutting dogma – that fared best in the aftermath of the crisis.

The welfare state played a crucial role in promoting economic growth and social equality in the second half of the 20th century. The same is true today. The World Economic Forum (WEF) *Global Competitiveness Report* ranks countries on 12 pillars of competitiveness such as infrastructure, health care, education and technological readiness. Governments contribute heavily to these pillars, so the national ability to deliver them depends largely on tax revenues. Of the WEF's four most 'competitive' countries in 2011, two – Sweden and Finland – were among the countries worldwide with the highest tax levels and social expenditure.[46]

To recap, it was only with the post-crisis recession and bank bail-outs that deficit-to-GDP and debt-to-GDP ratios exploded across Europe; but the same happened in a number of developed nations (first and foremost, in the United States). So what caused the financial crisis to become a 'sovereign debt crisis' in Europe, and Europe alone – and only in certain European countries?

It's the Trade Imbalances, Stupid

There is a growing body of evidence that the root of the euro crisis – the reason Europe has been affected by the financial crisis more profoundly, and for a longer period of time, than any other continent – lies in the way that the monetary union was created. To understand the euro, and its flaws, it is necessary to understand the political context in which it was conceived and created.

The euro was never just about economics. For the European elites, it was a historical and highly symbolic landmark in the continent's 60-year-long march from war and chaos towards ever-greater peace, unity and democracy. As Paul Krugman writes, the 'European elites were so enthralled with the idea of creating a powerful symbol of unity that they played up the gains from a single currency and brushed aside warnings of a significant downside'. The major downside was that, with little inter-European labour mobility and the lack of a central government and/or a coordinated economic policy, there was little to stop highly competitive economies (like Germany) and less competitive ones (like Greece or Spain) from becoming increasingly economically divergent.[47] Krugman was one of the economists who participated in the debate over the creation of the euro. He recalls:

> When one asked how Europe would handle situations in which some economies were doing well while others were slumping – as is the case for Germany and Spain, respectively, right now – the official answer, more or less, was that all the nations of the euro area would follow sound policies, so that there would be no such 'asymmetric shocks,' and if they did somehow happen, 'structural reform' would render European economies flexible enough to make the necessary adjustments. What actually happened, however, was the mother of all asymmetric shocks. And it was the creation of the euro itself that caused it.[48]

When the euro officially came into existence in 1999 (though it only materialised as cash in people's pockets three years later), it immediately had a fateful effect. It made investors feel safe in putting their money into countries that had previously been considered risky. Prior to the euro, interest rates on government bonds in southern Europe had historically been substantially higher than rates in Germany, because investors demanded a premium to compensate for the risk of devaluation. With the introduction of the euro, the spread collapsed and interest rates rapidly converged across the European board, as investors started to view southern European government bonds as almost as safe as German ones.

At that point it made sense for commercial banks to accumulate the bonds of weaker countries, because they offered slightly higher interest rates but there was perceived to be little or no additional risk. As money started to flow into the periphery, the cost of borrowing money in those countries dropped dramatically. As we have seen, this led to huge housing and consumption booms which quickly turned into huge bubbles (especially in Greece, Ireland and Spain). While these countries enjoyed housing and consumption booms on the back of cheap credit, thus becoming less competitive, Germany, which was struggling with the burdens of reunification, undertook a series of structural reforms – mostly based on wage moderation – that made the country increasingly competitive.

This was the result of a set of decisions made by Schröder's social-democratic government (and continued by Merkel's conservative government) which emphasised the export sector as the main motor of the economy. The core of Schröder's 'revolution' was the 2003–04 'Hartz IV' labour reform, which merged unemployment benefits and welfare at a lower level and expanded the low-wage sector. It led to a proliferation of low-paid, low-skilled jobs, also known as 'mini-jobs'.[49] A recent study by the Deutsches Institut für Wirtschaftsforschung (DIW), one of Germany's leading economic research institutes, emphasises the heavy price paid by German workers. Today the lower decile (the 10 per cent at the bottom of the social scale) earns a meagre €259 a month, and the second decile makes no more than €614 a month.[50] According to DIW, 80 per cent of the active German population saw a decrease in purchasing power between 2000 and 2010, while returns on capital grew dramatically.

The reforms had serious social effects, exemplified in the fact that life expectancy fell from 77 to 75 years.[51] But by squeezing wages and incomes, Germany drastically cut costs for its exporters, who benefited as a result.

The inflows of capital to the south, on the other hand, fed booms that led to rising wages, (although it should be stressed that the productivity increases from 1991 to the mid-2000s exceeded the increase in real wages in all Western EU countries except Portugal). In the decade after the euro's creation, unit labour costs (ULCs) rose about 35 per cent in southern Europe, compared with a rise of only 9 per cent in Germany.[52]

As a result, periphery countries lost competitiveness in comparison with Germany. Germany came to dominate trade and capital flows within the currency bloc, as exports from the north became cheap for the south. Germany's total export trade value more than tripled between 2000 and 2007, greatly improving the country's balance of trade.[53]

The balance of trade is one of the most important parameters of a country's economic performance – especially in today's globalised, export-driven world. It can be summed up as the relationship between a nation's imports and exports. If a nation exports more than it imports (meaning that it earns more than it spends, broadly speaking), it has a trade surplus; if not, it has a trade deficit. As a result of Germany's increase in exports, between 2000 and 2007 its trade surplus increased from €60 billion to €195 billion.[54] All the periphery countries (with the exception of Ireland), on the other hand, witnessed a dramatic worsening of their trade balance over the same seven-year period. Italy went from a €1.9 billion surplus to an €8.6 billion deficit; Spain's deficit more than doubled, from €44.3 billion to €99.2 billion; Greece, which in the 1980s had had a trade balance, saw its deficit go from €23.5 billion to €38.4 billion; and Portugal's deficit went from €16.9 billion to €19.7 billion. Ireland stands out as the only periphery country that managed to retain a constant trade surplus in the years following the creation of the euro. Figure 3.4 shows the massive rise of trade imbalances within the EMU after the introduction of the euro. One line shows Germany's current account balance (a broad measure of the trade balance); the other shows the combined current account balances of the PIIGS.

Obviously, it is not a coincidence that Germany's surplus is mirrored by the PIIGS' deficit. Although a significant proportion of Germany's impressive post-euro trade surplus increase is accounted for by trade with extra-EU countries, its trade surplus with the rest of the European Union grew from €46.5 billion to

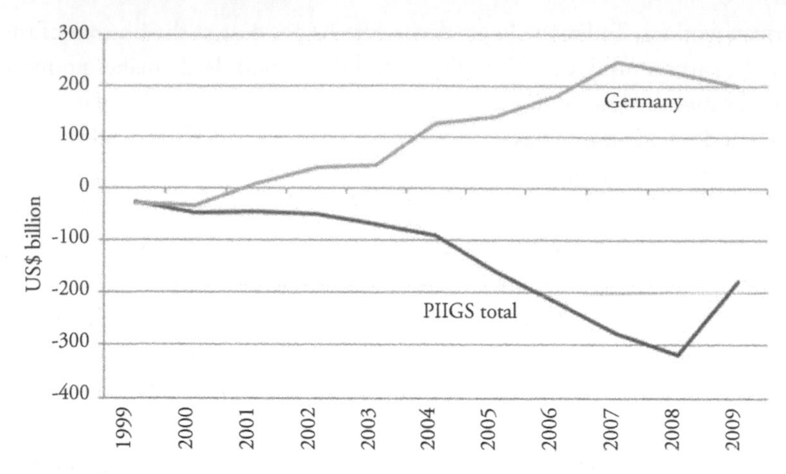

Figure 3.4 Current account balance of Germany and PIIGS countries, 1999–2009

Source: IMF.

€126.5 billion during those seven years. A large proportion of this came from trade with the countries of the Mediterranean. Between 2000 and 2007, Greece's annual trade deficit with Germany grew from €3.4 billion to €5 billion; Portugal's more than doubled, from €1.2 billion to €2.5 billion; Italy's almost tripled, from €5.9 billion to €16.5 billion; and Spain's almost tripled as well, from €10.7 billion to €25.8 billion. Ireland is the only periphery country to have constantly registered a surplus with Germany over the 2000–07 period, but the amount plummeted from €6 billion to less than €1 billion. In other words, although Europe had seen a more or less balanced trade between its countries since the 1980s, from 2000 onwards the countries became increasingly divided into creditors and debtors.

Many experts consider this widening spread – a direct consequence of the way the monetary union was created – to be at the heart of Europe's problems. The reasons are easily explained. In the pre-euro system of multiple currencies, a trade deficit would have caused a country's currency to depreciate, making its exports cheaper, while a surplus would have caused its currency to rise, or appreciate, making its exports more expensive and its imports cheaper. So there was a natural corrective mechanism to prevent continuing deficits and surpluses. In the euro system, on the other hand, the value of the currency is determined by the combined performance of its major economies. Therefore, there is no way for countries within the system to adjust the value of their currency relative to each other. Imports from EMU countries with sustained trade surpluses (such as Germany) do not become more expensive for the countries with sustained deficits, and nor do the exports to such countries become cheaper.

A wide body of evidence points to the fact that a system of fixed exchange rates can only work properly if unit labour costs (ULCs) converge and eliminate the need for exchange rate flexibility.[55] The easiest way to achieve this is to ensure that in all member countries the ULCs increase in line with the commonly agreed inflation target, which is 2 per cent for the EMU.[56] Since the euro's inception, though, member countries have done the exact opposite. It is certainly true that periphery countries overshot their target, by letting their wages rise more than they should have – and thus were, in this sense, 'living beyond their means' – but it is also true that Germany *undershot* its target by an even greater degree, as progressive economists Costas Lapavitsas and Heiner Flassbeck note. It did this, as we have seen, by exerting enormous pressure on wage negotiations to improve the country's international competitiveness, both inside and outside the EMU, despite its growing trade surplus .[57]

Germany's increased competitiveness was largely a result of this policy of wage compression, not of a growth in productivity. Its productivity growth rate was actually lower than Greece's over the 2000–08 period.[58] In economics, this is known as 'beggar-thy-neighbour' policy: simply put, a country that has a great deal of trade with its neighbours is able to achieve huge economic gains if it 'beggars' these neighbours by robbing them of significant market shares in regional and global trade. In short, despite all the talk of 'European solidarity' which accompanied the creation of the euro, by creating a monetary union without a proper fiscal and economic union, let alone a common industrial policy, its member states were effectively pitted one against the other in a highly competitive (and, to some extent, rigged) arena. The emergence of winners and losers crystallised and exacerbated the tensions and imbalances of European capitalism, sowing the seeds of the crisis.

These imbalances exploded in 2008. As we saw, the countries of the periphery that had sustained their growing trade deficits – and had allowed their banks to fuel huge housing and consumption booms – by borrowing cheap money from abroad, became increasingly unable to obtain finance in the commercial markets. In Ireland, Spain and elsewhere, the same institutions that had poured in huge amounts of capital pulled their money out as soon as the booms they had helped create went bust. These countries were left with inflated, uncompetitive wages, and their economies ground to a halt. The crisis had nothing to do with higher social spending: on the whole these countries had lower welfare budgets than their northern neighbours.[59]

These booms-gone-bust also highlight the risks of unregulated capital flows. Simply put, there was nothing to control the flow of money either in or out of an individual country. As we have seen, this was a consequence of the policy of financial liberalisation spearheaded by Europe in the 1980s and 1990s and then institutionalised in the EMU's architecture.

After the introduction of the euro there was a major increase in cross-border bank activity. The vice-president of the ECB, the Portuguese Vítor Constâncio, recently acknowledged the problems this exemplified:

> The European rules on free movement of capital, the objective to create a level-playing field for different banking sectors, and the belief in the efficiency of supposed self-equilibrating financial markets, all conspired to make it very difficult to implement any sort of containment policy.[60]

The situation this led to was more typically 'characteristic of emerging economies'. A sudden stop – or, even worse, a reversion – of cross-border flows could easily happen, with disastrous consequences for the country involved – and it did.

Even in the face of demand-crushing austerity at home, countries that devalue in order to improve their competitiveness can normally count on foreign demand to pick up some of the slack caused by a lack of domestic demand. A good example is Iceland, which still has its own currency. After its economy collapsed it devalued its currency, giving a boost to local producers and exporters. Since 2011 Iceland's economy has started to grow again, while its unemployment rates and public debt levels have been falling. Within a common currency, though, the option of devaluation is not available unless the currency bloc as a whole takes this route. So it is much more difficult for member states facing a trade deficit to accomplish the transition to a surplus.

Countries that are shackled to the euro have two options to improve their competitiveness. They can either leave the euro and readopt their own currency (an option discussed later), or they can slowly and painfully force down real costs through deflation. Deflation – also known as 'internal devaluation' – is economic jargon for lower wages. Basically, if two countries have the same currency, and one country's wages grow too high compared with the other (as is the case with Spain and Germany, for example), the easiest way (from a purely economic perspective, ignoring any human cost) for the inflated country to become competitive again is to push its workers into accepting lower wages. Hence the solution offered by Germany and the EU-ECB-IMF troika to countries in trouble: lower wages and German-style labour reforms, coupled with drastic government spending cuts.

As we have seen, Germany was quick to blame the post-crisis high deficit/debt levels of the PIIGS on excessive government spending. In much the same way, it put the blame for their trade deficits on their lack of competiveness. This was claimed to be a result of the 'laziness' of their workers. This crisis-related myth too is largely unfounded. OECD data shows that Greek workers put in more hours per year than those in any other European country, while from 1995 to 2005 labour productivity growth in Greece was way ahead of the EMU average.[61]

This post-crisis narrative of the virtuous masses of the core and the deficient minority of the periphery has been described as 'neoliberal economic populism' by Victoria Stoiciu of the Bonn-based Friedrich Ebert Foundation. It aims at demonising some sections of the European population 'so as to avoid questioning the popular legitimacy of [the austerity regime's] own draconian policies'.[62] Germany played a major role in imposing and enforcing these 'draconian policies' on other countries (through the troika), and the assumption underlying this was that Germany was the only country in the EMU that had got its policy right, so what was needed was for the other member states to improve their competitiveness by following the German wage-slashing model.

This is based on a flawed and ideologically based reading of the crisis, as we have seen: in reality Germany was as much, if not more, a violator of the commonly agreed target as anyone else. More importantly, under the current architecture of the eurozone it would be impossible to restore all the economies of the EMU to health by following these policies.

While most Germans believe that their country's recent relative success is entirely owing to the labour reforms introduced under Gerhard Schröder, the reality is that Germany's export-led growth story would not have been possible without the credit-fuelled booms in the countries of the periphery (and the artificially low value of Germany's currency). Germany certainly benefited from an efficient industrial base and (except for those reduced to poverty wages) from its labour market reforms, but this would not have been sufficient without an export market. In other words, the necessary counterpart to Germany living within – or below – its means was that others were living beyond their means. It is economically impossible for all European states to be in surplus unless the EMU as a whole runs a trade surplus with the rest of the world. And that is technically impossible in the long run, not to mention politically hazardous, as it would also greatly increase the risk of trade disputes (which have historically been the prelude to all-out military conflicts, hence the term 'currency war'). In light of this, Germany's insistence that the countries of southern Europe all develop a trade surplus of their own is at best naïve, especially considering that Germany and other northern countries, through their financial sectors, actively contributed to the bubbles in the countries of the periphery.

As a consequence of Germany's emphasis on exports, its banks accumulated huge amounts of euros – mostly from the countries of the periphery. Rather than using this money to increase demand in Germany (which would have stimulated not only the German economy, but the whole European economy), the German banks channelled their export earnings straight back into the countries of the periphery, in the form of debt. It was this that enabled those countries to keep on buying from the north. As a New Economics Foundation paper sums up this self-perpetuating (but ultimately unsustainable) economic cycle, '[s]urplus and savings on one side were matched by deficits and debts on the other'.[63] In other words, to a large extent, 'Germany self-financed its own so-called economic miracle', as the American banker and economist Daniel Alpert put it.[64] That money directly contributed to the housing bubbles in Spain and other countries: since local banks didn't have nearly enough deposits to support all the lending they were doing, they borrowed funds, on a massive scale, mainly from banks in France and Germany. By the end of 2009, according to the Bank for International Settlements, German banks had amassed claims of $720 billion on Greece, Ireland, Italy, Portugal and Spain – much more than the German banks' aggregate capital.[65] (German banks are the most highly leveraged in the eurozone, as we saw in Chapter 1.) Irresponsible borrowing, in short, was made possible by irresponsible lending.

The banks of the core, though, did not just lend massively to the banks of the periphery. They also lent huge amounts of money to the governments of those countries, especially Greece. For example, in mid-2010, when Greece received its first bail-out loan, French and German banks accounted for 60 per cent of the foreign exposure to Greek public debt. This money was also used to buy goods from the lending countries, as we shall see.[66]

Between 2006 and mid-2007 there was a significant increase in the money being loaned by core European banks to the Greek government. The loans peaked in the run-up to the financial crisis, with a 33 per cent increase between mid-2007 and mid-2008 (from $120 billion to $180 billion), and then continued to run at a very high level (around $120 billion) throughout the rest of 2008 and 2009.[67] This is easily explained. As the ECB started to flood the banks with cheap loans in the aftermath of the financial crisis, and Greek interest rates started to rise (since Greece could not obtain finance on similarly cheap terms), it became increasingly profitable for the banks to invest in Greek bonds.

It is not so much that the banks underestimated the risks involved in lending to Greece; it is rather, it seems, that they didn't care about them. Ever since the accession of Greece to the eurozone, there has been an understanding among Western European bankers that the most powerful European countries would come to their aid in the eventuality of a crisis – especially if their own banks were threatened. So far, they have been proven right. The banks might have made a wrong bet, but they did not lose financially as a result, as we shall see. Moreover, Western governments had every reason to play along with their banks' reckless lending to the Greek government. Historically, Greece has always invested heavily in defence (largely because of the perceived threat from Turkey), and the United States, Germany and France are major arms-exporting countries (see Figure 3.5). Their defence industries have benefited greatly from Greece's ability to buy their products.

Greece has been Europe's main military spender (in proportion to its size) for most of the past four decades, spending twice as much of its GDP on defence as the EU average.[68] No other area has contributed as heavily to the country's debt mountain. According to economist Angelos Philippides, if it were not for Greece's decades of formidable military spending, 'there would be no debt at all'.[69] Germany scolded Greece for its excessive government borrowing and spending in the aftermath of the crisis, but during the five years up to the end of 2010 Greece

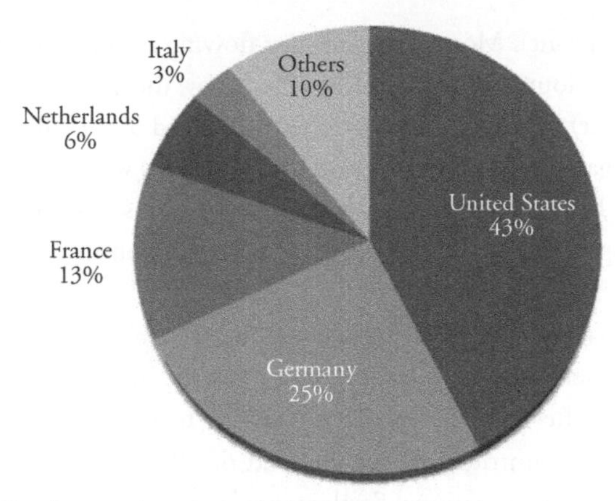

Figure 3.5 Greek arms imports, 2002–11

Source: SIPRI.

purchased 15 per cent of Germany's arms exports, more than any other country.[70] Since the onset of the financial crisis Germany's share of Greece's military expenditure has increased dramatically, reaching 58 per cent in 2010, according to the Stockholm International Peace Research Institute (SIPRI).[71] The country's overall military expenditure fell in this period, but it is hardly surprising that many suspect there was a private agreement that if Germany and France supported the bail-out, Greece would make it a priority to continue to buy military hardware from them.[72]

This is more than just a telling demonstration of the hypocritical attitude of northern countries to the issue of periphery debt and 'uncompetitiveness'. It is a crucial factor in understanding Germany's response to the euro crisis. Following the financial crash, German banks found themselves massively exposed to the banks (and to a lesser extent, the governments) of periphery countries. Understandably (in a short-term sense), Germany wanted to protect that exposure.

Bailing Out Germany (and Not Only Germany)

The bail-outs of Greece, Ireland, Portugal and Spain are often framed as loans handed out to the poor, irresponsible countries of the periphery by rich, responsible countries like Germany. They might come with very harsh conditions attached, but their aim is nonetheless to help the recipients. But is that really the case? A closer look actually reveals a more disturbing side to the bail-outs, which begs the question: is it the debtors or the creditors that ultimately are being rescued?

As we have seen, with the notable exception of Greece, the build-up of debt in the countries of the periphery in the run-up to the crisis was caused by an accumulation of mostly private – not public – debt. The banks in these countries borrowed huge amounts of money from foreign banks, which they lent on to builders and aspiring homeowners, encouraging massive debt-fuelled booms (while earning the foreign banks a nice profit). Most of this money flowing into the periphery came from the banks of just four countries: France, Germany, the United Kingdom and Belgium (in that order).[73] German banks alone had loaned $720 billion to Greece, Ireland, Italy, Portugal and Spain by the end of 2009. This was certainly far more than was prudent. Two of Germany's largest private banks, Commerzbank and Deutsche Bank, together loaned $201 billion to these countries, according to figures compiled by *Business Insider*.[74]

The result was that consumers in these countries were able to import an ever-growing amount of German goods, leading to a dramatic increase in the country's trade surplus. In the aftermath of the crisis German banks yanked $420 billion out of other euro area countries between the end of 2008 and the end of 2010, according to the Bank of International Settlements.[75] But the debt of the periphery countries did not disappear, of course. In most cases it was transferred from banks to governments, as these stepped in – in at least one case (Ireland), under direct pressure from the ECB – to save their over-leveraged banks from failing, ultimately forcing a number of them to ask for financial assistance from the troika.

It takes two to tango, as they say: irresponsible borrowing could not have happened without irresponsible lending. And yet the clean-up costs for the economic devastation wrought by these booms-gone-bust have not been equally borne by all parties. Of course, given that the lion's share of the bail-out loans came from the rich countries of the core (first and foremost Germany), we could be forgiven for viewing this as the lender countries extending a helping hand to their troubled brethren. When speaking of Europe's sovereign bail-outs, though, we have to ask: who has benefited the most from the bail-outs? And more importantly, where did the money go?

Let's take Spain. In mid-2012, the year of its €100 billion bail-out, Spanish banks owed their German peers more than €40 billion.[76] Add in the exposure of German banks to Spain's corporates and governments (national and local), and the total debt amounted to €113 billion.[77] So it is quite realistic to see the bail-out of Spanish banks – backed initially by the Spanish taxpayers, and then by the European Stability Mechanism (ESM) – as effectively 'a back-door bailout of reckless German lending', as an *International Financing Review* article put it. It took Spain's German and other creditors off the hook, while sending Spanish public debt levels through the roof.[78]

Jens Sondergaard, former senior European economist at Japanese investment bank Nomura, makes much the same point. 'The Spanish bailout in effect is a bailout of German banks .... If lenders in Spain were allowed to default, the consequences for the German banking system would be very serious.'[79]

Germany is the main contributor to the ESM, providing almost €200 billion of the fund's €700 billion capital, meaning that to a large degree, German banks were saved from losses on their risky loans by their own government. But all EMU countries, including Spain (the fourth-largest contributor), participate in the fund. So all of the EMU, Spain included, played a part in ensuring the German creditor banks did not lose out.

The Spanish bail-out is paradigmatic of all the post-crisis European sovereign bail-outs. Ireland's over-leveraged banks were indebted mostly to British, German and French banks, in that order. When the Irish government was pressured by the ECB into offering a blanket guarantee to its creditors, that did not benefit Ireland; it benefited those foreign banks. And it was because of that guarantee that the Irish government was ultimately forced to turn to the European Union and IMF for 'help'.

Much the same as applies to loans to banks also applies to loans to periphery country governments. According to a study made by Attac Austria, at least 77 per cent of the €200+ billion disbursed by the troika as part of the two 'rescue packages' for Greece went to the financial sector. In other words it was paid to the country's creditors: mostly banks and investment funds, many of them based in core countries, and to a lesser degree Greece's own banks.[80] Another study estimated that more than 80 per cent of the second €130 billion bail-out went to banks outside Greece and to the ECB (in interest payments).[81] As the German magazine *Die Gazette* wrote: 'The billions of taxpayer euros are not saving Greece. They're saving the banks.'[82]

The same opinion is shared by Peter Böfinger, economic advisor to the German government, who stated that the Greek bail-outs 'are first and foremost not about the problem countries but about our own banks, which hold high amounts of credit there'.[83] The shift in liabilities from European banks to European taxpayers has been staggering. One study found that the public debt of Greece to foreign governments, including debt to the EU-IMF loan facility and debt through the TARGET2 interbank payment system (which calculates debts between the EMU's central banks), increased by €130 billion, from €47.8 billion to €180.5 billion, between early 2010 and late 2011.[84] The same is true for the other PIIGS. At the same time, the combined exposure of foreign banks to Greek entities – public and private – fell from over €200 billion in 2009 to around €80 billion in early 2012.[85] Meanwhile Greece's public debt – and that of the EMU as a whole – kept skyrocketing.

In this light, the troika bail-outs can be seen as 'phase two' of the bail-out of Europe's financial sector. The first, more straightforward stage took place in the immediate aftermath of the 2008 crash, when governments stepped in to guarantee bank debts and extend loans to their banks. In the second, more subtle stage (some have called it a 'back-door bail-out') which began in 2010, the EU establishment and core countries stepped in and 'strongly encouraged' the periphery countries to take on government loans from the troika rather than consider alternatives such as debt restructuring, which would have ensured that the banks paid some of the price for their excessive lending. The funds were then, to a large degree, channelled back to the creditor countries.

This entailed a double shift in liabilities: from the banks of the periphery to the governments (and citizens) of the periphery; and from the banks of the core to the governments (and citizens) of the eurozone as whole, since most of the troika bail-out funds came from EMU countries, with Germany at the forefront. In other words, bank-to-bank (Spanish bank to German bank, for example) and government-to-bank (Greek government to German bank, for example) debt was converted into government-to-government debt (Greek and Spanish governments to other EMU governments, including the German government). In this sense, strictly 'nationalistic' readings of the crisis are to a certain extent misleading: to varying degrees, the banks' debts have been transferred to all the citizens of the EMU.

Germany also benefited from a more subtle (and mostly ignored) form of bail-out by its European partners, in what amounts to yet another shift in liabilities from banks to taxpayers. Because of the way in which the eurozone's TARGET2 interbank payment system works, when German banks pulled money out of Greece, the other national central banks of the EMU collectively offset the outflow with loans to the Greek central bank. These loans appeared on the balance sheet of the Bundesbank, Germany's central bank, as claims on the rest of the euro area. This mechanism, designed to keep the currency area's accounts in balance, made it easier for the German banks to exit their positions. The Bundesbank's claims were now only partly the responsibility of Germany. If Greece defaulted on its debt, the losses would be shared among all euro area countries, according to their shareholding in the ECB, and Germany's stake would be about 28 per cent.[86] As a Bloomberg editorial noted, '[i]n short, over the last couple of years, much of the risk sitting on German banks' balance sheets shifted to the taxpayers of the entire currency union'.[87] Figure 3.6 shows how Germany succeeded in reducing its exposure to Greece by almost 80 per cent between mid-2010 (when Greece entered the first 'rescue programme') and mid-2012.

US economist Robert Reich has argued that things might be even more complicated, and that the Greek bail-out actually benefited the creditors of the creditors: that is, Wall Street. While US banks were owed only about €5 billion by Greece, they had a much more significant exposure to German and French banks. This accounted for almost half of Wall Street's total exposure to the eurozone of about $2.7 trillion – and of course, the banks' exposure to Greek debt made them vulnerable.[88] US banks had also insured or bet on all sorts of derivatives emanating from Europe. Thus, if a German or French bank were to go under, the ripple effects – and its impact on Wall Street – would be incalculable. Reich's conclusion leaves little to the imagination:

> Make no mistake. The United States wants Europe to bail out its deeply indebted

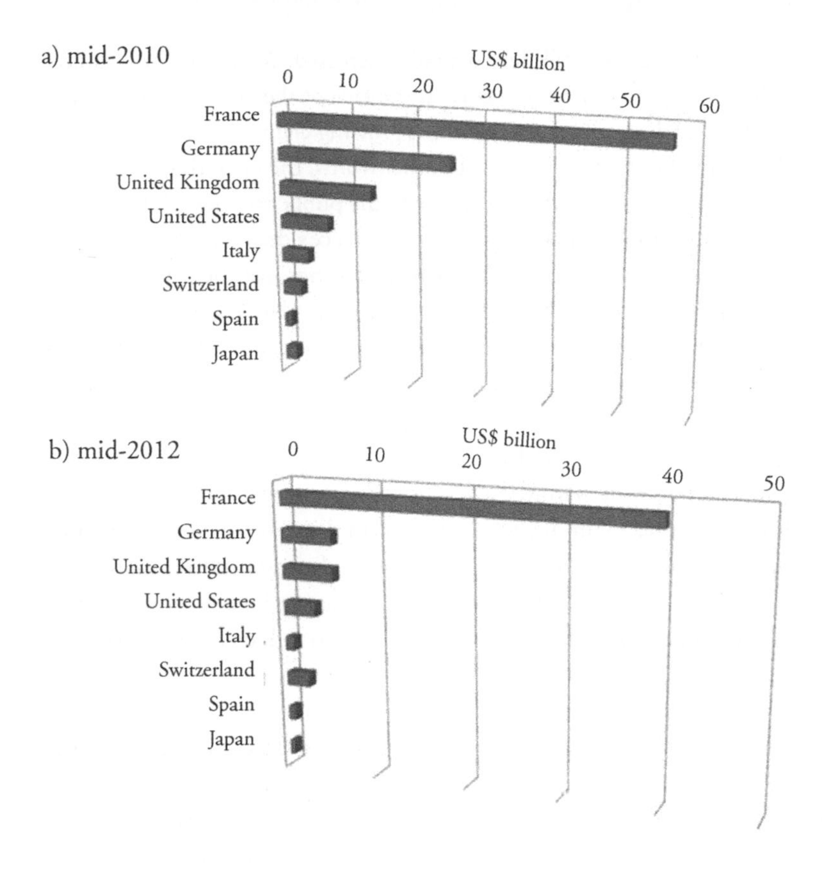

Figure 3.6 Countries most exposed to Greek debt (in US$ billion), mid-2010 and mid-2012

Source: Bank of International Settlements.

> nations so they can repay what they owe big European banks. Otherwise, those banks could implode – taking Wall Street with them .... In other words, Greece isn't the real problem. Nor is Ireland, Italy, Portugal, or Spain. The real problem is the financial system – centered on Wall Street. And we still haven't solved it.[89]

True, the second Greek bail-out called for the banks to accept a 50 per cent write-off or haircut. That might sound like a lot, but a number of commentators have argued that the banks got a much sweeter deal (and Greece a much rougher one) than is commonly understood. The €110 billion haircut on privately held bonds was matched by an increase of €130 billion in the debt owed by Greece to its official creditors – the European Union, ECB and IMF. And a significant part of that went to bail out private creditors, as we have seen. In other words, while private creditors were able to massively offload Greek sovereign bonds (which had already lost 65–75 per cent of their value)[90] from their balance sheets and shift the risk to the public sector, Greece's overall debt actually increased. Moreover, any future haircuts – which will probably be necessary in the face of the country's mounting public debt – will fall disproportionately on the growing claims of Greece's official creditors: that is, the European taxpayers. In other words, the operation amounted to yet another shift in liabilities from the private to the public sector, with European taxpayers now liable for more than 70 per cent of Greece's debt (see Figure 3.7).

Even more shamefully, the Greek bail-out benefited not just the private banks, but also the European Central Bank. In mid-2013 the Greek government was forced to borrow €4.2 billion from the ESM to pay back around €2 billion in interest to the ECB,[91] as well as to the various countries participating in the loans. When the first loan of €110 billion was adopted Christine Lagarde, then the French finance minister, announced that France was lending to Greece at 5 per cent while at the same time borrowing at a much lower rate, so far from being generous, it was profiting comfortably from its part in the deal.[92] The situation was so scandalous – with similarly exorbitant interest rates also applied to Ireland from November 2010 and to Portugal from May 2011 – that the lending governments and the European Commission decided in mid-2011 to reduce the rates paid by these countries.

Trade imbalances, and the divergence between creditor and debtor countries, are only part of the problem, though. The euro crisis cannot be understood unless we understand the perversely unique, and radically neoliberal, economic-monetary arrangement that countries were more or less consciously signing up to when they joined the eurozone.

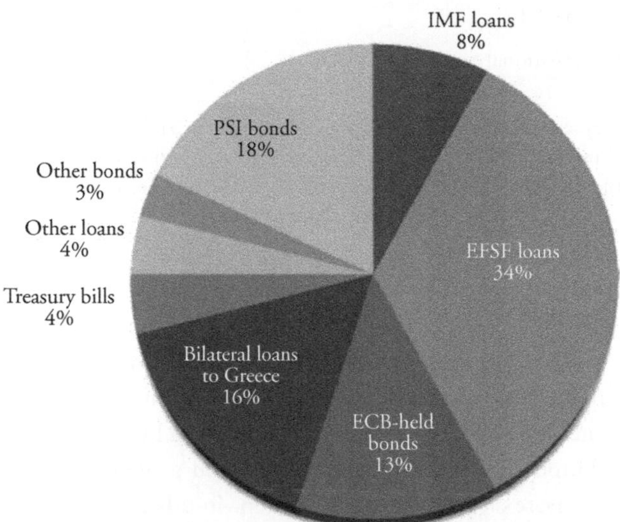

Figure 3.7 Composition of Greek public debt, end of 2012

Source: Goldman Sachs Economic Research.

The EMU: An Experiment in Pure Neoliberalism

Following the collapse of the Berlin Wall, the countries of Europe were faced with the prospect of a newly reunited Germany. Considering that twice in the 20th century most European countries had gone to war to stop the expansionist aims of a united Germany, most of them – and France, Germany's historical adversary, in particular – saw this as a potentially troubling development. The only alternative that these governments saw to the emergence of a new German superpower in the heart of Europe was to integrate Germany into the emerging economic and monetary union, commonly known as the eurozone. The German political and monetary establishment, though, set down some stringent conditions. First and foremost, it required a financial authority to be set up and put in charge of managing the euro. The European Central Bank was to be entirely independent of national governments.

The concept of independent central banking was not new in the early 1990s. The central bank is the authority in charge of managing a country's monetary policy by controlling (in theory at least) how much money gets printed and injected into the system, usually through the banks. In the 1980s – in line with the rise of neoliberalism, with its innate distrust of government intervention in the economy – many economists began to believe that that a central bank which is too susceptible to political direction or pressure may encourage economic boom-and-bust cycles. They argued that politicians may be tempted to boost economic activity in advance of an election, to the detriment of the long-term health of the economy and the country. Thus, they argued that the best way to ensure optimal monetary policy was to make central banks independent of the rest of executive government. This argument was broadly accepted by those in power, and those central banks that did not yet have independence began to gain it.

The financial crisis has proved that the idea is largely a myth. In 2008 the global economy was brought to the brink of meltdown precisely by one of the colossal booms-gone-bust that independent central banks were supposed to prevent.

At the same time as control of the money supply was being transferred from the supposedly untrustworthy hands of elected politicians – flawed, as we all know, yet accountable (at least in theory) – into the supposedly more 'competent' hands of non-elected technocrats (the central bankers), the ability of private commercial banks, unaccountable by definition, to create money out thin air was being dramatically increased. This happened through financial deregulation, and credit securitisation in particular, as we saw in Chapter 1. It is worth remembering that of all the money in circulation, it is estimated that less than 3 per cent is tangible cash; the other 97 per cent is digital money created by commercial banks. In such a context, making central banks independent of national governments has little influence on boom–bust cycles, simply because the money supply is largely out of the central banks' control. A number of commentators now view the failure of governments to constrain the private financial system's creation of private credit and money as one of the root causes of the financial crisis.

Whatever the obvious flaws of the theory, the idea that it was beneficial for central banks to be independent held a lot of sway in the early 1990s, when the rules of the EMU were established with the signing of the Maastricht Treaty. In fact the central banks of Europe (along with those of most advanced economies) were already independent to varying degrees by that time. But the Maastricht Treaty brought the concept of independent central banking to a new and historically unprecedented level. It is one thing to put an individual country's monetary policy into the hands of an independent entity charged with acting in that country's best economic interest. It is quite another to put its monetary policy into the hands of a body that acts on behalf of a number of different countries with different economies, and as a result, with different requirements from their economic policy.

As we have seen, the economies of the eurozone might be intended to converge, but in reality they have diverged. A single monetary policy cannot meet the interests of every one of them.

But this is just one aspect of the problem. Another condition made by Germany was that the sole objective of the ECB should be to keep inflation down. In other words, its main, if not its only, criterion for acting would be to ensure price stability. This too was unprecedented in the history of central banking. It might sound like a technical point, but it is actually crucial in understanding the euro crisis.

All central banks have an 'inflation control mandate', as does the ECB. That is, they aim at maintaining price stability and keeping inflation from rising above a certain level. But most of them, such as the US Federal Reserve, also have an 'employment mandate'. So another explicit aim of their policy is to guarantee the maximum employment of the country's workforce. To this end, they reserve the right to act as lenders of last resort to their countries' governments by intervening directly on sovereign bond markets. (However they do not purchase government bonds directly from governments – most central banks in the developed world are prohibited from doing that – but from private banks.) The primary purpose of this power, as far as governments are concerned, is to ensure that sovereign borrowing costs are kept under control. If financial markets refuse to buy bonds or ask for excessively high yields, the central bank can always step in and buy the bonds itself with newly 'printed' money. The ECB, on the other hand – until it partially reversed its policy as a reaction to the euro crisis – was prohibited by its mandate from financing governments or lowering their borrowing costs through the purchase of government bonds. In this it differs from every other central bank in the world.[93]

In short, by joining the monetary union, member countries did not just give up control of their central banks (which were already independent). They gave up entirely on having a central bank which could act as a lender of last resort. This meant that member states would have to rely solely on loans from the financial markets for their financing needs, with no control over their borrowing costs and no one to go to for help if things went wrong. This went hand in hand with another condition, also strongly influenced by Germany. The Stability and Growth Pact (the forerunner to the Fiscal Compact) aimed at imposing financial discipline on member states by allowing a maximum deficit-to-GDP ratio of 3 per cent and debt-to-GDP ratio of 60 per cent. This was based on the deeply flawed and ideologically biased notion that limiting public sector deficits was all that was needed to keep the EMU's economies from diverging. (In more general terms, it also reflected the idea that 'high' levels of public debt are inherently bad.) In fact, as we have seen, labour costs and cross-border capital flows are much more important determinants of intra-EMU imbalances.

In short, the very pillars of the eurozone were forged according to the (fallacious) neoliberal myth that governments cannot be trusted with money and should interfere in the economy as little as possible (hence the independence of the ECB and the Stability and Growth Pact), and that only markets can guarantee an efficient and functioning economy. Moreover, by explicitly prohibiting the ECB from acting as lender of last resort, thus subjecting governments to the supposed 'discipline' of the markets, the EMU marked the coronation of a neoliberal dream: the definitive financialisation of public finance.

Recently Angela Merkel coined a rather ominous term for such system: 'market-conforming democracy'. Trade union adviser Ronald Janssen described this as the idea that 'the competence of national democracies should be subordinated to what the economic and financial elite considers necessary'.[94] As the euro crisis would make clear, though, financial markets are just as incapable of efficiently assessing and managing the public finances of countries as they are of disciplining or correcting themselves (as was extensively documented in Chapter 1). In fact, the financialisation of public finance – coupled with the monetary orthodoxy of the ECB – played a crucial role in the onset, and worsening, of the euro crisis.

As we have seen, the establishment of the EMU made the interest rates on government bonds converge across the monetary union, causing money to flow from Europe's core to its periphery. This in turn led to huge housing and consumption booms that quickly turned into huge bubbles (especially in Greece, Ireland and Spain). When the crisis hit, and the institutions that had fuelled those booms pulled their money out, the implications of the EMU structure hit home. Those countries in a slump could not resort to currency devaluation. Because they did not have the right to print their own money, or a central bank willing to act as lender of last resort (and because they borrowed huge amounts of money to bail out their banks), they became exposed to the risk of sovereign default, or 'national insolvency'. As Merkel stated in late 2011, '[t]he top priority is to avoid an uncontrolled insolvency, because that wouldn't just hit Greece, and the danger that it hits everyone, or at least a number of other countries, is very big'.[95]

The notion of 'national insolvency' is fairly recent, and the term is potentially very misleading, notes Stephen Kinsella, senior lecturer in economics at the University of Limerick.[96] Developed countries that control their own currency have no reason to default. Even if they borrow too much, they can always push the debt into the future by rolling it over (as long as they have a central bank willing to keep borrowing costs down), or they can pay for it by printing money, in a process known as 'debt monetisation' (which is discussed later). Failing that, they can default on some or all of the debt. In other words, there are always alternatives to 'national insolvency', and thus it is never essential to accept austerity in order to avoid it. To pretend otherwise, as the EU elite has done in the aftermath of the financial crisis, is very dangerous, says Kinsella:

> If politicians and policy makers believe their country is, literally, insolvent, then they behave differently towards their creditors. For politicians of debtor states, suddenly vast privatisations make sense, because of course you're selling some of your remaining assets. Suddenly the will of the people of the debtor nation becomes secondary to the will of the nation's creditors. Suddenly democracy is an expensive irrelevance in the face of an overwhelming technocratic desire for a speedy, and market-friendly, solution.[97]

As a prominent US investment banker wrote at the height of the euro crisis, 'the less solvent you are, the more sovereignty you have to give up'. That is precisely what has happened to a number of European countries which were termed 'insolvent' by the markets.[98] But this, says Yale professor of economics Robert J. Shiller, is 'nonsense'.[99] More precisely, it is a deception made possible solely by the eurozone's flawed and hyper-financialised design. That has created the conditions for something very close to national insolvency, because of the lack of a 'real' central bank willing to act as lender of last resort. This in turn has been used to 'reduce the grip a people have on their sovereignty' and has paved the way to a 'more or less autocratic system of coercion', as Kinsella writes.[100] To a certain extent, the EMU's architecture transformed its member states into banks. They became susceptible to bank-run-style self-fulfilling panics in which investors are led to shun sovereign bonds, or demand higher interest rates, for fear that the country in question might default – increasing the risk that it will do just that. 'It turns out that countries that lack their own currency are highly vulnerable to self-fulfilling panic, in which the efforts of investors to avoid losses from default end up triggering the very default they fear', writes Paul Krugman.[101]

The EMU's architecture implies, and its founders probably believed, that financial markets can correctly assess the solvency of states and that they act in an entirely rational way. But markets are in reality fundamentally irrational and their traders are very prone to panic attacks, as was seen in the financial crisis. The assessment of financial markets about the eurozone countries has repeatedly proved to be wrong, as it swung from unwarranted optimism in the years following the creation of the eurozone – treating the debt of periphery countries as almost as safe as German debt, so pumping disproportionate amounts of money into them, and fuelling huge housing and consumption bubbles – to unjustified panic in the wake of the crisis.

In line with the view that the assessment of market operators regarding a country's public finances always reflects an objective reality, when the interest rate on Greek bonds rose to more than 10 per cent in mid-2010, almost everyone – from financial operators to policy makers to media analysts – concluded that the risk of default genuinely was high. If investors demanded a huge risk premium, this could only mean that the danger was extreme. This revealed, at best, a deep and widespread ignorance about the true nature of financial market assessments. The future price of an asset (such as a government security) is by no means predetermined, and an assessment, as the name implies, is nothing more than 'a belief, a bet on the future', in the words of the *collectif* of Appalled Economists.[102]

Even assuming that markets always act in good faith, it is inherently dangerous for eurozone countries to be entirely dependent on their judgements. Experience has shown that these are not always moderate and rational. But as the financial crisis has made clear, markets rarely act in the interest of anyone or anything but themselves. So the situation exposed the governments of the EMU to an even greater danger than instability: speculation.

Biting the Hand that Feeds: The Role of Speculation in the Euro Crisis

Beginning in early 2010, various countries in the eurozone started to come repeatedly under attack from speculators. This phenomenon seriously exacerbated the euro crisis in its initial phase.

The most straightforward form of speculation is betting on rumours about the economic situation of a country. The speculator waits to buy the bonds of a government in trouble until the interest rates offered are large enough to make them attractive. Banks engaged in this activity on a massive scale throughout the first two years of the euro crisis, aided by the credit rating agencies, which (more or less deliberately) exacerbated the post-crisis panic by rapidly downgrading country after country.

Because of the dependence of eurozone member states on financial markets for their financing needs, a downgrade can have devastating effects on a country's bond markets. By discouraging investors, it cuts governments off from crucial sources of funding, and drives up interest rates. This is what happened, with the interest rates of periphery countries soaring throughout 2010–11 – to the sole benefit of the banks, which were able to use the money loaned from the ECB at record-low rates to buy the bonds of distressed countries at record-high rates. To get an idea of the kind of money that banks were making by exploiting the unfolding euro crisis – and the extent to which the ECB's policy, throughout the euro crisis, has privileged the interests of financial markets over those of member states – when a country has to borrow money at an interest rate of 6, 7 or 8 per cent from a bank that is borrowing it at 0.1 per cent, it is paying 60 to 80 times more for its borrowing than the bank is paying.

Another way banks speculate on sovereign debt is by resorting to the same instruments that they use to speculate on pretty much anything (such as subprime loans): the now-infamous credit default swaps, or CDSs. Through so-called 'naked' CDSs, banks can 'insure themselves' against the default of governments even when they do not actually own any bonds. The implications are obvious: if the banks have nothing to lose, and everything to gain, from a country's default, they have every reason to hope for – or even worse, contribute to – just that. It would be as if dozens of people took out fire insurance on your own flat, and then played with a box of matches. This is precisely what was happening to Greece and other countries in 2010–11, with the speculative attacks against the weaker members of the union reaching such alarming proportions that some commentators started to allege that the attacks were part of a wider plan to destabilise the euro.[103]

In light of this, it is baffling that the top priority for European politicians throughout the entire euro crisis has been – and continues to be – that of 'reassuring the markets'. It is widely agreed that some financial players (mostly but not only American), aided by the credit rating agencies, were conspiring to push certain countries off the 'fiscal cliff' in order to trigger the payment on their swaps.[104] The idea of 'reassuring the markets' rests on the widely held view that financial markets are akin to a sort of collective consciousness of all the entrepreneurs and smart people that make our economies move – hence the assumption that 'what's good for the markets is good for everyone'. As the speculative attacks on the euro have shown, though, markets often reflect the interests of a very narrow group of financial players. The most obvious example is the elite 'Wednesday club' revealed by *The New York Times*, which comprises nine super-banks that control most of the derivatives trade.[105]

Further down the financial pyramid, things are not much better. A groundbreaking study by the Swiss Federal Institute of Technology (ETH) – the first-ever investigation into the complex architecture of international corporate ownership – has revealed that a large part of the global economy is controlled by what the authors call an economic 'super-entity'. This comprises 147 incredibly powerful transnational corporations that control 40 per cent of the entire network. Of the top 50 most powerful companies, 45 are financial firms. The list includes Barclays (the most influential corporation in the world, according to the study), JPMorgan, Merrill Lynch, Goldman Sachs, Deutsche Bank and other familiar and less well-known names. Twenty-four companies are US-based, followed by eight in Britain, five in France, four in Japan, and Germany, Switzerland and the Netherlands with two each. Canada has one.[106]

The authors noted that although no study has demonstrated that this international 'super-entity' has ever acted as a bloc, 'this is not an unlikely scenario'.[107] To a large extent this 'super-entity' is what is meant by 'the markets'. This is the body whose wishes politicians like Angela Merkel would like our democracies to 'conform to': a handful of banks acting very probably like a bloc, as the ETH study concludes, and ruthlessly pursuing their own interests, as banks do.

This is the reason that, as the speculative attacks against the periphery countries of the eurozone became increasingly violent throughout 2011 and 2012, a growing number of commentators and organisations (including the IMF) started to call upon the ECB to act as a real central bank and intervene to defend the member states from speculators. They noted that by refusing to do so it was violating its mandate obliging it to contribute, if not to the welfare of European citizens, at least to 'the stability of the financial system'.[108]

Finally, on 2 August the ECB announced its Outright Monetary Transactions (OMT) programme: unlimited outright purchases of government bonds on secondary bond markets which were aimed 'at safeguarding an appropriate monetary policy transmission and the singleness of the monetary policy'.[109] As we have seen, the ECB was already intervening in secondary bond markets before the creation of the OMT programme, through the now-terminated Securities Markets Programme (SMP). In that case, though, it had set a pre-announced limit to the size of its intervention, thus playing into the speculators' hands. By declaring that 'no ex ante quantitative limits are set on the size of Outright Monetary Transactions', the ECB sent a much clearer signal to the markets. The implication was that if markets demanded excessively high interest rates the ECB would step in and buy the bonds itself, theoretically putting an end to the speculators' game.

As of late 2013, the OMT programme has succeeded in tackling speculation, stabilising interest rates on Spanish and Italian bonds at a much lower level (although it is still high compared with non-euro countries, for reasons that we shall see further on). Other measures introduced by the European Union to tackle speculation include a limited ban on 'naked' CDS trading (November 2011)[110] and tighter controls on credit rating agencies (November 2012).[111]

Does this means that the ECB has finally become a full-fledged lender of last resort and thus a 'normal' central bank? Far from it, regrettably. The OMT programme (as with most things EU- and ECB-related) comes with a lot of strings attached. As the ECB's press release states, a 'necessary condition for Outright Monetary Transactions is strict and effective conditionality'. Intervention is attached to an ESM structural adjustment programme including a host of economic and social reforms (liberalisation of labour markets, reduction of labour costs: the usual agenda) on the macroeconomic level, and cost-cutting reforms on the fiscal level.[112] In other words, governments in crisis or under attack by speculators will be offered the minimum help necessary to keep their bond yields below an unacceptable level, but in exchange will be forced to implement recessionary troika-style austerity programmes.

In short, the OMT programme is just a troika programme in a different guise, based on the same economic and ideological fallacy that is driving fiscal austerity: the idea that fiscal profligacy is at the root of the problem, and that the reason investors are demanding high yields from periphery countries is that they are not cost-cutting hard enough, fast enough. This is a gross misconception of the nature of the crisis, argues Larry Elliott, economics editor of the *Guardian*:

> The reason investors demand high interest rates when they lend to Italy and Spain is their concern about the impact of permanent recession on public finances and banks. A rescue plan that has at its core more demand-destroying measures will do more harm than good.[113]

This is the same conclusion reached by a January 2012 IMF report, which states that 'further tightening during a downturn could exacerbate rather than alleviate market tensions through its negative impact on growth'.[114]

In other words, the neoliberal notion underpinning the OMT programme – that it should be up to private bond markets to set yields, and that governments should live in fear of these markets – is not only ethically dubious but economically flawed – and ultimately self-defeating, even purely in terms of bond yields. Thus, the plan falls very short of transforming the ECB into a 'real' central bank. Rather than a lender of last resort, it effectively makes the ECB a 'dealer of last resort', with the power to exploit the economic difficulties of countries to blackmail them into implementing neoliberal and austerity-driven reforms, as EU policy analyst Protesilaos Stavrou notes.[115]

This is the exact opposite of what other central banks do. When the US Federal Reserve buys US government bonds it ties its purchase to economic variables such as improvements in the labour market, not political variables, like the ECB does. The ECB's policy, on the other hand, is more akin to the 'help' offered by the World Bank and the IMF to developing countries. The strict conditionalities attached to OMTs may help explain why, as of late 2013, no country has yet asked the ECB for 'help' or applied for an OMT programme. It is also why a number of commentators have argued that the OMT programme – precisely because it does

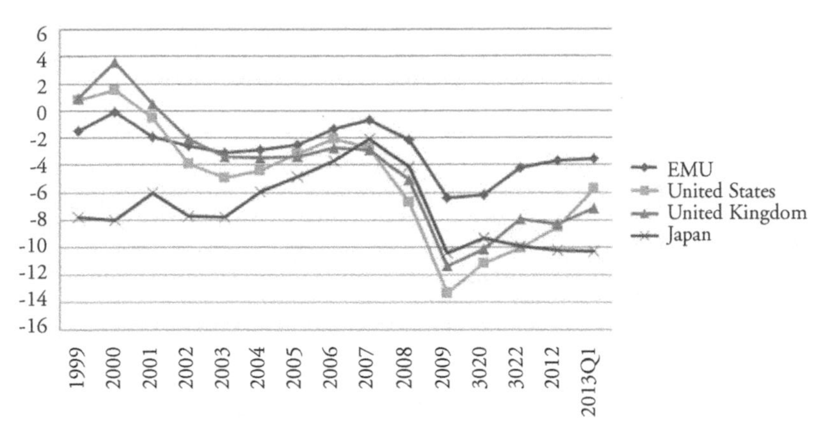

Figure 3.8 Deficit-to-GDP ratio of the EMU, the United States, the United Kingdom and Japan, 1999–2013

Sources: Eurostat, IMF and OECD.

not address Europe's real problems: unemployment, recession and widening core–periphery socioeconomic divergences – will fail, just as the troika programmes have failed, in both economic and social terms. In fact it could be argued that is already failing, resulting in what Paul Krugman calls the 'euro penalty', in which countries that use the euro face higher borrowing costs than countries with similar, or worse, economic and fiscal outlooks that retain their own currencies.[116]

Given all the babble about the 'European debt crisis', we could be forgiven for thinking that Europe is the most indebted region in the world. In fact, from a fiscal standpoint, the position of eurozone is no worse – and in many respects rather better – than that of the United States, the United Kingdom or Japan. As of mid-2013, the budget deficit for the euro area as a whole is considerably lower than that of the United States, the United Kingdom or Japan, while the EMU's overall post-crisis debt-to-GDP ratio, about the same as the level of the United Kingdom, is considerably lower than that of the United States, not to mention Japan, one of the most indebted countries of the world.

Despite this, eurozone countries on average pay a higher interest rate on ten-year government bonds (3 per cent, as of mid-2013) than the United States or the United Kingdom pay, and almost four times more than Japan pays (0.8 per cent, as of mid-2013).[117] Japan also pays half the interest that Germany, Europe's economic powerhouse, pays, and that the EMU's less indebted economies – such as Finland and the Netherlands – pay.[118] What is the cause of such massive, and apparently unjustified, spreads, and why are Japan, the United States and other non-euro countries not facing a crisis of the kind the euro area is, despite higher debt levels? The answer, once again, lies in the role of the ECB.

The ECB's reluctance to intervene in sovereign bond markets, and the condi-

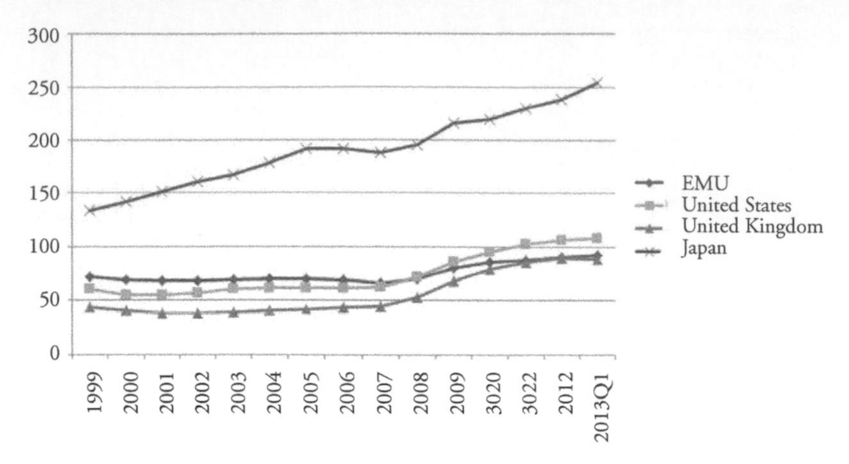

Figure 3.9 Debt-to-GDP ratio of the EMU, the United States, the United Kingdom and Japan, 1999–2013

Source: Eurostat and IMF (2013Q1 data for Japan is based on IMF's projection).

tions – unacceptable to many – that it imposes for doing so, mean that it does not act in the way a conventional central bank acts. It still leaves member states ill-equipped to deal with financial crises and pursue growth-spurring policies, and over-reliant on market assessment for their bond yields. It need not be that way. As advanced non-euro nations show, countries that have a full-fledged central bank have the power to exercise their authority over markets and set their own bond yields. And rightly so. Europe deserves nothing less.

As we have seen throughout this chapter, the root cause of the euro crisis lies not in the alleged profligacy of governments, but in the fundamental economic imbalances that have resulted from three decades of financial deregulation and neoliberal economic policies. These have been exacerbated by the neoliberal architecture and highly financialised economy of the eurozone. Yet, as we shall see in Chapter 4, the crisis has been (indeed, is being) exploited (and in some cases 'engineered') by Europe's political-financial elite to do away with the last remnants of the welfare state and complete the neoliberal project.

CHAPTER FOUR

From Economic Crisis to Economic Shock

'Large-scale growth-enhancing national reforms seldom happen without the specter of a crisis, involve compromises, and take time. Market pressure may succeed where other approaches have failed'—IMF report, November 2010 (my emphasis)[1]

The Age of Austerity

Until the start of the euro crisis, the word 'austerity' did not mean much to most European citizens. It has since become the most talked-about word in the continent's modern history, earning it the title of Merriam-Webster's 2010 'Word of the Year' because of the number of web searches generated that year. It has also become one of the most hotly debated issues in recent history (not only in Europe) – hailed by politicians and bureaucrats across the European Union as a panacea to all the eurozone's problems; slated by non-mainstream economists, unions and social movements as a grave threat to labour and social rights, and the major obstacle to economic recovery. In most people's minds, the word has become inextricably – almost naturally – linked to the word 'crisis'. The politicians' austerity-justifying mantra – expressed for the first time at the end of 2010 by Wolfgang Schäuble, Germany's minister of finance, in his widely distributed article, and then repeated *ad nauseam* by the establishment in the following months and years – can be summed up as follows:

- The recklessness of the financial system was not the real cause of the crisis – it was merely a trigger.
- The real cause is excessive government debt.
- This was caused by excessive government spending by countries that have 'lived well beyond their means'.
- The deficit/debt needs to reduced 'at once' before it is too late.
- Spurring growth through government investment is not an option.
- The only way to reduce the deficit/debt is to reduce welfare spending.
- Eurozone reform should be focused on imposing 'fiscal discipline' on member states.

- Countries must learn 'to live within their means and strengthen their competiveness'.
- The priority of governments must be that of 'reassuring the markets', whatever the social or economic cost.

In one word: austerity. Even though (as demonstrated in the previous chapters) this is an extremely partisan, ideological and ultimately fallacious reading of the crisis, which ignores the true root causes of Europe's political and economic crisis – a self-serving and unregulated financial sector, a monetary union producing structural imbalances, and reverse redistribution of wealth – it soon became conventional wisdom among most European politicians, commentators and bureaucrats, influencing policy responses all throughout Europe. As Krugman says, 'deficit scaremongering took over the debate'.[2]

The austerity 'cure' was first force-fed by the troika to the countries that were unlucky enough to require a bail-out (Portugal, Ireland, Greece, Spain), then followed, more or less willingly, by other European countries such as Italy, France and the United Kingdom. In total, dozens of austerity plans were approved and implemented across Europe between 2010 and early 2013 (more than 40 in the eurozone alone), with more planned for the years ahead.[3] As we have seen, the countries of the periphery (and particularly those under explicit troika programmes) – along with non-periphery countries which also came under heavy market pressure, such as various Eastern European member states – have been the ones to implement the harshest measures. Greece, Ireland and Portugal have adopted so-called 'fiscal consolidation' plans (the fancy term for austerity) amounting on average to 16.2 per cent of GDP by 2015, while a host of other countries, including Spain and Italy, have adopted plans ranging between 6 and 9.1 per cent of GDP. Even the OECD acknowledges these to be 'very large by historical comparison'.[4] To varying degrees, all EU countries without exception have taken (indeed, are taking) or are considering austerity measures. So have a few other advanced countries, most notably the United States, with OECD countries as a whole committing to austerity measures amounting on average to 5.5 per cent of GDP over the 2010–15 period.[5]

The measures taken include:

- a reduction in welfare benefits
- a reduction of the minimum wage
- public-sector pay reductions or freezes, and the reduction of salary bonuses
- pension cuts and increased retirement age
- a reduction in severance pay
- a reduction in vacation days
- an easing of restrictions on layoffs
- a reduction in duration and amount of unemployment benefits

- the curtailing of collective bargaining agreements
- the expansion of part-time and temporary work
- tax increases (mostly on consumption and labour)
- the privatisation of public services and assets.

We assessed in Chapter 2 the nefarious short-term effects that austerity has had on individual countries. Now we shall take a wider, more systemic look at the issue, and see, more than three years after Europe was first prescribed the austerity cure, how well the patient is faring.

The Social Effects of Austerity

In mid-2013, according to official statistics, unemployment in the eurozone was at a record-high 12 per cent – and rising – with almost 20 million unemployed across the currency bloc. This amounts to an almost 50 per cent increase on pre-crisis levels, when the unemployment rate was less than 7 per cent.

The outlook is especially bleak for young people, with youth unemployment rising above 24 per cent in the eurozone and 23 per cent in the European Union – meaning that one in four people under 25 in Europe are jobless. In the three countries that have suffered the deepest austerity-driven cuts and crisis- and austerity-induced recessions – Greece, Spain, Portugal and Italy – the situation is now verging on a social and humanitarian crisis, according to a wide range of sources.

Greece, the original test country (or guinea pig)[6] for Europe's new austerity regime, is the country in Europe that has suffered the deepest and harshest fiscal consolidation measures and neoliberal reforms. The budget cuts and tax hikes amounted to €32 billion throughout the 2010–13 period, and are estimated to

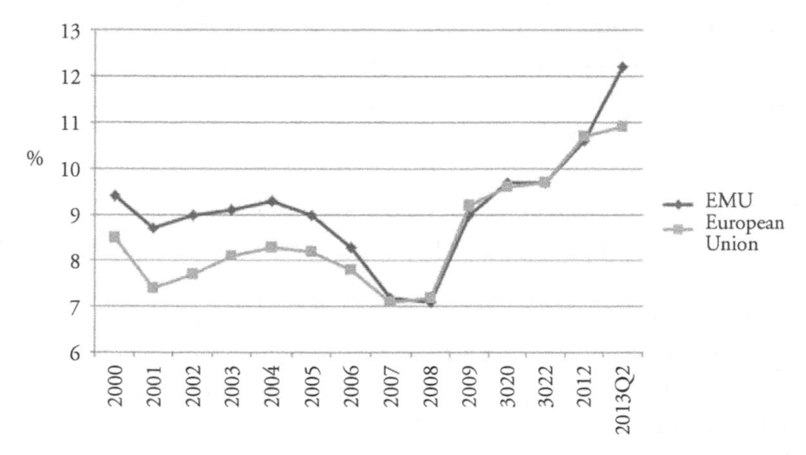

Figure 4.1 EU and EMU unemployment rates, 2000–13

Source: Eurostat.

total €42 billion (half of which are spending cuts), equivalent to 18.5 per cent of GDP, by 2015.[7] The measures taken or planned include:

- A reduction in the government's operational spending of €430 million by 2014, estimated to reach €1 billion by 2015.[8]
- Domestic public investment cuts of €800 million.[9]
- A reduction in social security funds and social spending of €2.5 billion by 2014, estimated to reach €4.3 billion by 2015.[10]
- A reduction in health-care and pharmaceutical spending of over €1 billion by 2014. This includes the firing of 35,000 doctors, nurses and other health workers, and a 14 per cent reduction in the salaries of nurses compared with 2009. It is despite a rise in public hospital admissions of 24 per cent from 2009 to 2010, and a further 8 per cent in the first half of 2011 compared with the same period of 2010. The cuts are estimated to reach almost €2 billion by 2015, with demands by the troika that public spending on health be capped at 6 per cent of GDP.[11]
- The effective dismantling of 'universal' health care, with unemployed Greeks now receiving benefits only for a maximum of a year.[12]
- The reduction of public-sector wages by 15 per cent, with cuts to the public-sector wage bill amounting to €2 billion by 2015.[13]
- A 2.3 per cent decrease in nominal wages over the 2009–12 period, with the average salary down by 23 per cent that same year.[14]
- A 30 per cent reduction in the minimum wage between 2009 and 2012.[15]
- The replacement of 13th- and 14th-month salaries with an annual lump sum.[16]
- A massive public-sector layoff, including the reduction of 150,000 public-sector jobs through hiring freezes and the elimination of temporary contracts.[17]
- The slashing of unemployment benefits.[18]
- The suspension of a poverty-support scheme introduced in 2009.[19]
- Drastic cuts in benefits for large families.[20]
- Plans to end collective bargaining and impose individualised contracts instead.[21]
- The legalisation of extended very low-paid or unpaid internships.[22]
- An increase in indirect taxation, with VAT raised from 19 to 23 per cent and special taxes on fuels, alcohol and tobacco introduced.[23]
- An increase from 9 to 13 per cent of the lower VAT rate (applied to staple goods, electricity, water and similar commodities).[24]
- The reduction of tax exemptions for a number of categories.[25]
- An increase in income tax for the middle brackets.[26]
- Plans to privatise ports, airports, railways, water and electricity supply companies, financial firms and the lands owned by the state, including a number of the country's islands.[27]

- Cuts and freezes in pensions, with an increase in the legal retirement age from 61 to 65, and spending on pensions capped at a maximum level of 2.5 per cent of GDP, resulting in the reduction of supplementary pensions by 10–20 per cent.[28]
- An increase by 30 per cent in all public transport fares.[29]

Such an assault on the social, economic and labour rights of the Greek population – part of a radically neoliberal overhaul of the country's economy – has brought the nation, and an increasing percentage of its population, to its knees (exactly as various non-mainstream economists predicted). In mid-2013, unemployment in Greece hit 27 per cent, with the youth unemployment rate rising above 60 per cent – the highest rate in the developed world.

In 2011, 31.4 per cent of the population, or 3.4 million people, lived on an income below 60 per cent of the national median disposable income, according to EU data. At the same time, 27.3 per cent (that is, more than one fifth) of the population, or 1.3 million people, were at risk of poverty – and things are estimated to have become dramatically worse since, with UNICEF reporting in mid-2013 that one in three children in Greece are now living in poverty.[30] Using further EU indicators, a large proportion of Greek households currently live in conditions of 'material deprivation'.[31] A little more than 15 per cent live in 'extreme material deprivation', which means they are without enough heating, electricity, and use of either a car or a telephone.[32] The number of homeless people has also risen to unprecedented levels, with unofficial estimates putting them at 40,000. At the same time the suicide rate has doubled from pre-crisis levels (when it was the lowest in Europe).[33]

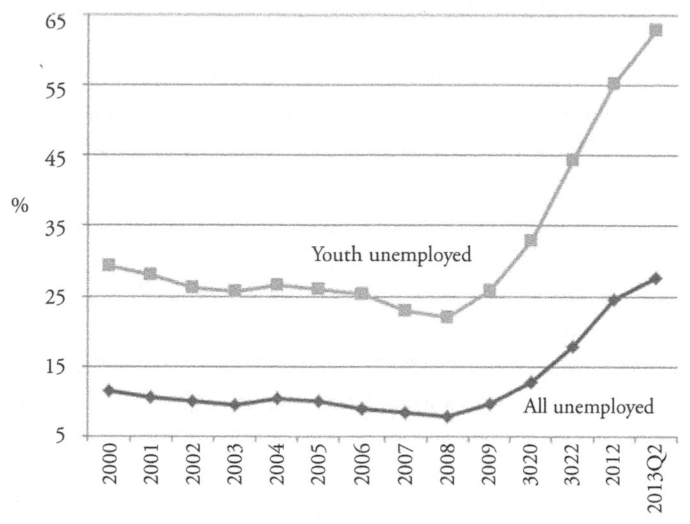

Figure 4.2 Greece's unemployment rates, 2000–13

Source: Eurostat.

Moreover, as a result of the massive cuts to the health-care system, HIV rates have jumped by 200 per cent, and the country has seen its first malaria outbreak since the 1970s.[34] Greece has also witnessed a sudden surge in the popularity of right-wing and neo-fascist movements, with the neo-Nazi party Golden Dawn being elected for the first time to the Hellenic parliament in the mid-2012 elections. This has been accompanied by a dramatic increase in racist and homophobic attacks.[35] As the Greek journalist Alex Politaki wrote in the *Guardian* in early 2013, 'Greece is currently in the centre of a humanitarian crisis'; and, even worse, 'the current state of affairs has been brought about by the so-called economic "rescue" of Greece'.[36]

Spain, while not subject to an outright troika programme, has also introduced a series of very harsh austerity measures, enacting the biggest budget cuts in the country's history, most of them in health care, education and other public services. Fiscal consolidation measures amounted to €77 billion throughout the 2010–13 period (of which €51 billion was spending cuts), with an extra €5 billion planned for 2014 – totalling 7.3 per cent of GDP.[37] The measures include:

- Public infrastructure investment cuts of almost €13 billion.[38]
- Cost-cutting and 'streamlining' in the health-care system throughout all of the country's 17 semi-autonomous regions amounting to €7 billion. Catalonia, for instance, announced in 2011 a 10 per cent reduction in the health-care budget, cuts to the salaries of some 40,000 public health professionals, and the closure of a third of its hospital beds and 40 per cent of its operating rooms.[39]
- The part-privatisation of health care, making the previous 'universal' health-care system dependent on employment status.[40]
- The limitation of illegal immigrants' access to the health-care system.[41]
- Massive cuts to public education – including the halving of public university funding – amounting to €7.5 billion. The aim is to bring education costs down to 3.9 per cent of GDP (the same level as 1987), well below the EU average of 5.5 per cent.[42]
- A 50 per cent increase in tuition fees for public universities.[43]
- Increased working hours for teachers and professors.[44]
- Social security cuts – including the elimination of a €2,500 childbirth allowance – amounting to €4.2 billion.[45]
- A huge increase in the standard VAT rate from 16 to 21 per cent, and in the lower VAT rate on public transport, hotels and processed foods from 7 to 10 per cent.[46]
- Income tax increases totalling €12 billion.[47]
- A 5 per cent cut and indefinite freeze in public-sector pay, with total cuts to the public-sector wage bill amounting to €16 billion.[48]
- The elimination of the Christmas bonus for public-sector employees.[49]

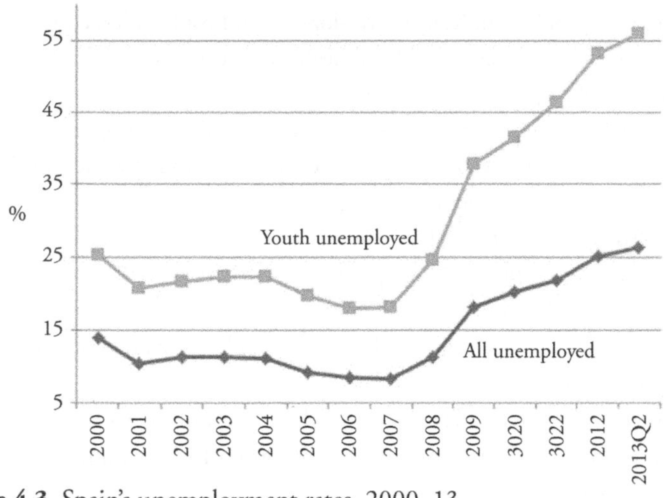

Figure 4.3 Spain's unemployment rates, 2000–13

Source: Eurostat.

- The slashing of unemployment benefits from 60 to 50 per cent from the sixth month without work.[50]
- A 20 per cent reduction in subsidies to political parties and trade unions.[51]

The effects of the cuts on Spanish society have been nothing short of devastating. The country's unemployment rate, at 26.3 per cent (according to mid-2013 data), is just below Greece's level. Its youth unemployment rate, at 56.1 per cent, is even more staggering.

According to Eurostat figures, at the end of 2012 only Bulgaria and Romania had a higher percentage of people deemed at risk of poverty – a grim reality which many argue is already tearing the country's social fabric apart.[52] In a damning report, Oxfam said that previous crises in Latin America and Asia point to serious long-term damage if austerity measures remain in place. 'Poverty and social exclusion may increase drastically', it says. 'By 2022, some 18 million Spaniards, or 38 per cent of the population, could be in poverty.'[53] In the country's poorer regions, such as the Canary Islands, Andalucía and Extremadura, almost a third of the population is below the at-risk-of-poverty line, according to the national statistics institute.[54] Eviction-related suicides are also dramatically on the rise.[55] Despite all this, Mario Draghi's assessment at the end of 2012 was that '[t]hings are improving in Spain', according to Spanish translations of his words.[56]

In Portugal, the austerity measures imposed by the troika as a condition for its bail-out loan – totalling €20.5 billion in budget cuts and tax increases, with an estimated cumulative impact of 12.2 per cent of GDP[57] – include:

- Expenditure reductions amounting to €11 billion.[58]

- Cuts of over €1.5 billion in health care alone, with hospitals forced to cut their overtime costs by 20 per cent and local health-care centres facing a 15 per cent budget reduction.[59]
- Cuts to social welfare programmes – including income support allowance, senior citizens' pension supplements, and survivor and disease subsidies – amounting to almost €2 billion.[60]
- Public investment cuts of over €2 billion.[61]
- A 3–7 per cent cut in public sector pay.[62]
- The freezing of civil service recruitment.[63]
- Eimination of holiday and Christmas bonuses for public servants and retirees.[64]
- The elimination of four public holidays.[65]
- Plans to make public-sector employees work an extra hour per day.[66]
- Voluntary redundancy programmes for 30,000 of the country's 600,000 public-sector workers.[67]
- The easing of restrictions on layoffs.[68]
- The reduction of unemployment benefits.[69]
- An increase in the VAT rate by 2 per cent.[70]
- A 3.5 per cent surcharge tax on everyone's earnings.[71]
- The reduction of tax-deductible items such as mortgages and health care.[72]
- Income tax increases amounting to €2 billion.[73]
- Plans to increase social security contributions from 11 to 18 per cent of workers' pay.[74]
- A reduction in pension benefits of between 3.5 and 40 per cent.[75]
- Plans to raise the retirement age by two years to 67.[76]
- The privatisation of public state holdings in a number of companies.[77]

In April 2013, the Portuguese constitutional court rejected some of the troika-imposed measures – such as the cuts to public sector wages and state pensions – as unconstitutional, on the basis that the burden of the cuts was unfairly distributed.[78] The communication sent out by the European Commission two days later rejected the judgement completely, expressed its approval that Lisbon was continuing with the agreed treatment and refused any renegotiation.[79]

Sweeping cuts to the country's health-care system were blamed for a thousand extra deaths in February 2012, 20 per cent more than usual.[80] During the winter of that same year, the death toll for over-75s increased 10 per cent over the previous year.[81] Reportedly, more than 40 per cent of pensioners living alone cannot heat their homes adequately because of the cuts.[82] Overall, even after social transfers, 24 per cent of the population were still at risk of poverty and/or social exclusion, according to Eurostat.[83] In 2011, emigration increased by 85 per cent (in relation to the previous year). In both 2011 and 2012 it is estimated that more than 100,000 people left the country annually, with the majority being young people and/or highly skilled workers.[84] As of mid-2013, 18 per cent of the country's workforce, and more than 40 per cent of its youth, were unemployed.

Italy passed three major austerity budgets following the ECB's 'secret letter' of mid-2011 urging the government to introduce 'a major overhaul of the public administration' including the full liberalisation of local public services, large-scale privatisations, reduction of labour costs and more stringent criteria for pension benefits. The measures are projected to total €100 billion (more or less equally divided between expenditure reductions and revenue enhancements), equivalent to 6.1 per cent of GDP, over the 2011–14 period.[85] The fiscal consolidation measures, either implemented or planned, include:

- Cuts to social welfare programmes, such as the reduction of expenditure on disability programmes.[86]
- Cuts to health-care expenditure.[87]
- Wage cuts and/or freezes in the public sector.[88]
- A reduction in the number of employees in the public administration.[89]
- The reduction of transfers to local administrations.[90]
- Cuts to 'structural economic policy' funds.[91]
- A massive tax hike, including the reintroduction of the property tax on primary residencies and an increase in other property-related taxes, which alone raised more than €23 billion in 2012.[92]
- A 2 per cent increase in VAT to 23 per cent, with a further 0.5 per cent increase planned for 2014.[93]
- An increase in the gasoline tax.[94]
- An increase in women's retirement age to bring it on a par with men's.[95]

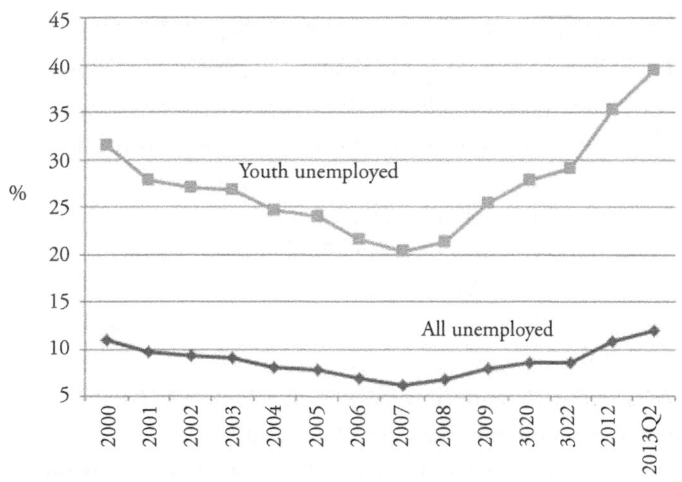

Figure 4.4 Italy's unemployment rates, 2000–13

Source: Eurostat.

- A pension reform requiring Italians to work 41 years before retirement.[96]
- The privatisation of state-controlled entities and buildings.[97]
- The liberalisation of formerly protected industries.[98]

As a result of these measures, and of their destructive effects on the wider economy (outlined below), millions of Italians are now struggling to make ends meet, according to a number of sources. In mid-2013, the youth unemployment rate almost hit 40 per cent – the third-highest rate in Europe, after Greece and Spain.

According to the country's national statistics institute Istat, in southern Italy one in three young people aged 15–29 were unemployed by mid-2013.[99] Just over half of new graduates were currently employed, with the Europe-wide average standing at 77.2 per cent.[100] Moreover, 14 per cent of Italy's population – 8.6 million people – were living on food assistance, a number that had doubled over the previous two years, according to the report.[101] Even more shockingly, some 15 million people – 25 per cent of the population – were living in families that met three or more poverty indicators (with those meeting more than four considered to be seriously deprived).[102] Italy, like Greece and Spain, has also seen a sharp increase in 'economic suicides'.[103]

Ireland – the second country to receive an EU-IMF bail-out after Greece – was also the country to undergo the second-largest fiscal consolidation programme in relation to GDP (again, after Greece), amounting to €32 billion by 2015, equivalent to a colossal 18 per cent of GDP.[104] The measures, either implemented or planned, include:

- Across-the-board budget cuts totalling almost €13 billion.[105]
- Cuts to the health-care budget of €750 million in 2011 alone, with more planned in the coming years.[106]
- Cuts in public-sector wages by an average 13.5 per cent.[107]
- A large-scale public-sector layoff, including the reduction of almost 25,000 public-sector jobs over peak 2008 levels.[108]
- An average 10 per cent cut in unemployment and welfare benefits, for a total of more than €3 billion by 2015.[109]
- A €150 million reduction in child benefits.[110]
- An increase in income taxes by more than €7 billion.[111]
- A 2 per cent increase in the VAT rate, from 21 to 23 per cent.[112]
- A one-year increase in the pension age to 66, with plans to raise it to 67 by 2021 and 68 by 2028.[113]
- A 0.7 per cent decrease in nominal wages over the 2009–12 period.[114]
- The reduction of the minimum wage by 12 per cent.[115]
- Increased 'labour market flexibility' and reallocation of labour within and across sectors.[116]
- The introduction of water metering by 2014.[117]

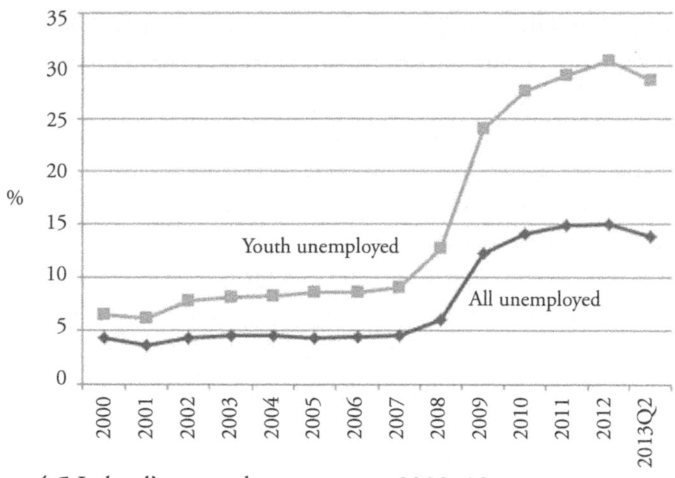

Figure 4.5 Ireland's unemployment rates, 2000–13

Source: Eurostat.

- Plans to privatise various state-owned companies.[118]

It is widely agreed that these measures have exacerbated the effects of the post-crisis recession in Ireland. In mid-2013, unemployment stood at 13.8 per cent, up from a pre-crisis rate of 4.6 per cent, while the youth unemployment rate was 28.6 per cent, up from a pre-crisis rate of 9 per cent.

Poverty is also dramatically on the rise: at 38 per cent, Ireland has the highest rate of children at risk in Western Europe and the fifth-highest in the European Union.[119] According to a 2012 report by the Irish League of Credit Unions, 61 per cent of people have less than €100 left at the end of the month once essential bills are paid, 36 per cent have less than €50 and 20 per cent have nothing at all.[120] Another survey showed that 56 per cent of Irish homes have been forced into debt to pay household bills.[121] Moreover, the Irish Central Statistics Office reported that almost one quarter of the population – over one million people – experienced two or more types of deprivation in 2011.[122] This poverty has manifested itself in hunger, with 10 per cent of the population – or 450,000 people – now in food poverty, according to 2010 data.[123]

Even though the above countries are the ones that have undergone (indeed, are undergoing) the harshest fiscal consolidation processes and neoliberal 'structural reforms', austerity has been far from limited to periphery countries. A number of Eastern European member states – such as the Slovak Republic, Slovenia and the Czech Republic – have implemented wide-ranging consolidation measures, all in the range of about 6 per cent of GDP, despite comparatively low deficit-to-GDP and debt-to-GDP ratios.[124] Major austerity budgets were also passed in the countries of the core. In mid-2010, Germany – in line with the idea that the country should 'set a positive example for other eurozone countries' – announced plans for an ambitious €80 billion consolidation programme, equivalent to 3 per cent of GDP.[125] However Germany's plan pales in comparison with the French one, totalling almost €100 billion by 2015 and including health-care and welfare cuts of €16 billion and the cutting of 150,000 public-sector jobs between 2009 and 2013.[126] Smaller but nonetheless significant fiscal consolidation measures were also approved in Belgium and the Netherlands.[127]

Austerity has not been limited to euro countries. The largest austerity programme underway in the continent, in absolute terms, is the United Kingdom's, estimated to total £130 billion, equivalent to 7 per cent of GDP, by 2015–16. This includes cuts to all administrative budgets between 33 and 40 per cent, the slashing of 710,000 public-sector jobs by 2015–16, drastic welfare cuts, an increase in the standard VAT rate from 17.5 to 20 per cent, and the raising of the pension age to 66 for men and women by 2020, and to 67 between 2026 and 2028.[128]

To varying degrees, the effects of austerity are being felt all across Europe – from Brussels to London, from Paris to Ljubljana – as an entire generation wrestles with unemployment, dwindling social services, and a general sense of hopelessness and precariousness – and comes to grip with the fact that, for the first time in the post-1945 period, they can expect to grow up poorer than their parents. As we have seen, though, it is not just hopes and expectations that are being destroyed. Increasingly, lives are being lost. Public health experts David Stuckler and Sanjay Basu explain in *The Body Economic: Why Austerity Kills* how by resorting to budget-crushing austerity measures many countries have turned their recessions into all-out epidemics. The authors estimate that more than 10,000 additional suicides and up to a million extra cases of depression have been recorded in Europe and the United States since governments started to introduce austerity programmes.[129] 'Had austerity been run like a drug trial, it would have been discontinued, given evidence of its deadly side-effects,' says Stuckler.[130] A recent article in the prestigious medical journal *The Lancet* also places the blame for the post-crisis deterioration of health levels across Europe on the austerity measures demanded by the troika, concluding that 'although recessions pose risks to health, the interaction of fiscal austerity with economic shocks and weak social protection is what ultimately seems to escalate health and social crises in Europe'.[131]

In short, few people would seriously dispute that austerity is exacting a very high social and human toll on the people of Europe. Is it at least delivering in economic and budgetary terms?

The Economic Effects of Austerity

In mid-2013, the EMU's economy made a very timid upturn, technically putting an end to a recession that had dragged on since the end of 2011 (given that reces-

Figure 4.6 EMU GDP growth rate, 2007–13 (percentage change over the previous quarter)

Source: ECB.

sions are commonly defined as two subsequent quarters of shrinking GDP). This was the longest recession since the Second World War, following a mild recovery in 2010–11. But as a number of commentators pointed out, there was little to rejoice about. Overall, the EMU's economy was 'weaker than ever since the start of the crisis'. The mild upturn was largely the result of improved conditions in core countries, at the expense of periphery states (an indication of the profoundly asymmetric nature of the 'recovery', something discussed in more depth later). Growth, unemployment and debt levels were still abysmal in many countries.[132]

Most agree that this is a direct consequence of austerity. As we saw in the previous chapters, immediately following the economic crash of 2008 governments had no other choice but to resort to deficit spending to finance the holes in public budgets that resulted from unemployment benefits shooting up and tax revenues falling. From a social and economic standpoint this made a lot of sense. It functioned as a circuit-breaker and allowed the European economies to recover rather swiftly from the post-crisis crash, as testified by the mild growth rates registered in the 2010–11 period.[133]

In fact, temporary economic stimulus was 'probably the most important reason we didn't have a full replay of the Great Depression', Paul Krugman writes.[134] Then in 2010, as austerity became the order of the day, these stimulus policies were dramatically reversed, while the warnings of some (admittedly not many) economists that austerity would derail the recovery process were ignored. As the then president of the ECB, Jean-Claude Trichet, confidently asserted, '[t]he idea that austerity measures could trigger stagnation is incorrect.'[135]

Trichet was probably referring to Harvard economists Alberto Alesina and Silvia Ardagna's much-quoted 2009 paper on 'expansionary austerity'. This claimed that fiscal consolidation, if focused on spending cuts, leads to economic expansion.[136] Their conclusion was categorically disproved the following year by the IMF. The Fund's review of Alesina and Ardagna's study reached the conclusion that the authors' measure of fiscal policy was seriously flawed and that fiscal consolidation is typically contractionary.[137]

As it turned out, Trichet was kind of right. Austerity has not triggered stagnation (that is, slow or no economic growth); it has triggered an all-out recession, short-circuiting the recovery and plunging Europe into a deadly economic vicious circle. In mid-2013, despite the mild upturn, the EMU's GDP was still almost 1 per cent lower than the previous year, and 3.1 per cent below its pre-crisis peak. Nor is there much sign of recovery in the near future.

The correlation between austerity and recession (or a worsening thereof) is rather intuitive. Basic economic theory suggests that other things being equal, cutting government spending causes the economy's overall output to fall, tax revenues to decrease and spending on welfare benefits to increase; almost invariably, the end result is slower growth (or a recession/depression). This self-reinforcing trend is known as 'pro-cyclicality'. Considering that throughout the 2010–13 period eurozone governments as a whole have engaged in fiscal consolidation programmes amounting to 3 per cent of GDP (according to the IMF's rather conservative estimates), that means that through cuts in public-sector wages, investments and social expenditures, and tax increases, they have taken roughly €300–400 billion of demand and purchasing power out of the economy in just a few years. The resulting disaster was predictable, especially if account is taken of the latest research into the so-called 'fiscal multiplier'.[138]

The fiscal multiplier measures the negative impact of fiscal consolidation on growth, and specifically how much a country's economic output changes for each euro of budget cuts and/or tax increases. The multiplier typically used by the IMF and other international organisations in 2010 to forecast the impact of austerity on economic growth was 0.5, meaning a 0.5 per cent reduction in GDP for every 1 per cent of fiscal consolidation.

This in itself should have been a reason for concern, given that in early 2010 Europe was still reeling from the post-crisis economic shock. Late 2012 and early 2013, though, marked the beginning of a growing ideological divergence between the IMF and the other two members of the troika, the European Commission and the ECB. Two IMF officials, chief economist Olivier Blanchard and economist Daniel Leigh, admitted that the Fund had wildly underestimated the impact that the radical austerity measures prescribed to the countries of the periphery would have on economic growth. They estimated that in the case of the European austerity and structural adjustment programmes started in 2010, the multiplier was between 0.9 and 1.7, meaning that in some cases 1 per cent of fiscal consolidation resulted in GDP contracting by as much as 1.7 per cent.[139]

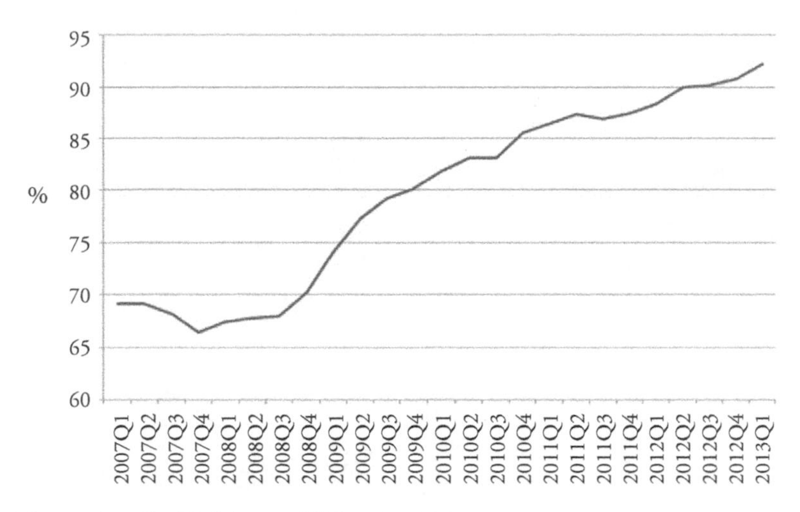

Figure 4.7 EMU debt-to-GDP ratio, 2007–13

Source: Eurostat.

As we have seen, a number of countries in the EMU have adopted fiscal consolidation plans between 6 and 18.5 per cent of GDP. The implication is that the destructive impact of austerity on the economies of these countries (and of Europe as a whole) has surpassed even the most pessimistic expectations. On the basis of Blanchard and Leigh's findings, a study by global advisory firm Oxford Economics has concluded that, had the peripheral economies of the EMU implemented fiscal austerity only half as severe over the 2010–13 period, Greek GDP would be nearly 14 per cent higher, Spain's GDP would be nearly 10 per cent higher, whilst Portugal's and Ireland's economies would have shrunk by 5.5 per cent and 3.5 per cent less respectively. The study also concludes that across the five PIIGS, the number of unemployed would be 1.2 million lower if fiscal austerity had been less severe.[140]

Austerity fails most spectacularly, even on its own narrow terms, when the effect on debt is considered. Less growth also means higher debt-to-GDP ratios. Since government debt is calculated as a percentage of GDP, if GDP declines (as it does in a recession), the debt-to-GDP ratio shoots up. In mid-2013 the eurozone's debt-to-GDP ratio stood at a record-high 92 per cent, compared with a pre-austerity level of 79.3 per cent at the end of 2009.

In other words, austerity is making it ever more difficult, if not nearly impossible, to reduce public debt-to-GDP ratios – especially when high debt levels are used to justify even harsher austerity measures, or force countries to request sovereign bail-outs that come with strict austerity-driven 'conditionalities' (while, of course, directly increasing the debt burden). As might be expected from the above data, those countries that have implemented the harshest austerity measures are also the ones that are showing the most adverse economic effects and the highest increases in debt levels.

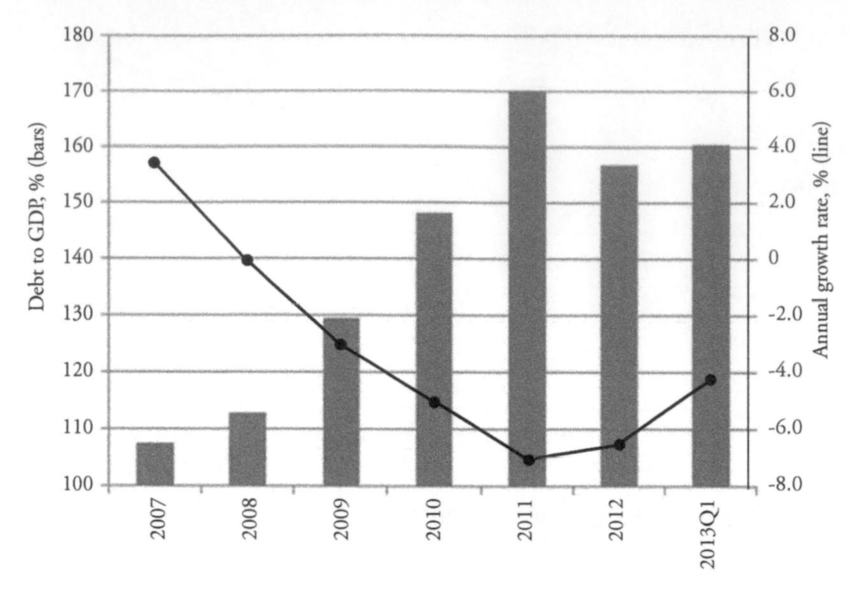

Figure 4.8 Greece's annual growth rate and debt-to-GDP ratio, 2007–13

Source: Eurostat.

Nowhere is this more obvious than in Greece. The country's debt-to-GDP ratio was 160 per cent in mid-2013, up from 145 per cent in 2010 – the year the European Union and IMF intervened to 'help' Greece cope with its excessive public debt – and from just above 100 per cent before the financial crisis.

In short, one of the most fierce austerity programmes ever tried in a Western country – ostensibly prescribed as a cure for Greece's ballooning debt – has had the effect of increasing by almost 50 per cent the country's pre-crisis debt-to-GDP ratio. This is a consequence of both the bail-out loans and of the wider devastation wrought on the Greek economy by the austerity policies, with Greek GDP declining by almost 20 per cent since 2008. The near-complete failure of the Greek bail-out – even according to the troika's dubious aims – was recently admitted by none other the IMF, in a damning report released in mid-2013. The report noted that many IMF board members had serious misgivings about offering Greece such a huge loan in relation to the size of its economy, insisting that it would make Greek public debt – which, according to the report, was still sustainable at the time – ultimately unsustainable. Ostensibly, the Fund argued for an early write-down (or 'haircut') of the Greek debt, but the other two members of the troika – the European Commission and the ECB – vigorously opposed any losses for the bondholders. They opted instead to save bondholders at the expense of the Greek people. Recently leaked classified documents and notes from a dramatic meeting of the Fund on 9 May 2010 – when the governing board of the IMF approved the first Greek bail-out – reveal that some member states had serious doubt about the real aims of the programme. As the Brazilian representative uncompromisingly stated:

> The risks of the program are immense .... As it stands, the program risks substituting private for official financing. In other and starker words, it may be seen not as a rescue of Greece, which will have to undergo a wrenching adjustment, but as a bailout of Greece's private debt holders, mainly European financial institutions.[141]

When the European Union and ECB were forced to agree to the 'haircut' in the summer of 2011, the damage was already done. As a result, says the IMF, the plan has been a failure on all fronts: 'Market confidence was not restored, the banking system lost 30 percent of its deposits and the economy encountered a much deeper than expected recession with exceptionally high unemployment.'[142] The implications of the IMF's report are unequivocal. The complete destruction of the Greek economy, the suffering of millions and the death by suicide and deprivation of countless citizens was not the inevitable outcome of the economic crisis, but was a direct result of the criminal – murderous might not be too harsh a term – policies imposed on the country by the European Union-ECB-IMF troika.

In Spain the situation is just as bleak: after two years of tax increases, spending cuts and bank rescues, the country's economy is contracting at a rate of almost 2 per cent, while its debt-to-GDP ratio has soared to a record-high (in its modern history) 88 per cent, as of mid-2013. Even though, as of late 2013, the Spanish government has not yet asked for an ECB bail-out under the new OMT

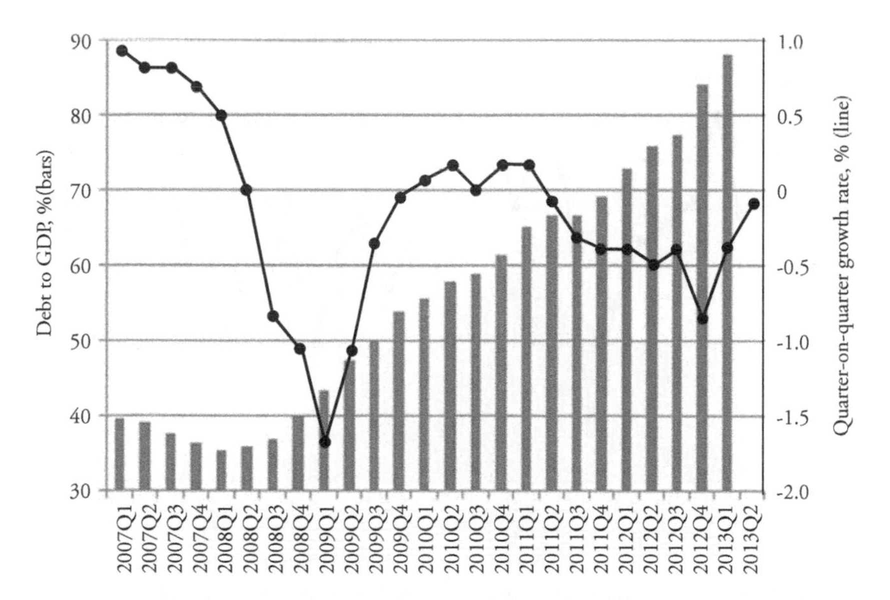

Figure 4.9 Spain's quarter-on-quarter growth rate and debt-to-GDP ratio, 2007–13

Source: ECB and Eurostat.

programme – probably in order to avoid the even deeper austerity that it would entail – many analysts believe it is just a question of time before it does.

As for Portugal, despite having complied completely with the austerity demands associated with its bail-out (or, as many would argue, precisely because of that), its economy is shrinking at a rate of 2 per cent year-on-year (despite a mild quarter-on-quarter recovery in mid-2013) and its debt is growing: in mid-2013 it was standing at 125 per cent of GDP, up from 108 per cent when it was bailed out by the troika.

Italy, another country that has seen the introduction of harsh austerity measures under Monti's technocratic government (subsequently confirmed by the new government elected in February 2013), is in a severe recession. Moreover, at the end of 2012, the Italian central bank announced that the country's public debt had risen to an all-time high of over €2 trillion, with its debt-to-GDP ratio also standing at a record 127 per cent, as of mid-2013, up from 113 per cent in 2009.

The same goes for Ireland: while the country is suffering from a milder recession than other periphery countries, its debt-to-GDP ratio is ballooning, having increased fivefold, as of mid-2013, from pre-crisis levels.

So wherever it has been tested, austerity has not only generated devastating social outcomes – with a number of countries in the midst, or on the verge, of outright humanitarian crises – it has also crippled the economies and destroyed the productive capacity of those countries, resulting in record-high unemployment levels and ballooning debt-to-GDP ratios. It's a deadly vicious circle, akin to trying to pay

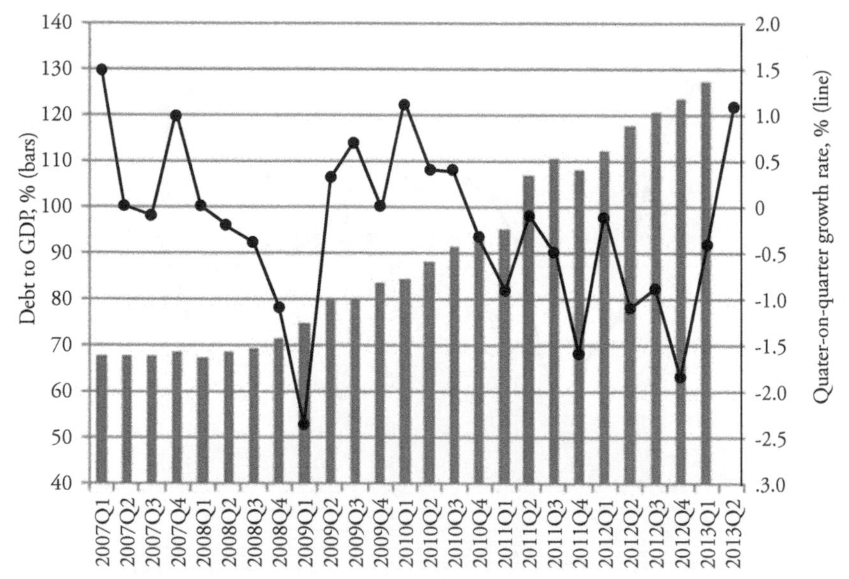

Figure 4.10 Portugal's quarter-on-quarter growth rate and debt-to-GDP ratio, 2007–13

Source: ECB and Eurostat.

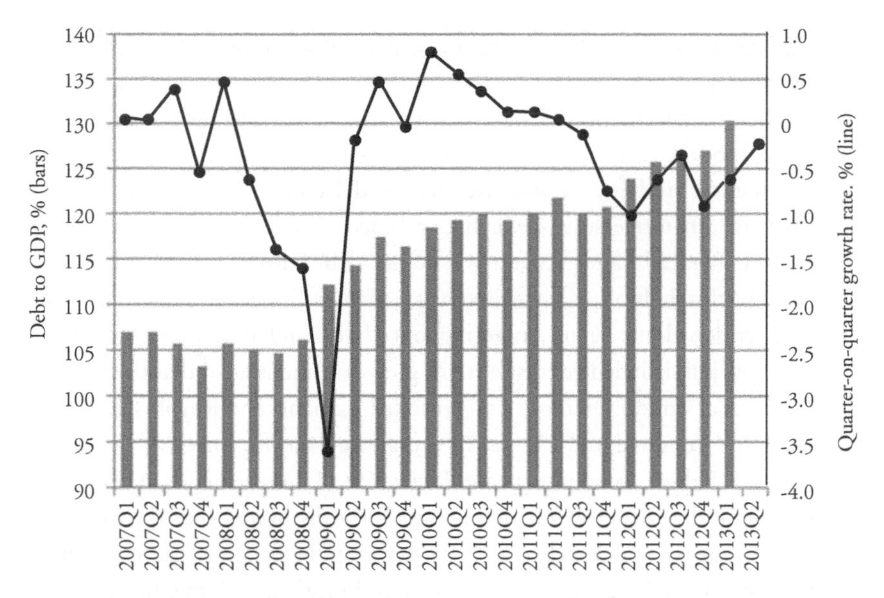

Figure 4.11 Italy's quarter-on-quarter growth rate and debt-to-GDP ratio, 2007–13

Source: ECB and Eurostat.

down a large credit card balance after taking a pay cut: you can slash expenses, but with lower earnings it is hard (if not impossible) to set aside money to pay off debt.

These dismal figures highlight one of the fundamental fallacies of the pro-austerity ideology (and of the entire EMU architecture, for that matter): the idea

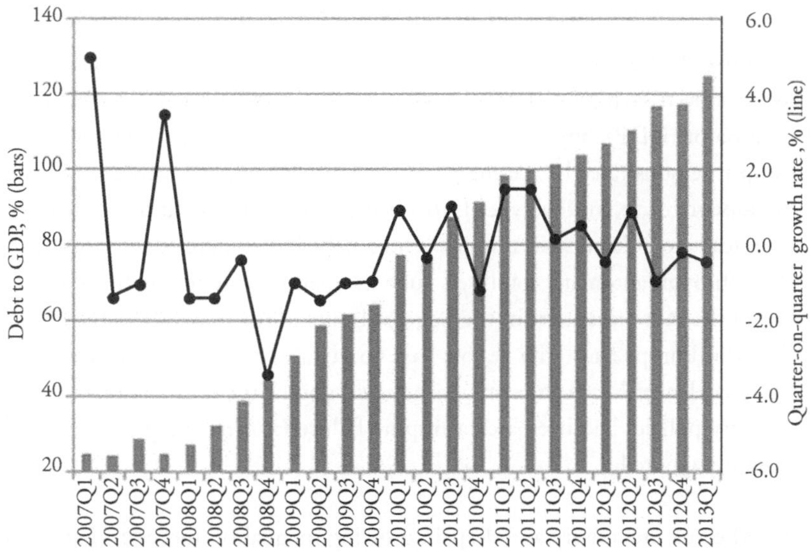

Figure 4.12 Ireland's quarter-on-quarter growth rate and debt-to-GDP ratio, 2007–13

Source: ECB and Eurostat.

that 'high' levels of public debt inevitably lead to slower growth (and thus have to be avoided at all costs), when it is actually the other way round. One of the most oft-cited theoretical justifications for fiscal austerity and debt reduction in the aftermath of the financial crisis, in both Europe and the United States, was a hugely influential study by Carmen Reinhart and Kenneth Rogoff. The authors conducted an exhaustive survey which concluded that economic growth starts to decline dramatically after a country's public debt surpasses the 90 per cent debt-to-GDP threshold.[143] Many economists, such as Robert J. Shiller and Paul Krugman, criticised the report, pointing out that Reinhart and Rogoff never explained how public indebtedness restrains growth – and argued that there could be other forces at work. Even those who criticised Reinhart and Rogoff's notion of a debt-to-GDP threshold, though, assumed that the data was correct.

In mid-2013 three economists at the University of Massachusetts Amherst set out to replicate the Rogoff-Reinhart findings. They discovered that their conclusion was the result of – an Excel error.[144] By factoring the data into the spreadsheet correctly, the new study found that the average real GDP growth rate for countries carrying a public debt-to-GDP ratio of over 90 per cent is actually 2.2 per cent, not -0.1 per cent – thus transforming high-debt countries from recession to growth! In a damning reanalysis of the Reinhart and Rogoff study, Arindrajit Dube of the University of Massachusetts Amherst confirmed that there is indeed a statistical correlation between high debt-to-GDP ratios and slow GDP growth, but that the causation is running in the reverse direction to the one suggested by Reinhart and Rogoff: it is slower growth that leads to higher debt-to-GDP ratios, and not vice versa.[145]

Of course, Dube simply provides statistical backing to what Keynesian economists have been saying for decades: since the ratio has a numerator (debt) and a denominator (GDP), any fall in GDP will automatically make it larger (as has been amply demonstrated by the euro crisis). That is why austerity, by exacerbating the recessionary cycle, inevitably leads to a rise in debt-to-GDP ratios. Moreover, a recession leads to a decrease in revenues and a debt-based increase in government spending through automatic stabilisers such as unemployment benefits – and, in the case of the more recent crisis, the huge bail-outs of the financial sector.

What did Europe's austerity zealots have to say about this scathing rebuttal of their core evidence? Much the same as they said about the IMF's admission that the austerity policies had been a catastrophic failure (and not only in Greece). It was blatantly ignored.

Social and economic misery and despair, growing inequality (more on that later), dwindling public services, loss of hope and ballooning debts: this is austerity's scorched-earth legacy. Perhaps the saddest thing about this whole story, though, is that this outcome could easily have been predicted (and a few economists did indeed predict it), simply by looking at the many instances in which countries have resorted to austerity – or, more commonly, have been forced into it – in the past.

Austerity: Lessons from the Past

As we saw in Chapter 1, the forces that gave rise to the various subprime crises, the Great Recession and the euro crisis were similar to the ones that led to the crash of 1929 and the subsequent Great Depression: radical free-market capitalism, minimal financial regulation and widening inequalities. And the unregulated capital flows that generated huge imbalances within Europe (as well as between Europe and the United States) during the 1920s – dividing the continent in creditor and debtor nations, and ultimately paving the way for war – closely resembled the ones tearing Europe apart today. (The roles then were reversed, with Germany in the role of the boom-to-bust country.)

In the mid-1920s, after the excessively punitive schedule of war reparation payments and transfers of property and equipment imposed on Germany under the Treaty of Versailles was revised, its French and American creditors started to pour huge sums of money into the battered German economy, attracted by the prospects of rapid growth that it offered. The massive inflow of capital helped fund Germany's sovereign obligations and led to soaring wages. Consequently, Germany underwent a credit-driven boom very similar to the ones which developed in the European periphery in the mid-2000s.[146]

When the speculative bubbles in both Europe and the United States burst in the aftermath of the Wall Street crash of 1929, both continents (to varying degrees, and more or less willingly) turned to austerity as a perceived 'cure' for the excesses of the previous decade. In the United States, President Herbert Hoover, a year after the crash, declared that 'economic depression cannot be cured by legislative action or executive pronouncements' and that 'economic wounds must be healed by the action of the cells of the economic body – the producers and consumers themselves'.[147] At first Hoover and his officials downplayed the stock market crash, claiming that the economic slump would be only temporary and that it would actually help clean up corruption and bad business practices within the system. When the situation did not improve, Hoover advocated a strict *laissez-faire* policy, dictating that the federal government should not interfere with the economy but rather let the economy right itself. He counselled that 'every individual should sustain faith and courage' and 'each should maintain self-reliance'.[148]

Even though Hoover supported a doubling of government expenditure on public works projects, he also firmly believed in the need for a balanced budget. As Nouriel Roubini and Stephen Mihm observe, Hoover 'wanted to reconcile contradictory aims: to cultivate self-reliance, to provide government help in a time of crisis, and to maintain fiscal discipline. This was impossible.'[149] In fact it is widely agreed that Hoover's inaction was responsible for the worsening of the Great Depression.

If the United States' reaction under Hoover can be described as 'too little, too late', Europe's reaction in the late 1920s and early 1930s actively contributed to the downward spiral of the Great Depression, setting the stage for the Second World War. Austerity was in fact the dominant response of European governments during the early years of the Great Depression. As the historian Steven Bryan writes, then as now, '[g]overnments and the major media deemed finance more important than industry and employment and government policy reflected that choice'.[150] That choice would have disastrous consequences, especially for Germany.

In 1929, in response to the financial panic gripping the markets, investors rapidly pulled their money out of the country. Suddenly deprived of foreign capital, and unable to rely on exports for growth because of the inflated wages left behind by the boom now gone bust, Germany turned to austerity to meet its debt obligations – just as the countries of the periphery have done in recent years. Germany also faced the same problem that today's less competitive countries of the eurozone face: since its exchange rate was fixed by the gold standard, it could not resort to currency devaluation to boost its exports. This meant that competitiveness could only be restored through a slow and painful decline in wages, despite skyrocketing unemployment levels – the same solution envisaged today by Germany and the EU elites for the periphery countries of the EMU.

As the effects of the financial crisis started to ripple across the continent, banks everywhere came under pressure. In 1931 the failure of Austria's largest bank, Credit-Anstalt, triggered a loss of confidence that quickly spread, rapidly leading to an all-out European banking crisis. As pressure built in Germany, the leaders of the largest economies repeatedly met to discuss the possibility of assisting the flailing economy. But the French, in particular, would brook no reduction in Germany's debt and reparations payments. Refusing to accept a restructuring of Germany's debt, the country's creditors – in another similarity with the events unfolding in Europe today – tried to set up a fund to lend to governments and banks in need of capital, in order to avoid at all costs a German default. (This was not unlike today's ESM bail-out fund.) Unlike today, though, the plan fell through. And so the dominoes fell.

As the crisis worsened, Danatbank, at the time the second biggest bank in Germany, went bust some two months after Credit-Anstalt, triggering yet another wave of massive runs on every other German bank. The government was forced to introduce capital controls and suspend gold payments, effectively unpegging its currency. At that point Germany's economy collapsed, and the horrors of the 1930s began. By 1933 Hitler had gained power and was set on bringing full employment to Nazi Germany in a different way – by arms production, rapid expansion of the military, and imperialist conquest. This, as everyone knows, was followed by the Second World War, with five years of destruction and the deaths of over 60 million people.

Various historians and economists see the rise of Hitler as a direct consequence of the austerity policies indirectly imposed on Germany by its creditors following the economic crash of the late 1920s. Ewald Nowotny, the head of Austria's national bank and a member of the ECB's governing council, recently sent shockwaves across the European establishment by stating that it was precisely 'the single-minded concentration on austerity policy' in the 1930s that 'led to mass unemployment, a breakdown of democratic systems and, at the end, to the catastrophe of Nazism'.[151] Historian Steven Bryan agrees: 'During the 1920s and 1930s it was precisely the refusal to acknowledge the social and political consequences of austerity that helped bring about not only the depression, but also the authoritarian governments of the 1930s.'[152]

As Europe descended into chaos, the United States, under the newly elected President Franklin D. Roosevelt, chose to tackle the Great Depression in a radically different way. As we saw in Chapter 1, Roosevelt understood that the roots of the crisis laid in out-of-control, unfettered capitalism, which called for radical reforms of the US financial system. He also understood that financial reform, albeit necessary, was not enough. Partly inspired by the writings of British economist John Maynard Keynes, he did away with Hoover's let-the-markets-sort-themselves-out approach, and implemented a huge government stimulus plan to kick-start the economy. In 1938 he famously stated that 'if private enterprise did not provide jobs this spring, government would take up the slack'.[153]

In the 1920s and 1930s Keynes spearheaded a revolution in economic thinking, overturning the older ideas in economics which held that free markets could automatically provide full employment, as long as workers were flexible in their wage demands. Keynes instead argued – this is spelled out at length in his masterpiece, *The General Theory of Employment, Interest, and Money*, published in 1936 – that aggregate demand determined the overall level of economic activity, and that inadequate aggregate demand could lead to prolonged periods of high unemployment. Thus, he advocated the use of debt-based expansionary fiscal and monetary measures – the exact opposite of austerity – to mitigate the adverse effects of economic recessions and depressions, first and foremost by creating jobs that the private sector was unable to provide, by investing in public works. Once the economy had started growing again, the increased revenues would allow governments to pay back any outstanding debts.

In the following decades, fiscal policy became the weapon of choice when dealing with economic downturns. Keynes's ideas provided inspiration for Roosevelt's New Deal, during which the government funded countless public projects and social programmes, including Social Security. The amount of construction undertaken during Roosevelt's New Deal remains impressive to this day. It included 24,000 miles of sewer lines, 480 airports, 78,000 bridges, 780 hospitals, 572,000 miles of highways, and upwards of 15,000 schools, court houses and other public buildings.[154] Roosevelt's policies gave the United States three decades of relative social and economic stability, from the 1940s until the 1970s, during which inequality fell sharply, median incomes grew rapidly, and the working and middle classes experienced a sharp rise in their living standards.

After the Second World War, Europe and other countries (Canada and Japan, for example) followed suit, abandoning *laissez-faire* capitalism in favour of strongly state-regulated economies, known also as mixed economies. The war ended with a clear determination in the West to pursue policies and create international institutions to make impossible any repetition of the deadly 1930s mixture of high unemployment, national aggression and beggar-thy-neighbour trade and austerity policies. In 1944 the International Labour Organization (ILO) adopted the Declaration of Philadelphia, outlining rules on salary, working time and the fair and equitable sharing of salaries and dividends to be respected in each country and in global trade. In 1945 the United Nations was set up to support policies aimed at the attainment of full employment, labour rights and rising living standards on a world scale.

In spite of the Cold War, much of this economic agenda was achieved. Until the 1970s, developed countries enjoyed 25 years of mostly low levels of unemployment, greater economic stability and higher levels of economic growth than ever before. Living standards rose, and – especially in Europe – a variety of policies and institutions for welfare and social protection (also known as the 'welfare state') were created, including sustained investment in universally available social services such as education and health. All this was an unmistakable demonstration that there clearly were alternatives to the austerity policies and economic depression of the 1930s.

We saw in Chapter 1 how this model started to crumble in the 1970s, under the weight of the neoliberal counter-revolution. By the start of the 1980s, the two most important countries of the West were ruled by free-market fundamentalists: Margaret Thatcher in Britain and Ronald Reagan in the United States. The new social order established in the centre was then exported to the periphery. The advocates of neoliberalism, though, understood that a clean break with the post-war social democratic model would have proved politically unfeasible in the West. Hence, they turned to developing countries as a testing ground for their pure breed of *laissez-faire* capitalism.

Developing countries seeking finance from the IMF and the World Bank were forced to adopt the new neoliberal policies, which included harsh austerity measures – similar to the ones being imposed today on the periphery countries of the eurozone – as a condition of international support. The programmes of structural adjustment and austerity imposed by the IMF on developing countries in the 1980s and 1990s undermined many of the achievements of the previous growth model, driving living standards down and poverty levels up.[155] By the mid-1990s, no less than 57 developing countries had become poorer in per capita income than

15 years earlier – and in some cases than 25 years earlier.[156] In almost all countries where free-market, austerity-driven policies were imposed, poverty and unemployment grew, labour rights deteriorated, inequality soared, and financial and economic instability increased.[157]

In 2003 even the IMF's independent evaluation office, in a study which analysed 133 IMF-supported austerity programmes in 70 (mostly developing) countries, acknowledged that policy makers had consistently underestimated the disastrous effects of rigid spending cuts on economic growth.[158] It found that targets for fiscal consolidation were mostly missed, for the same (and rather obvious) reasons as the policies are failing in Europe today. 'Absolute levels of revenue respond to growth, with shortfalls in growth leading to corresponding shortfalls in revenue', the paper concluded.[159] Another IMF study, which looked at 173 episodes in which advanced economies undertook budgetary measures aimed at fiscal consolidation over the past 30 years, reached the same conclusions, finding that economic contraction and increased unemployment were the consistent results.[160]

Austerity is proving to be a colossal failure of economic policy, not to mention a cause of immense human suffering. Moreover, there is overwhelming historical and analytical evidence that whenever and wherever it has been tested, in both developed and advanced countries, it has worked terribly in an economic as well as a social sense. A number of historians consider the austerity policies pursued in Europe and the United States in the 1920s a leading cause of the Great Depression of the 1930s, which set the stage for (and to a certain extent directly contributed to) the horror and destruction of the Second World War.

And yet, since the onset of the euro crisis, the EU establishment – with the IMF's support, even more incredibly given the number of studies by the Fund itself which disprove the supposed benefits of austerity – has blindly pursued these disastrously flawed policies. This begs the question, why? The reasons suggested are numerous and often overlapping: ideology, lobbying and vested interests are among the main ones. This is how John Maynard Keynes, reflecting on the 'victory' of the neoclassical model – the precursor to neoliberalism – in the early 20th century, explained its success:

> It must have been due to a complex of suitabilities in the doctrine to the environment into which it was projected. That it reached conclusions quite different from what the ordinary uninstructed person would expect, added, I suppose, to its intellectual prestige. That its teaching, translated into practice, was austere and often unpalatable, lent it virtue. That it was adapted to carry a vast and consistent logical superstructure, gave it beauty. That it could explain much social injustice and apparent cruelty as an inevitable incident in the scheme of progress, and the attempt to change such things as likely on the whole to do more harm than good, commended it to authority. That it afforded a measure of justification to the free activities of the individual capitalist, attracted to it the support of the dominant social force behind authority.[161]

Paraphrasing Keynes, we could say that the power of austerity resides in the fact that it 'explains much social injustice and apparent cruelty as the inevitable consequence of the crisis', which obviously 'attracts to it the support of the dominant social forces'. After all, are we really to believe that the European Union's insistence on pursuing austerity – which is proving to be a colossal failure even by mainstream economic standards, while at the same time hugely benefiting 'the dominant social forces behind authority' in Europe – is purely a case of political and ideological short-sightedness? Vicente Navarro, professor of public policy at Johns Hopkins University, writes (the italics are mine):

> The arguments put forward, even by people from the Left to explain why [austerity policies continue to be pursued despite their devastating impact on the economy], is that economists who manage or advise on these austerity policies are incompetent or ignorant. But these arguments are not credible. Another argument that has been used is that these economists are imbued with an ideology, a neoliberal ideology that they practice and promote with a faith that lacks an empirical base. But this argument ignores the fact that *this faith exists because it benefits those that promote and sustain it.* There are very powerful interests – for which such economists work – supporting austerity.[162]

This raises another possible, and even more disturbing, explanation of current European policies: that austerity was never about 'saving' the distressed economies of the eurozone and promoting growth. Viewed in this light, the policies pursued by the EU elites since the onset of the euro crisis, far from being 'short-sighted', 'blind', 'self-defeating' or 'flawed', suddenly appear surprisingly coherent. After all, when we say that austerity has 'failed', we have to ask, who has it failed? Has it really failed everyone?

Austerity: Just Another Name for Class Warfare

As for the officially stated aims and the sectors of society that austerity has failed, the list is long: it has failed to spur growth, plunging Europe back into recession (or depression, depending on who you talk to); it has failed workers, and in particular young people, with unemployment rates at the highest levels in modern European history; it has failed small and medium-sized businesses, strangled by the recession and still mostly cut off from credit; it has failed to restore market confidence, with little productive investment in the continent's economies; it has failed the weakest sectors of society, as vital systems of social support (the welfare state) are systematically dismantled; it has even failed to ease the continent's debt-to-GDP ratios, which are dramatically on the rise. So who has austerity not failed? As you have probably guessed by now, it has not failed the continent's creditors – that is, the banks and big investment funds – or more generally the wealthy elite. The reason is simple, some argue: that was its intended purpose all along. Paul Krugman writes (my italics):

> If you look at what [the advocates of austerity] want – fiscal policy that focuses on deficits rather than on job creation, monetary policy that obsessively fights even the hint of inflation [...] – all of it in effect *serves the interests of creditors*, of those who lend as opposed to those who borrow and/or work for a living. Lenders want governments to make honoring their debts the highest priority.[163]

How conscious politicians are of the vested interests that their policies serve (rather than simply buying into the neoliberal ideology that predates them) is a matter of debate, but given the cosiness between the financial industry and the EU elite, it is hardly surprising that the interests of lenders were given precedence over those of citizens and workers. To better understand how austerity serves the interests of creditors, at the expense of citizens, it is important to understand the different ways in which a country can assess its budget.

When we talk about a country's budget, we have to distinguish between the 'primary budget' and the 'secondary budget'. The *primary budget*, also known as the 'primary balance', refers to how much a government earns, minus what it spends, not including interest payments on the existing debt. The *secondary budget* refers to the interest on the existing debt, also knows as the 'debt service'. The two combined form the total government 'budget balance', which can be either in deficit or in surplus. In the years following the financial crash of 2008, there was a lot of talk about 'exploding government deficits' – hence the need for drastic austerity measures to atone for years of government profligacy, or so the official story went. As we saw in Chapter 3, though, this was largely a myth: prior to the crisis, the overall fiscal deficit (including interest payments) of the eurozone was in line with, or very close to, the parameters of the Maastricht Treaty (which set the maximum deficit-to-GDP ratio at 3 per cent). The same goes for the PIIGS countries (some of which, such as Spain and Ireland, had among the lowest deficit ratios in the entire EMU).

There was indeed a sharp increase in government deficits in the years following the financial crash, but again, this was not caused by excessive government spending but by the combined effects of the massive bank bail-outs, the fall in government revenues (because of the post-crash recession) and the government stimulus programmes necessary to avoid an all-out depression. In any case, beginning in 2010, deficit and debt reduction became the eurozone's mantras. Today, as a result of the drastic budget cuts and tax hikes (mostly on the lower and middle classes) imposed across Europe, the deficit levels (in the eurozone as a whole, and in most periphery countries) are starting to decrease again.

This is often cited by the pro-austerity camp as a demonstration that austerity 'is working'. Technically that is true, but only on the basis of the austerity regime's biased and ideologically driven assumptions: that is, that budget deficits are inherently bad, and therefore governments should always aim for a balanced budget, even in a recession. In reality, as we have seen, these deficit reductions have come at a huge social and economic cost. Not only are they triggering all-out humanitarian crises in a growing number of countries, as vital systems of social support are systematically dismantled; they are directly responsible for deepening the recession and driving the continent's economies into recession, as testified by the IMF itself. The logical conclusion is that the deficits will start to grow again as a result of the dramatic collapse in revenues, as many experts predict, which will in turn be used as an excuse to implement further budget cuts, further deepening the recessionary spiral. And yet the EU establishment insists that Europe needs 'more austerity' – while graciously offering countries a little more time to reach their deficit-reduction targets. Is this obsession with 'sound public finances' just another case of neoliberal ideological short-sightedness, or is there more to it?

It is a common misconception that when we talk of 'budget deficits' we are talking uniquely of government revenues minus expenses: that is, governments spending more than they collect in taxes. (Supposedly this is one of the main issues austerity addresses, even though it is bound to fail even on these terms, for the reasons explained above.) However the overall budget balance includes the interest payments on the existing debt. A country's public finances (revenues minus expenditures, excluding interest payments), on the other hand, are defined by the primary budget. So how is Europe faring in this respect?

According to data by the European Commission, between 1992 and 2008 the eurozone has constantly registered a primary surplus – that is, on average, it has consistently earned more than (or as much as) it has spent, if we exclude interest payments. By mid-2013, following the post-crisis rise in deficits, it was estimated to have regained a primary budget balance (see Table 4.1).

In other words, Europeans – far from being the money-guzzlers the pro-austerity camp accuses them of being – are among the most fiscally responsible people in the world, and have largely been living well within their means for the past decade and a half. Even if we look at the PIIGS countries – supposedly the most profligate of all – we can see that, prior to the financial crisis of 2008, three countries (Italy, Ireland and Spain) had primary budget surpluses (that is, they earned more than

Table 4.1 Average EMU government annual primary balance as a percentage of GDP (excluding interest payments)

Year	Percentage	Year	Percentage
1992–6	+0.2	2009	-3.5
1997–2001	+2.5	2010	-3.4
2002–06	+0.6	2011	-1.1
2007	+2.3	2012	-0.6
2008	+0.9	2013 (forecast)	+0.2

Source: European Commission.

Table 4.2 Periphery countries: government annual primary balance as a percentage of GDP (excluding interest payments)

	Italy	Greece	Portugal	Ireland	Spain
1992–6	+2.9	+1.6	+0.9	+3.9	-1.0
1997–2001	+5.0	+3.6	-0.6	+5.0	+1.8
2002–06	+1.3	-1.0	-1.8	+2.4	+2.7
2007	+3.4	-2.0	-0.2	+1.1	+3.5
2008	+2.5	-4.8	-0.6	-6.0	-2.9
2009	-0.8	-10.5	-7.3	-11.8	-9.4
2010	+0.1	-4.9	-7.0	-27.7	-7.7
2011	+1.2	-2.4	-0.4	-10.0	-7.0
2012	+2.5	-5.0	-2.0	-3.9	-7.7
2013 (forecast)	+2.4	0.0	-1.1	-2.4	-3.2

Source: European Commission.

they spent) and one (Portugal) had a near-balanced primary budget. Greece was the only country with a serious primary budget deficit. Moreover, all the PIIGS (with the exception of Spain) had managed to drastically reduce their post-crisis rise in primary deficits by 2013, with Italy regaining a surplus and Greece coming very close to a near-balanced budget (see Table 4.2).

It would a mistake to consider these 'improvements' in the fiscal position of the PIIGS as unambiguously positive: they have been achieved at a huge social and economic cost, are one of the main contributing factors to Europe's deepening crisis, and are bound to be short-lived. But they do put to shame the EU establishment's assertions that Europe needs 'more austerity', and most of all, that the purpose of austerity is to put the fiscal house of European countries in order.

If this was the case, most member states (including those of the periphery) would have no reason to keep implementing austerity measures, and would be able to launch massive employment- and growth-spurring stimulus programmes without further indebting themselves by virtue of their close-to-balanced or even surplus primary budgets. The problem is the interest payments on the existing debt. When these are factored in, the numbers change dramatically (Table 4.3).

So to the extent that the eurozone as a whole was – and still is – running an

Table 4.3 Average EMU government annual budget balance as a percentage of GDP (including interest payments)

Year	Percentage	Year	Percentage
1992–92	-5.3	2009	-6.4
1997-01	-1.7	2010	-6.2
2002-06	-2.5	2011	-4.2
2007	-0.7	2012	-3.7
2008	-2.1	2013 (forecast)	-2.9

Source: European Commission.

Table 4.4 EMU: primary balance versus budget balance as a percentage of GDP (2012 data)

Primary balance	-0.6
Budget balance	-3.7
Interest expenditure	+3.1 (€400 billion/year)

Source: European Commission.

overall budget deficit, it is entirely because of interest on previous debts. According to the European Commission, in 2012 the eurozone as a whole spent 3.1 per cent of its GDP – or roughly €400 billion, more than the combined GDPs of Greece and Ireland – solely on servicing its debts, or in other words, repaying banks and investment funds (see Table 4.4). The contrast is even more stark in the case of the PIIGS, which all register overall budget deficits which exceed by far their primary budget levels (Table 4.5).

So with the exception of Spain, these countries are registering relatively high overall deficits despite their massive cost-cutting largely because of the huge interest on their existing debt. European Commission data shows that the periphery countries of the eurozone are using a higher percentage of their GDP to service their debts than during the past 15 years because of higher refinancing interest rates (see Table 4.6).[164]

In these shocking numbers we find the most plausible explanation of the pain and suffering currently being imposed on the people of Europe. In times of crisis – when countries cannot collect enough money through revenues to fund their expenditures *and* service their debt interest – governments have to choose how to use their limited resources. They could choose to roll over their debt (although that requires a central bank willing to buy government bonds, keeping interest rates down: something the eurozone still doesn't have, the OMT programme's bond buying in exchange for austerity notwithstanding); they could choose to monetise their debt by printing money, which usually increases the rate of inflation, eroding the real value of the debt and freeing up resources for the funding of public

Table 4.5 Periphery countries: government annual budget balance as a percentage of GDP (including interest payments)

	Italy	Greece	Portugal	Ireland	Spain
1993–2007	-4.3	-6.2	-4.6	+0.7	-0.1
2008	-2.7	-9.8	-3.6	-7.3	-4.5
2009	-5.5	-15.6	-10.2	-13.9	-11.2
2010	-4.5	-10.7	-9.8	-30.8	-9.7
2011	-3.8	-9.5	-4.4	-13.4	-9.4
2012	-3.0	-10.0	-6.4	-7.6	-10.6
2013 (forecast)	-2.9	-3.8	-5.5	-7.5	-6.5

Source: European Commission.

Table 4.6 Periphery countries: primary balance versus budget balance as a percentage of GDP (2012 data)

	Italy	Ireland	Greece	Portugal	Spain
Primary bal.	+2.5	-3.9	-5.0	-2.0	-7.7
Budget bal.	-3.0	-7.6	-10.0	-6.4	-10.6
Interest exp.	+5.5	+3.7	+5.0	+4.4	+3.0
Interest exp., € billion/year	86	6	9.5	7.2	31

Source: European Commission.

services (a policy the ECB is firmly opposed to); they could choose to restructure or renegotiate their debt, which also frees up public money; they could choose to default on their debt altogether; or they could choose to increase taxes and cut expenditures – in other words, to pursue austerity – to free up money to pay the interest. Even if they choose this last option, governments can mitigate the burden on the weakest sectors of society by hitting the better-off the hardest – something European countries have consistently and shamefully refused to do, as we shall see.

Historian Steven Bryan writes:

> All societies make these choices, whether they admit it or not. Depressions and recessions have their own winners and losers, as do inflation and deflation. It is perfectly logical for bondholders to take whatever moves they view as likely to cause repayment of those bonds – even if this means the economy in general is weaker or someone else goes without a job.[165]

Salvatore Babones, senior lecturer in sociology and social policy at the University of Sydney, puts it even more bluntly: 'Austerity is nothing more than a way to make sure that banks and vulture funds get paid. It's about deciding who deserves more of society's limited resources and who deserves less.'[166] In other words, the purpose (or at least, one purpose) of the austerity policies was never to help the troubled countries of the eurozone, but simply to re-establish their debt-servicing capacity. The cuts and tax hikes did not make European governments any richer, or their public finances any more sustainable; the money 'saved' by cutting back on crucial public services went straight into the pockets of the creditors – and in Ireland's case, the bailed-out banks.

Ireland's problems over its bank bail-out were outlined in Chapter 1 (page 6). By 2013 the government was finding it increasingly difficult to justify continuing to pay out the enormous sums required – with the yearly €3.1 billion instalment roughly equivalent to the value of the austerity measures implemented by Dublin that year – and in February it reached an agreement with the ECB to replace the promissory notes with long-term government bonds. This meant that the state would be able to make more gradual repayments – providing some respite, in theory at least, to the Irish people and economy.[167]

It is particularly telling that in all periphery countries except Ireland the cuts implemented between 2010 and 2013 amounted to less than was spent on interest payments (see Table 4.7).

So in essence, austerity has resulted in a huge transfer of resources from the public to the private sector. It might seem outrageous that we should sacrifice the social support systems millions of people in Europe rely on just to pay back the big banks, but many EU and government officials have made it clear in recent years that this is their policy. It was perhaps best captured in a document said to have been circulated by German officials in early 2012 as part of the now-abandoned German proposal to force Greece to accept a 'budget commissar' to supervise its spending in exchange for a new 'bail-out' (at this point, quotation marks are obligatory): 'Greece has to legally commit itself to giving absolute priority to future debt service .... State revenues are to be used first and foremost for debt service, only any remaining revenue may be used to finance primary expenditure' – such as paying police salaries or purchasing hospital supplies.[168]

The document stated that under no conditions would Greece be allowed to default on its debt: 'If a future tranche [of the bail-out] is not disbursed, Greece can not threaten its lenders with a default, but will instead have to accept further cuts in primary expenditures as the only possible consequence of any non-disbursement.' Finally, 'Greece has to ensure that the new surveillance mechanism is fully enshrined in national law, preferably through constitutional amendment.' The sheer explicitness of this statement of priorities is a powerful reminder of the fundamentalist ideology currently dominating the EU establishment.

This also explains the need for 'more austerity'. From the point of view of the creditors, it is not enough for countries to achieve a primary surplus; they must have enough revenue to cover debt repayments as well. This is the officially stated aim of the Fiscal Compact. This means further reductions in the primary budget – public-sector expenses, welfare benefits, public investments and so on – to free up funds for debt servicing, which amounts to a further transfer from the 'real economy' to the financial sector.

Taking a wider, more systemic look at the issue, James Petras, retired professor emeritus of sociology, sees the events unfolding today in Europe as the last stage in the evolution of financial capitalism, in which the aim is 'to convert the entire state apparatus into an efficient press to continuously extract and transfer tax revenues

Table 4.7 Yearly average interest expenditure of the PIIGS, 2010–13

	Italy	Greece	Portugal	Ireland	Spain
Interest as % of GDP (yearly average)	+5.1	+5.4	+3.9	+3.8	+2.7
Interest (€ billion)	315	44	26	24	113
Fiscal consolidation (€ billion)	96	38	20	27	77

Source: European Commission and OECD.

and income from workers and employees to bond holders'.[169] In other words, the purpose of political institutions comes to be to serve, more or less explicitly, the interests of financial institutions.

This is not only highly unethical. In the context of a recession and without the aid of a central bank willing to lend to governments or at least to keep interest rates down, it is also politically unsustainable, and almost if not completely impossible to achieve. On the basis of 2013 data, in order to achieve an overall balanced budget, on top of the draconian austerity measures already implemented, EMU countries would have to make further budget cuts and tax increases amounting on average to 2.9 per cent of their GDP. PIIGS countries would have to go even further: Greece would have to slash expenses by another 3.8 per cent of GDP; Spain by 6.5 per cent, Ireland by 7.5 per cent, and so on.

Assuming a fiscal multiplier of 1.3 (the median of IMF chief economist Olivier Blanchard's range), this would mean a further drop in GDP of 3.7 per cent on average for the eurozone as a whole, and of 5 per cent for Greece, 8.4 per cent for Ireland and 9.7 per cent for Spain. All the misery that implies, on top of what has already been suffered, simply to pay back creditors!

If countries cannot afford to pay the interest on their debt, given the EMU's current monetary-political arrangement, their only alternative is to borrow more money and use it to pay their creditors. Debt-to-GDP ratios are soaring everywhere in Europe (and especially in the countries of the periphery) not only because GDP is shrinking but also because the debt itself is increasing (see Tables 4.8 and 4.9).

This exemplifies how unsustainable the current policy is. But perhaps more than anything else, it unmasks the shameless hypocrisy of the EU establishment's approach to public debt. Borrowing money to fund schools and hospitals, or to pay for care for the elderly is denounced as wasteful, reckless and irresponsible. But handing over even more money to the banks that caused the crisis in the first place is positively encouraged. (Of course, the fact that the periphery countries' biggest creditors tend to be the banks and governments of the core plays a significant role.)

The situation is made all the more absurd by the interest rate situation. As we saw in Chapter 3, EMU countries pay a higher interest rate on government bonds than non-euro countries in worse fiscal positions, largely because of the structure of the EMU itself. To be fair, Greece did see its debts reduced through the 2011

Table 4.8 Total EMU government debt, 2009–13 (in € billion and as a percentage of GDP)

Period	€ billion	% of GDP	Period	€ billion	% of GDP
2009	7.136	80	2012	8.600	90
2010	7.831	85	2013 (Q1)	8.750	92
2011	8.225	87			

Source: Eurostat.

Table 4.9 Periphery countries: government debt (in € billion and as a percentage of GDP)

	Italy	Greece	Portugal	Ireland	Spain
2009 € billion	1.769	299	141	104	565
(%)	(116)	(129)	(83)	(64)	(54)
2010 € billion	1.851	329	162	144	644
(%)	119	(148)	(94)	(92)	(61)
2011 € billion	1.907	355	185	169	736
(%)	(121)	(170)	(108)	(106)	(69)
2012 € billion	1.988	303	204	192	883
(%)	(127)	(156)	(123)	(117)	(84)
2013 (Q1) € billion	2.035	305	208	204	922
(%)	(130)	(160)	(127)	(125)	(88)

Source: Eurostat.

haircut. But in relation to GDP the country's debt is still above 2010 levels, and growing. The formula used for assessing debt sustainability is that the real growth rate must exceed the real interest rate multiplied by the debt as a proportion of GDP. In other words, government revenues must be growing at a greater rate than the interest payments on the existing debt.[170] Using that formula, if Greece were growing in real terms at 2.4 per cent per year (the average over the 1992–2001 period), it could sustain a real interest rate of 1.5 per cent on its current debts. But the Greek economy is not growing but contracting – in mid-2013, at a rate of over 5 per cent a year – and the interest it pays is much, much higher than that. In mid-2013 its 10-year bonds paid 10 per cent.[171]

As Forbes wrote, '[it is like] providing food aid to a country suffering famine and then insisting they export the food back again'.[172] *The New York Times* described it as 'economic warfare', the modern equivalent of what happened to Venezuela in 1902. (Germany, Italy and the United Kingdom took military action because Venezuela had not settled debts incurred to them during a series of civil wars. Venezuela was ultimately forced to divert 30 per cent of its revenues from imports tariffs to paying the debts.) As the paper put it:

> There is no military force here, of course. But it appears the result may be about the same. Greece is being allowed to reduce what it owes, but the European powers of this era will make sure that the remaining debts have 'absolute priority' over any other obligations.[173]

To adapt a famous comment by the Prussian general Carl von Clausewitz, we could argue that austerity is merely the continuation of colonialism by other means. And as we have seen, developed countries have long been imposing these policies on developing countries. But now they have come to the heart of the West.

Ensuring that creditors and bondholders are repaid whatever the cost is certainly one aspect of the austerity agenda. But is it the only intention of those imposing these policies? I believe it is not. I believe that Europe's political and financial elite are exploiting (and in some cases have engineered) the crisis to impose an even more extreme neoliberal order on the continent. Their intentions go directly against the ideal of a democratic, social and ecological Europe.

This is not the first time that a crisis has provided political and economic elites with the opportunity to push through unpopular policies. In her 2007 book *The Shock Doctrine*, Naomi Klein explored the idea of 'disaster capitalism'.[174] Her central thesis is that in moments of public fear and disorientation it is easier to re-engineer societies. Dramatic changes to the existing economic order, which would normally be politically impossible, are imposed in rapid-fire succession before the public has had time to understand what is happening, and more importantly, react. Just this has happened in Europe in the years following the financial crash of 2008, and it is still happening as I write. We have seen how the European political-financial elite rewrote the history of the financial crisis, transforming a crisis of the markets – and in more general terms of neoliberalism – into a crisis of public spending, and have used this narrative to push through policies designed to suit the financial sector and the rich, at the expense of everyone else.

A report by the European Trade Union Institute (ETUI) sums up the paradigm shift that has occurred since the financial crash:

> We have moved, in the space of four years, from a financial capitalism judged non-compliant with the demands of democracy to a democracy judged non-compliant with the demands of the financial markets. Economic governance and social models are to be tailored, from now on, to investors' needs.[175]

Some argue that this plan has been in the making for a long time. 'For several years now, the Commission and some governments have been pushing for stronger enforcement of policies tailored to the needs of big corporations, including financial corporations, that neglect the needs of the majority', write Corporate Europe Observatory and the Transnational Institute. 'The crisis has provided them with an opportunity'.[176] As Noam Chomsky says, in his trademark straight-to-the-point manner, 'Europe's policies make sense only on one assumption: that the goal is to try and undermine and unravel the welfare state.'[177] Europe's very own shock doctrine can be summed up as the combination of several mutually reinforcing elements.

The first of these is, of course, the imposition on the great majority of European countries (especially those of the periphery) of unprecedentedly harsh austerity measures, or 'structural adjustment programmes', consisting of the slashing of wages, social services and workers' rights, and privatisation of public services – precisely what neoliberal pundits have always argued for.

Second is a dramatic curtailing of democracy at both national and EU level. This has included the imposition of unelected technocratic governments in Italy (Mario Monti, 2011–13) and Greece (Lucas Papademos, 2011–12); and Greece, Ireland and Portugal (and to a lesser extent Spain and Cyprus) effectively putting their finances in the hands of the EU-ECB-IMF troika. No one on this body was directly (or even indirectly) elected. The European Union has effectively become a sovereign power with the authority to impose budgetary rules and structural reforms on member states outside democratic procedures and without democratic control.

This suggests that 'the competence of national democracies should be subordinated to what the economic and financial elite considers necessary to save the single currency', as Ronald Janssen writes. It is in line with the European Union's long-standing belief in the need for states to be disciplined by, and conform to, the will of the markets.[178] This became evident in October 2011, when the Greek prime minister decided to hold a referendum on the latest round of austerity measures, and the EU powers (the leaders of France and Germany, with the troika behind them) forced him to cancel it. They made it clear that the terms of the Greek bail-out were not only not negotiable, they were not allowed to be subject to democratic scrutiny.

Third is the way in which neoliberal policies have been institutionalised and crystallised through the Fiscal Compact and other binding treaties. Policies introduced as 'emergency' measures have now been enshrined in the European Union's new system of economic governance. This threatens the very survival of the European welfare state. Angela Merkel left little doubt that the intention was to prevent governments and citizens from changing these policies in the future: 'The debt brakes will be binding and valid forever. Never will you be able to change them through a parliamentary majority.'[179] It looks as if here the neoliberals have achieved the long-standing right-wing aim of putting economic policy beyond the reach of democratically elected institutions, for fear that they will not act in conformance with elite interests.

Another aspect is the increasingly violent repression of public dissent. The police have made widespread use of violence against anti-austerity demonstrators in Spain, Greece, Italy, Portugal and elsewhere.

Some might think that these policies are simply the product of a misplaced but well-meaning neoliberal faith in the virtues of the free market. However an increasing number of commentators are interpreting them as signs of a class war, waged by Europe's ruling elite against the continent's poor, working and middle classes. 'Fiscal consolidation is not the true end goal', argues Aaron Pacitti, assistant professor of economics at Siena College:

> The primary objective is power consolidation among the world's economic elite who look to cement their position atop the economic hierarchy by extracting wealth from

> those beneath .... [D]eficit reduction functions as political cover for ideologically driven policy changes that would otherwise be extremely unpopular and punitive. Austerity policies are part of a one-sided class war being waged by the wealthy against the elderly, poor, and middle class.[180]

The same argument has also been made by Noam Chomsky: 'The only argument I can see for [reconciling austerity policies with their economic consequences] is class war', he said in a recent interview.[181] Paul Krugman too recently reached the conclusion that '[t]he austerity agenda looks a lot like a simple expression of upper-class preferences, wrapped in a facade of academic rigor'; in other words, a 'policy of the 1 percent, by the 1 percent, for the 1 percent'.[182]

Behind this stance is the fact that the austerity regime's budget-slashing policies have not only produced a long list of losers: ordinary citizens, workers, young people and so on. They have also delivered a clear set of winners – and not just creditors and bondholders. As is often the case with those promoting neoliberal economic reforms, the line between ideology and self-interest is often blurred. A perfect example is the massive privatisation of public services and national assets – what some have called 'the great European fire sale'[183] – which the troika has made a key condition for bail-out loans.

Modern Europe's universal health-care systems, based on the idea that everyone, regardless of their economic status, has a basic right to access medical services, are one of greatest and most humane of the achievements of our era. The right have always resented the cost of the service, and neoliberals have claimed that their attempts to introduce market-based reforms were intended to limit that cost. But these attempts have always been met with strong popular opposition. In this sense, '[t]he economic crisis of 2008 opened a historic window of opportunity for those who would move away from universalism', writes Adam Gaffney, a member of the US-based Physicians for a National Health Program.[184] In Europe, those opposed to public, universal health-care reform found a powerful new ally in the troika.

In November 2011, Spain used a royal decree (avoiding a parliamentary debate) to effectively part-privatise the health-care system. What had been a universal system became dependent on employment status. One effect (and arguably a specific intention) was to seriously limit the ability of illegal immigrants to access the system.[185]

Greece was also forced to sharply limit access to public health services. Unemployed Greeks now only have full access to the health-care system for a maximum of a year. After that they have to pay for their medication – except that they are unlikely to be able to afford to do so – so an increasing number of people cannot access the health care they need.[186]

These reforms certainly have a strong ideological drive. Privatisation is based on the neoliberal assumption that markets are more efficient than governments in providing goods and services to the public, and the exclusion of immigrants and the unemployed derives from a belief that those who access the service should, in a broad sense, pay for it. But it should also be borne in mind that powerful private interests have a lot to gain from the privatisation of public services. Many large companies are looking to expand into sectors of the economy that had previously been regarded as best retained in the public sector because they are fundamentally unsuited for profit making. And they often manage to buy public assets at fire-sale prices in the process.

Of course, it is not just health-care systems that are being put up for sale. The state assets targeted for privatisation (especially, but not only, in periphery countries) include water services, government-owned buildings, national banks, energy companies, transport infrastructure and postal services. Greece is going as far as selling entire islands.[187] The argument behind these widespread privatisation plans is they will generate revenue to repay the debt. On past experience they are unlikely to resolve the fiscal crisis, however.

The arguments against such moves are not heard as loudly, but there are several. One is that this amounts to nothing more than another, albeit more subtle, form of socialisation of the debt, as publicly owned assets are sold off to those very markets that caused the crisis in the first place. A number of public interest groups, though, have argued that there may be a more sinister agenda at play. Questions have been raised, for example, concerning the role of financial groups and corporate interests in shaping these policies. Many suspect they have better access to the (often unelected) individuals dictating policy than do those who oppose neoliberalism.

In early 2012, the Brussels-based NGO Corporate Europe Observatory (CEO) set out to find out more about those lobbying the head of the EU Directorate-General for Economic and Financial Affairs, Commissioner Olli Rehn, who has been described as the 'austere guardian of budgetary discipline' in Europe.[188] Rehn has played a major role in shaping the EU influence in the troika dictating economic policy to countries in difficulty. CEO requested all the correspondence and minutes of the meetings between Rehn and his staff, and private sector and lobbying groups. It received only a part of what it hoped for, but the documents released detailed meetings between Rehn and his staff, and (for example) Goldman Sachs, the Belgian bank KBC, BBVA (the second largest bank in Spain), Moody's and Mason Capital Management, as well as the European Banking Federation. Rehn appeared to have had at least three meetings between late 2011 and late 2012 with Goldman Sachs heavyweights such as Lloyd Blankfein and Richard Gnodde. No minutes were provided, and many names of lobbyists were blacked out.[189]

CEO also exposed how BusinessEurope – one of the most powerful business lobbying groups in Europe – has been working with the European Commission to force through neoliberal reforms such as 'wage flexibility' in order to keep labour costs down.[190]

It is clear that there is a continuum of neoliberal policies: it would be a mistake to view the budget-slashing policies (supposedly aimed at re-establishing the debt-servicing capacity of countries) as separate from the wage-compressing labour market reforms and attacks on collective bargaining rights supposedly aimed at re-establishing the 'competitiveness' of countries, or from the privatisation policies supposedly aimed at restoring the 'sustainability' of public finances. A growing body of evidence suggests these are part of an overarching class-based strategy aimed at consolidating the power of Europe's political, financial and corporate elites at the expense of workers and ordinary citizens.

We can find further evidence of this class-based response to the crisis in the way the burden of austerity has been distributed. It could be argued that expenditure-side austerity measures – that is, government spending cuts – will always disproportionately affect the weakest, since they are most dependent on social welfare systems, so this is a 'painful but necessary' side-effect, not a deliberate policy of class warfare. That budget cuts always weigh down on the poor more than the rich is not entirely true, though. One sector of government expenditure that has suffered less budget cutting than others right across the European Union is military spending. Although it has been reduced in those countries most affected by the crisis, most states still spend as much or more on defence than they did ten years ago.[191]

Military expenditure in the European Union totalled €194 billion in 2010, equivalent to the annual deficits of Greece, Italy and Spain combined. This represents 1.6 per cent of Europe's GDP, second only to the $533 billion spent that year by the United States.[192] Four EU countries – the United Kingdom, France, Germany and Italy – make the 'top 15' list of biggest military spenders, with a combined expenditure of over $206 billion, about 12 per cent of the world total in 2011.[193] Military spending cuts, where they have come, have fallen almost entirely on people – reductions in personnel, lower wages and pensions – rather than on arms purchases. The budget for arms increased by more than 10 per cent in 2010 – from €38.8 billion in 2006 to €42.9 billion – while personnel costs went down from €110 billion in 2006 to €98.7 billion in 2010, a 10 per cent decrease which largely took place between 2008 and 2009.[194] A great deal of lobbying by powerful arms companies lurks behind these statistics.

However, revenue-side austerity measures – in other words, tax increases – are a better indicator than expenditure-side measures of where policy makers' priorities lie. Let us start by looking at taxes on labour – that is, taxes directly linked to wages and mostly withheld at source. These are the taxes that most affect most people's monthly and yearly budget. After a post-crisis decrease, these taxes started to rise in 2010, and by 2011 the EMU average was back at pre-crisis levels (see Table 4.10).

Since the crisis taxes on labour have increased as a percentage of GDP (see

Table 4.10 EMU: implicit taxes on labour as a percentage of earnings

1995	2007	2008	2009	2010	2011	change 2010–11
38.7	37.8	37.9	37.3	37.4	37.7	+0.3

Source: Eurostat.

Table 4.11). And perhaps most significantly, they have increased dramatically as a percentage of total taxation (see Table 4.12).

Taxes on labour did not rise significantly in absolute terms in the periphery countries except for Ireland and Portugal, but they increased dramatically everywhere (except for Greece) as both a percentage of GDP and a percentage of total taxation. So the tax burden on workers has become heavier compared with that on other sectors of society (9 percentage points more in Spain's case) (see Tables 4.13, 4.14 and 4.15).

This is happening, of course, at the same time as real wages are falling (and efforts are under way to cut nominal wages), the labour share (the share of national income represented by wages, salaries and benefits) is shrinking, and collective bargaining rights are increasingly being called into question, especially in periphery countries. After a post-crisis decrease, taxes on consumption also started to rise in 2010. A large part of the increase is accounted for by a sharp hike in VAT rates. (See Figure 4.13 and Table 4.16.)

Table 4.11 EMU: taxes on labour as a percentage of GDP

1995	2007	2008	2009	2010	2011	change 2007–11
21.4	20.1	20.6	21.0	20.8	20.9	+0.8

Source: Eurostat.

Table 4.12 EMU: taxes on labour as a percentage of total taxation

1995	2007	2008	2009	2010	2011	change 2007–11
54.0	50.3	52.0	53.8	53.4	53.0	+2.7

Source: Eurostat.

Table 4.13 Periphery countries: implicit taxes on labour as a percentage of earnings

	1995	2007	2008	2009	2010	2011	change 2007–11
Italy	37.8	42.3	42.9	42.5	42.7	42.3	0.0
Ireland	n/a	25.7	24.7	25.4	26.2	28.0	+2.3
Greece	n/a	33.3	32.9	30.0	31.5	30.9	-2.4
Portugal	22.3	23.7	23.6	23.9	24.0	25.5	+1.8
Spain	n/a	33.7	32.4	31.4	32.7	33.2	-0.5

Source: Eurostat.

Table 4.14 Periphery countries: taxes on labour as a percentage of GDP

	1995	2007	2008	2009	2010	2011	change 2007–11
Italy	18.1	20.8	21.6	22.0	22.0	21.8	+1.0
Ireland	13.4	10.8	11.3	11.7	11.7	12.1	+1.3
Greece	9.8	12.7	12.7	12.1	12.4	11.8	-0.9
Portugal	11.2	12.4	12.6	13.2	13.1	13.9	+1.3
Spain	16.1	17.0	17.0	17.0	17.4	17.2	+0.2

Source: Eurostat.

Table 4.15 Periphery countries: taxes on labour as a percentage of total taxation

	1995	2007	2008	2009	2010	2011	change 2007–11
Italy	45.5	48.8	50.7	51.3	51.7	51.2	+2.4
Ireland	40.9	34.2	38.0	41.5	41.2	41.9	+7.7
Greece	33.7	39.0	39.4	39.7	39.3	36.5	-2.5
Portugal	38.0	38.0	38.5	42.5	41.6	41.7	+3.7
Spain	50.1	45.7	51.5	55.5	54.0	54.8	+9.1

Source: Eurostat.

Consumption (or indirect) taxes are known to be regressive in nature, because they do not take into account the ability of the taxpayer to pay. In other words, everyone pays the same VAT on food and clothes regardless of income, which means that low-income households end up paying a larger proportion of their income in indirect taxes than higher-income households. The working and middle classes of Europe were thus doubly hit by the increase in both direct and indirect taxes.

On the other hand, how were the wealthier Europeans affected by the austerity

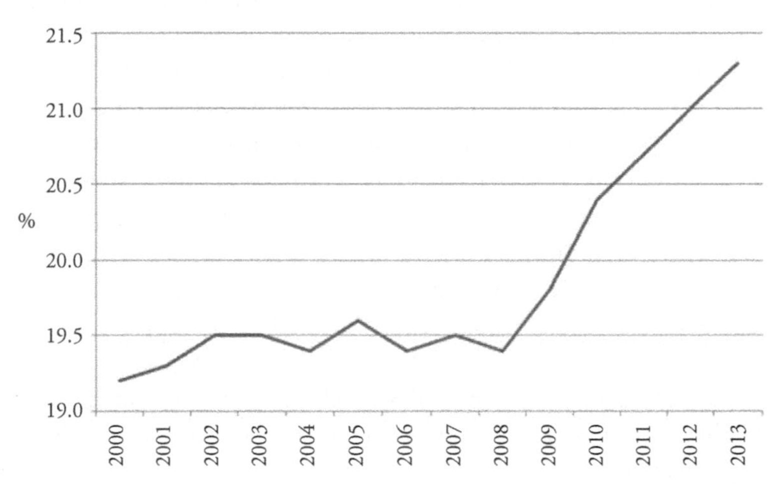

Figure 4.13 Development of the average standard VAT rate in the European Union, 2000–13

Source: Eurostat.

Table 4.16 Periphery countries: change in VAT rate 2007–13 (in %)

Italy	+2	Portugal	+2
Ireland	+2	Spain	+5
Greece	+4		

Source: Eurostat.

measures? As we saw in Chapter 3, Europe is an immensely rich continent, home to the second highest percentage of the world's richest 10 and 1 per cent, the majority of whom are concentrated in France, the United Kingdom, Germany and Italy. Even though the European Union's millionaires make up only 1.8 per cent of the population, they have known wealth equivalent to half of the European Union's total GDP – €7.6 trillion in 2012. Such high concentrations of wealth are in large part a result of the neoliberal anti-redistributive fiscal policies pursued by European governments from the 1980s onwards. There has been a drastic reduction in top income-tax rates, and in all but a few countries (France, Norway and Switzerland) wealth taxes on individuals have been abolished.[195] In 1990 half the OECD countries had wealth taxes, but by 2000 just over one third did so.

The collapse in revenues as a result of these policies is considered to be one of the leading causes of the growing indebtedness of both households and governments in recent decades, so after the crisis we might have expected governments to hit the richest the hardest. That did not happen. On average, top rates of income tax in the eurozone have increased from the level just before the crisis (especially in periphery countries), but they are still well below the 1995 level – not to mention the level of the 1970s and early 1980s. Over that same period (1995–2011) taxes on labour have decreased on average by a much smaller margin, and in some cases they have increased. Overall, Greece and Portugal stand out as the only two countries in the European Union (along with the United Kingdom) to have brought the top income-tax rate above the 1995 level. Elsewhere, little has been done to reverse the two decades long regressive and anti-redistributive trend in personal income taxes. In some countries (such as Ireland, the only country not to have raised the top income tax rate in the aftermath of the crisis) the inequality has actually worsened (see Table 4.17).

These figures are for income tax alone, so the change in burden is greater when we add in wealth taxes. Receipts from wealth taxes in those few countries that still have them have declined as a percentage of both GDP and total taxation since the crisis. Some countries (such as Iceland and Spain) have reintroduced annual wealth taxes on individuals, but mostly on a temporary basis, and these are exceptions to the more general trend.[196]

Falling national income from taxes on the rich is not just a consequence of neoliberal supply-side fiscal policies, though. Throughout the 1990s, the liberalisation of capital flows allowed the wealthiest individuals and corporations to

Table 4.17 Development of top income tax rate and taxes on labour in the EMU and the PIIGS, 1995–2011

	Top personal income tax rate, %			Taxes on labour, %		
	1995	2011	change 1995–2011	1995	2011	change 1995–2011
EMU	49.0	42.3	-6.7	38.7	37.7	-1.0
Italy	51.0	47.3	-3.7	37.8	42.3	+4.5
Ireland	48.0	41.0	-9.0	28.7†	28.0	-0.7
Greece	45.0	49.0	+5.0	33.8†	30.9	-2.9
Portugal	40.0	50.0	+10.0	22.3	24.0	+0.7
Spain	56.0	45.0	-11.0	30.5†	33.2	-2.7

† 2000 data.
Source: Eurostat.

stash their money in secretive tax havens, which are estimated to hold between $21 trillion and $32 trillion, avoiding even these relatively low tax rates. This tax-free money fuels an insatiable demand for financial products, at the expense of investments in goods and services, and so contributes to the kinds of economic bubble that led to the financial crash of 2008, and then to the euro crisis. And the estimated €1 trillion a year that European governments lose in unpaid tax as a result could clear the European Union's entire annual deficit in less than nine years. Richard Murphy, director of Tax Research UK, writes:

> [A]t a time of fiscal crisis we can no longer ignore the fact that tax evasion and tax avoidance undermine the viability of the economies of Europe and have without doubt helped create the current debt crisis that threatens the well being of hundreds of millions of people across Europe for years to come .... [I]t is clear that tackling this issue has to be the highest priority for governments seeking to recover their missing billions of lost tax revenues.[197]

There have been widely heralded international efforts to crack down on tax havens and financial secrecy, but little has actually been done, in stark contrast to the drastic action in other quarters.

Businesses and corporations have also done well. After a steady rise in the pre-crisis years, taxes on capital – defined as the overall taxes on capital and business income, profits, capital gains and stock – have also decreased dramatically since the financial crisis (see Tables 4.18 and 4.19).

In most periphery countries – and in the EMU as a whole – the reduction in the percentage of total taxation paid by businesses was matched very closely by the increase in the percentage paid by workers, amounting to yet another transfer of wealth from labour to capital (see Tables 4.20 and 4.21).

It could be argued that the overall capital tax rate applies to small and medium-sized businesses that have been badly hit by the post-crisis recession, and that by lowering it, European governments have given some respite to

Table 4.18 Implicit taxes on capital in the EMU and the PIIGS as a percentage of earnings

	1995	2007	2008	2009	2010	2011	change 2007–11
EMU	25.5	30.8	29.4	28.5	27.2	28.9	-1.9
Italy	26.6	34.7	34.5	36.5	33.0	33.6	-1.1
Ireland	n/a	n/a	n/a	n/a	n/a	n/a	n/a
Greece	n/a	n/a	n/a	n/a	n/a	n/a	n/a
Portugal	21.2	33.3	37.2	31.6	28.4	31.6	-1.7
Spain	29.3*	41.6	31.0	26.3	n/a	n/a	-4.7**

* 2000 data. ** Change 2007–09.

Source: Eurostat.

Table 4.19 Taxes on capital in the EMU and the PIIGS as a percentage of GDP

	1995	2007	2008	2009	2010	2011	change 2007–11
EMU	7.4	9.2	8.6	7.7	7.5	7.9	-1.3
Italy	11.0	11.5	11.0	10.9	9.9	10.0	-1.5
Ireland	6.5	9.5	7.5	6.3	6.3	6.7	-2.8
Greece	7.3	8.0	7.9	7.6	6.9	8.1	+0.1
Portugal	6.3	7.7	7.9	6.9	6.6	7.1	-0.6
Spain	7.7	11.3	8.3	7.3	6.8	6.6	-4.7

Source: Eurostat.

hard-working business owners. To a certain extent that is true. But there is a similar trend in the eurozone's average top rate of corporate taxation, which applies to the largest and most profitable businesses and corporate juggernauts. The average rate has fallen 0.9 percentage points from pre-crisis levels, and by no less than 10.9 percentage points between 1995 and 2013 (see Table 4.22).

The top rate is still well below the 1995 level in all periphery countries. Italy and Spain have drastically lowered it since the start of the financial crisis, while Ireland has left it unchanged. Most of these countries have cut the rate by more than average since 1995. In other words, big business has not only not shared the austerity, it has profited from tax changes.

Table 4.20 Taxes on capital in the EMU and the PIIGS as a percentage of total taxation

	1995	2007	2008	2009	2010	2011	change 2007–11
EMU	18.8	23.0	21.7	19.7	19.3	19.9	-3.1
Italy	27.8	26.8	25.8	25.2	23.3	23.5	-3.3
Ireland	19.8	30.0	25.1	22.4	22.3	23.3	-6.7
Greece	25.1	24.5	24.6	24.9	21.8	25.0	+0.5
Portugal	21.4	23.4	24.0	22.2	21.0	21.5	-1.9
Spain	24.0	30.5	25.3	23.8	21.1	21.0	-9.5

Source: Eurostat.

Table 4.21 Development of taxation on capital and labour in the EMU and the PIIGS, 2007–11

	Capital*	**Labour****
EMU	-3.1	+2.7
Italy	-3.3	+2.4
Ireland	-6.7	+7.7
Greece	+0.5	-2.5
Portugal	-1.9	+3.7
Spain	-9.5	+9.1

* Taxes on capital: percentage change in total taxation, 2007–11.
** Taxes on labour: percentage change in total taxation, 2007–11.
Source: Eurostat.

Table 4.22 Development of the top corporate tax rate in the EMU, 1995–2013

1995	**2007**	**2013**	**change 1995–2013**	**change 2007–13**
36.8	26.8	25.9	-10.9	-0.9

Source: Eurostat.

It is hard to imagine a better example of the European Union's class-based response to the crisis than this. The working and middle classes have been made to pay more tax on their earnings and more tax on their purchases, which was presented as a 'painful but necessary evil' to shore up government finances (although the primary aim was to enable governments to pay the large interest on their debts). Meanwhile the largest corporations operating in Europe – which already faced taxes that were half the US average before the crisis, and paid even less still through the process known as 'fiscal dumping' (estimated to cost governments an estimated €150 billion a year and to be a leading cause of their increased indebtedness) – received generous tax cuts after the crisis.

Are the politicians imposing these policies motivated solely by ideology, oblivious to the extent to which they are forwarding the interests of what Keynes called 'the dominant social forces behind authority'? Or is their deliberate aim to consolidate the power of the economic elites by extracting wealth from those below? Whichever is the case, austerity is effectively creating 'the single biggest transfer of resources from low and middle-income people to the rich and powerful in history', as Seán Healy, director of the independent think-tank Social Justice Ireland, writes.[198] In this sense, it is not an exaggeration to speak of 'class warfare'.

As we saw in Chapter 1, there is growing evidence that today's extreme levels of inequality – a consequence of 30 years of neoliberal anti-redistributive policies and financial deregulation – were a crucial factor behind the global economic and financial crisis since 2007/8. Yet the crisis (especially in Europe) has been used to

Table 4.23 Development of the top corporate tax rate in the PIIGS, 1995–2013

	1995	2007	2013	change 1995–2013	change 2007–13
Italy	52.5	37.3	31.4	-21.1	-5.9
Ireland	40.0	12.5	12.5	-27.5	0.0
Greece	40.0	25.0	26.0	-14.0	+1.0
Portugal	39.6	26.5	31.5	-8.1	+5.0
Spain	35.0	32.5	30.0	-5.0	-2.5

Source: Eurostat.

pursue an even more radical, anti-redistributive neoliberal agenda. In this sense, Europe's austerity policies can be seen as the final stage of the neoliberal project. James Petras describes it as the third and final stage of financial capitalism. As Salvatore Babones, senior lecturer in sociology and social policy at the University of Sydney, puts it, '[a]usterity programs in Europe today are based on the idea that ordinary and poor people should make sacrifices so that the rich and powerful can continue to make gains despite the economic downturn.'[199]

In 2011, the OECD documented that the gap between rich and poor in OECD countries had widened continuously over the three decades to 2008, reaching an all-time high.[200] In a new report, released in mid-2013, it showed that inequality had increased more over the 2008–10 period than in the previous 12 years, concluding that 'the pain of the crisis was not evenly shared'.[201] According to the OECD report, the top 10 per cent of the population did better than the poorest 10 per cent over this period in 21 of the 33 countries analysed. The differences were most acute in those countries where household incomes dropped the most. In Spain and Italy, for example, the income of the top 10 per cent was fairly stable while the income of the bottom 10 per cent fell about 14 per cent in Spain and 6 per cent in Italy. The report noted that tax-benefit systems, reinforced by fiscal stimulus policies, were able to absorb most of the impact and alleviate some of the pain, but that – as a result of the austerity measures – there was a 'growing risk' that inequality and poverty had increased even more drastically following 2010 and would continue to do so (though it did not have enough data to confirm this).[202]

A recent IMF study looked at the distributional effects of 173 episodes in which advanced economies have undertaken fiscal consolidation over the past 30 years, and reached the conclusion that the impact of austerity is not borne equally by all strata of society. It weighs down much more heavily on wage earners than on those receiving profits and rents. It typically leads to significant and long-lasting increases in poverty, unemployment and inequality, and equally long-lasting declines in low- and medium-level wages and in the wage share of income.[203]

The OECD's fears, and the IMF's predictions, were confirmed in another report released at the same time by the ILO. It reported a sharp increase in inequality in advanced economies beginning in 2010, and attributed it to declining and increasingly polarised wages (suggesting that there has been a 'hollowing in the middle' of the wage distribution), and a strong recovery of corporate profits.[204]

Nowhere has this process been more evident than in Europe. According to the European Trade Union Institute (ETUI), between 2009 and 2012, as a result of the European Union's increased influence on national wage policies, the majority of EU countries (15 out of 27) recorded falling real wages. The most dramatic declines took place in those countries that were subject to financial bail-out programmes, which also registered steep declines in real hourly minimum wages, as well as a drop in the share of GDP going to salaries, indicating a redistribution of income from labour to capital (see Table 4.24).[205]

This is, of course, a trend for low- and medium-level wages. Compensation for senior executives has returned to – and in some cases exceeded – pre-crisis levels.[206] A study conducted by the executive search firm Pedersen & Partners concluded that the total cash compensation of the top executives of the 100 largest corporations in Europe and the United States increased by 8.8 per cent in the 2011–12 period.[207] In some countries, the post-crisis increase in income for chief executives (CEOs) has been simply baffling. Executive pay for the CEOs of the 100 largest companies on the London Stock Exchange, for example, rose by 49 per cent in 2010.[208] The average compensation of a European or American CEO in 2012 was €1.31 million per year – 40 times as much as the average salary of a white-collar employee, and 100-plus times the average earnings in the economy.[209]

According to a 2013 report by the Federation of European Employers, in Italy and Spain – two of the most recession- and austerity-stricken countries in Europe – CEO salaries are higher than in any other part of the continent. An Italian CEO is likely to earn as much as €1,144 per hour, or more than €3 million per year, not including bonuses, share options and other extra payments.[210] And this not to mention the mind-boggling compensations and bonuses of bankers – a problem which the European Union only started to address in mid-2013, by introducing a cap which limits bonuses on anyone in the industry earning more than €500,000 per year to 100 per cent of annual salary, or twice if explicitly approved by shareholders.[211] Largely as a result of this process of bottom-up wealth redistribution, as austerity cuts swept Europe and the economy as a whole contracted, the number of

Table 4.24 Development of wages in the PIIGS, 2009–12

	Real wages, %	Change in adjusted wage share, %
Italy	-5.6	-0.3
Ireland	-7.2	-5.5
Greece	-4.8	-6.6
Portugal	-1.6	-4.7
Spain	-0.4	-4.3

Source: European Trade Union Institute.

people in Europe with wealth of more $1 million rose from 7.8 million in 2010 to 9.2 million in 2012. Over the 2012–13 period, the eurozone saw a further increase in the number of millionaires: France topped the list in the EMU by adding 287 millionaires, followed by Germany at 221, and Italy at 127. Spain also gained 47 new millionaires.[212]

The increase in executive compensation is related to the post-crisis recovery of corporate profits, which by 2011 had returned to pre-crisis levels – or exceeded them – thus continuing the almost uninterrupted rise in profit shares registered in developed economies since 2000.[213] It has not been a bonanza for everyone, though. As the ILO report notes, there is a growing polarisation between small and larger firms. The profit margin of smaller firms in 2011 was more than 40 per cent below the pre-crisis average, but for large firms it has been trending upwards since the crisis (despite a small dip in 2011), and by 2010 had returned to pre-crisis levels.[214] According to Pedersen & Partners, since the financial crisis the revenues of the 100 largest corporations in Europe and the United States have grown by 22 per cent, and their profits by 18 per cent.[215]

Of the 50 corporations worldwide with the fastest-growing profits over the 2010–11 period, ten were European.[216] The five biggest banks in Europe made profits of €34 billion in 2011.[217] Rising profit margins are also reflected in global stock indices, which by mid-2013 had come close to – or exceeded – historical highs in both Europe and the United States, prompting the *Economist* to claim that 'Wall Street is back'.[218]

Any reduction in the wage share is mirrored by an increase in the profit share. In this sense, wage moderation – though self-defeating in the long run even from the perspective of capital, because of the fall in demand – is arguably the crudest and most direct way in which Europe's austerity policies lead to a transfer of resources from labour to capital. (We saw in Chapter 1 how these trends have already led to extreme levels of inequality and household indebtedness, and to a large degree paved the way for the financial crisis.) The fact that these policies have disproportionately benefited large firms shows that the silent class war currently being waged in Europe is not simply one of capital against labour. It is also one of large-scale corporate-controlled capital (commonly known as 'big business') and finance against small- and medium-sized businesses.

Austerity, though, does not only lead to a transfer of wealth from the lower to the higher strata of society. '[I]t also influences the struggle between conflicting European capitalist interests', leading to a transfer of wealth from some countries to others, as the Italian economists Emiliano Brancaccio and Marco Passarella argue.[219] Chapter 3 looked at the implications of establishing a monetary union which allowed for the free flow of capital but locked countries into a fixed exchange rate, and did not incorporate a proper fiscal and economic union, let alone a common industrial policy. It showed how this led to a huge competitive gap between the countries of the core and those of the periphery, and how the troika, in the aftermath of the crisis, went about correcting these imbalances by imposing on deficit countries a policy of 'internal devaluation': in other words, lower wages. And wages have indeed fallen, to a degree that would have been considered politically impossible before the crisis.

In Greece, for example, by 2012 cuts to nominal wages had reached 2.3 per cent, with the average salary down by 23 per cent and the minimum wage down by 30 per cent. This represented an 11 per cent drop in hourly labour costs over the 2008–12 period.[220] To varying degrees, unit labour costs have been falling in all periphery countries except Italy over the 2009–12 period, as a result of nominal wages increasing very moderately compared with productivity, or even decreasing, as in Greece and Ireland.[221] This has led to a drastic rebalancing of intra-euro trade balances, with periphery countries registering a sharp decrease in their pre-crisis intra- and extra-euro trade deficits (and Italy even gaining a small surplus in 2013). This, though, was just as much a consequence of increased exports as it was of decreased imports, because of the drastic reduction in demand.

The benefits of increased exports for these countries are offset by the devastating effects on the wider economy of stagnating or falling wages. This is especially so since the export share of periphery economies is rather low, amounting to 27, 32 and 39 per cent of GDP in Greece, Spain and Portugal respectively, compared with 52 per cent in Germany. So 'the overall effect [of export growth] on the economy is moderated', as a report by the Dutch state-owned bank ABN Amro notes.[222]

A recent discussion note by the European Commission pointed to the risks involved in boosting exports solely through cost cutting:

> [T]he scope for restoring competitiveness through wage adjustment is limited by the risk that this may trigger a deflationary wage spiral across the EMU – thereby simultaneously leaving their international competitiveness unchanged and depressing domestic demand in all Member States concerned and in the Union as a whole.[223]

In other words, internal deflation is akin to killing the patients in order to cure them. The reason is that wage deflation policies are based on a fallacious and ideological reading of the crisis. As we saw in Chapter 3, it is logically impossible for all EMU countries to follow the German pattern: to a large degree, Germany's export-led success story would never have been possible without the booms in the periphery, which provided customers for German products. Competitiveness, in other words, is a relative concept: if all countries, in the years following the creation of the euro, had applied the same wage moderation policies as Germany, the whole continent would have likely plunged into recession. The same is true today: a long-term, economically and socially sustainable solution to Europe's crisis requires Germany to bear some of the burden, by boosting demand through increased wages, and reducing its surplus (or even running a deficit). Regrettably, the surplus countries of the core – first and foremost Germany – have so far been unwilling to boost demand, if not very moderately.

This problem was also acknowledged by the European Commission. In mid-2012 it warned that an 'orderly unwinding of intra-euro area macroeconomic imbalances is crucial for sustainable growth and stability in the euro area', and prodded surplus countries to 'contribute to rebalancing by removing unnecessary regulatory and other constraints on domestic demand'.[224] The IMF added its call for higher wages and prices in Germany, and for reform of parts of the country's economy to encourage more spending by its consumers (which would help generate demand that would soak up exports from other countries), stating that such adjustments were 'pivotal' to re-balancing the eurozone and global economy.[225] Paul Krugman writes: 'Even with such policies, the peripheral nations would face years of hard times. But at least there would be some hope of recovery.'[226]

Various commentators have therefore argued that the problem is that Germany has not just continued to shut off such an adjustment mechanism, it has done the exact opposite. It has refused to raise wages (if not marginally, relative to the country's huge trade surplus) and has passed its own set of yearly austerity budgets (albeit much milder than the ones imposed on the countries of the periphery), cutting expenditures rather than raising them, in order to achieve its target of a balanced budget by 2014.[227] In late 2013, Germany's trade policies were the subject of harsh criticism by none other than the US Treasury Department, which openly accused the European country's authorities of pursuing beggar-thy-neighbour policies which were dragging down its EMU partners and the rest of the global economy:

> Euro area deficit countries have sharply reduced their current account deficits, but euro area surplus countries have not reduced their current account surpluses .... Thus, the burden of adjustment is being disproportionately placed on peripheral European countries, exacerbating extremely high unemployment, especially among youth in these countries, while Europe's overall adjustment is essentially premised on demand emanating from outside of Europe rather than addressing the shortfalls in demand that exist within Europe .... Germany's anemic pace of domestic demand growth and dependence on exports have hampered rebalancing at a time when many other euro-area countries have been under severe pressure to curb demand and compress imports in order to promote adjustment. The net result has been a deflationary bias for the euro area, as well as for the world economy.[228]

This is unsustainable not only from an economic and balance-of-trade perspective but also from the debt perspective. Costas Lapavitsas and Heiner Flassbeck explain, drawing on Keynes's oft-forgotten lesson, that an 'indebted country can only service and repay its debt if the surplus country allows the deficit country to become a surplus country'. If the creditor country defends its current account surplus by all means, it becomes very difficult or even impossible for the debtor country to turn its current account deficit into a surplus, as required for a net repayment of its external debt.[229]

There are a number of reasons for this apparently self-defeating policy. Germany's historical fear of inflation – hence its unwillingness to pursue expansionary policies of any kind – certainly plays a role, but it would be naïve to ignore the short- and long-term benefits reaped by the country as a result of its post-crisis policies.

For starters, Germany has benefited from the dramatic increase in bond spreads since the onset of the financial crisis. As investors fled from debt-saddled countries to safer havens, especially Germany, the bond yield spreads between the former and the latter increased dramatically. By the end of 2011 Germany was estimated to have made more than €9 billion out of the crisis.[230] Other studies estimate that the savings on the reduced interest rate for Germany amount to as much as €63 billion.[231] German banks witnessed a similar inflow of capital,[232] and also benefited from the bail-out of periphery countries, as we saw in Chapter 3.

More importantly, though, Germany's response to the crisis can only be understood in the context of its commitment to a radically mercantilist export-led economic model. It is interesting to observe that although Germany's trade surplus with the rest of the EMU has shrunk considerably since the financial crisis (by more than 50 per cent), the country has almost doubled its surplus with non-EU countries. By 2012, more than 70 per cent of the German surplus came from extra-EU trade, while the country's overall surplus had almost returned to its record-high pre-crisis levels.

As George Soros writes, the current process of asymmetric adjustment – whereby countries in difficulty deflate but countries in a good position do not inflate; or to put it differently, deficit countries reduce their deficits but surplus countries defend their surpluses at all costs – will result in a eurozone increasingly dominated by Germany. The divergence between creditor and debtor countries will continue to widen. 'It would be a German empire with the periphery as the hinterland', he says.[233] This grim prediction is already becoming reality. The trade gap between the countries of the core and those of the periphery has narrowed, but the economic gap has widened. In other words, trade imbalances have given way to economic and social imbalances.

A recent ETUI study notes: 'Ill-conceived policy responses have contributed to exacerbating weaknesses in the economies, thereby setting the European Union on a path of diverging economic regimes, ultimately jeopardising the very existence of the single currency as well as the continuing pursuit of European integration.'[234] This is a process that has to be viewed through the lens of the unresolved inter-capitalist struggle between core-based and periphery-based capital. A good indicator of this is the increasing divergence in insolvency rates.

According to the German-based Creditreform, between 2010 and 2011 Germany and the Netherlands registered a 5.8 and 2.9 per cent decrease respectively in the number of insolvencies. Over the same one-year span there was an increase of 7 per cent in Ireland, 17 per cent in Italy and Portugal, 18 per cent in Spain and 27 per cent in Greece.[235] If left unchallenged, this process, Brancaccio and Passarella argue, will inexorably lead to the 'mezzogiornification' – otherwise known as 'southification' or 'Chinesification' – of the periphery countries of Europe, and to an increased concentration of capital in the hands of core countries. Capital in the periphery will tend to largely disappear or be absorbed by that of the core.[236]

'Mezzogiornification' is a term coined by Paul Krugman in a 1991 paper, in which he analysed the nexus between the process of economic and monetary integration and that of industrial concentration.[237] He theorised that once the single currency was established, Europe would experience a dramatic concentration of production and employment in certain countries (those with more competitive and better developed economies of scale, such as Germany), at the expense of others, since the former would benefit from the reduction in tariffs and barriers associated with the introduction of the single currency. Such 'convergence' would not be painless, Krugman warned: entire areas of the continent would be sentenced to productive desertification and worker outflow. The relative underdevelopment of areas like the south of Italy (the *Mezzogiorno*) would become paradigmatic of this increasingly imbalanced relationship.

This process is intrinsically tied to the growing hegemony of Germany in Europe. As Brancaccio and Passarella write:

> The peripheral economies of the continent will be progressively integrated within the German system. The industries of the southern Europe in competition with German industries will be gradually excluded from the market; the ones that are bought up, or that operate within German supply chains, will survive. Capital will be gradually concentrated in Germany and in the core countries of the Union, while the countries of the periphery will be increasingly populated by minority shareholders and low-wage workers.[238]

This, the authors argue, is part of a wider design aimed at transforming the monetary union into a huge German-style, export-led economic machine (as exemplified by the proposed EU–US free trade agreement). Such a project, though, is very likely destined to fail. Not only would it pit the countries and workers of Europe against each other in a self-destructive race to the bottom, it would also pit Europe against the rest of the world, with potentially very destabilising consequences. As Adam Posen, president of the Peterson Institute for International Economics, recently wrote in the *Financial Times*:

> '[L]ow wages are not the basis on which a rich nation should compete .... If Germany's economic model is the future of Europe, we should all be quite troubled. But that is where we seem to be going.'[239]

In this chapter we have seen how, far from being a necessary, albeit painful, and almost natural outcome of the current crisis, austerity consists of a complex, multi-level assault on the post-war European social and economic model. In the next chapter we shall see how the supposedly 'emergency' post-crisis austerity programmes are in the process of being institutionalised and formalised in the new system of European governance. This represents an attempt to change the social and political landscape of Europe – and our shared future – forever.

CHAPTER FIVE

Brave New Europe

At the end of 2012 the European Council unveiled its 'Roadmap for the completion of Economic and Monetary Union', which followed other reports prepared by the European Commission, the European Central Bank and the Eurogroup over the course of the second half of 2012.[1] The basic premise of all these reports is that the current architecture of the EMU – that of a 'currency without a state' – is untenable. That is, it is not realistic to maintain a monetary union with a centralised monetary policy but lacking a common fiscal and economic policy capable of addressing the systemic macroeconomic imbalances which are bound to arise between member states. So, in order to survive, the eurozone needs to swiftly move towards a banking, economic, fiscal and ultimately political union.

In other words, the proposal is for a full-fledged federal state loosely based on the US model, or what has been journalistically termed the 'United States of Europe'. This involves a game-changing transfer of sovereignty from the national to the supranational level.

In very general terms, a (limited) number of progressives would agree with the diagnosis, and with the proposed cure. The notion of European federalism, after all, harks back to the ideas of some of the most enlightened progressive thinkers of the 20th century (most notably the Italian Altiero Spinelli), who believed in a clean break with Europe's past and with the nation-states that had caused so much horror and destruction, and in the creation of a new supranational political system, through a radical restructuring of politics and extensive social reform, aimed at the creation of a US-style, democratic European federation.[2] In this sense, from a progressive standpoint, the problem is not federalism – or the notion of a single European state – as such, but how it is achieved, and what kind of state is the result.

For many years federalism was taboo, unmentionable in respected political circles. Then over the course of 2012, as the crisis worsened, the F-word slowly gained popularity. The first leading European politician to break the taboo was Angela Merkel, in a speech to an audience of young Europeans in the Neues Museum in Berlin in early 2012. On that occasion, she said that 'we definitely need more and not less Europe', and spoke of the need for a 'political union' to complement the economic and monetary union. In an argument that readers will be familiar with by now, she stated that such a union should first and foremost be about 'sound finances' and 'sound budgeting', for which 'we need more commitment' in order to overcome the main challenges facing Europe: 'huge national debts' and 'the [lack of] competitiveness of some of the states'.[3]

In light of this, and despite Merkel's acknowledgement that 'national responsibility goes hand in hand with European solidarity', we could be justified in wondering if Merkel's new-found 'European idealism' – after years of waging what *The New York Times* and numerous commentators have described as 'economic warfare' against Greece and the weaker countries of the periphery – is truly the result of a change of heart. Or is simply the next phase in the Berlin-Brussels establishment's neoliberal 'shock doctrine'? Is it aimed at providing a veil of democratic legitimacy to, as well as indefinitely institutionalising and crystallising, the supposedly 'emergency' austerity programmes imposed to varying degrees on the whole of Europe, and especially on the countries of the periphery? Or is it a case of Germany 'continu[ing] to do the minimum necessary to hold the euro together', since Germany is the country that benefits the most from the single currency, as George Soros writes?[4]

Following Merkel's speech, and in the face of a dramatic worsening of the euro crisis, the notion that the European Union, and especially the monetary union, needed to swiftly move towards a budgetary, banking and political union to survive became conventional wisdom. By the end of the year it had been formalised in a number of official 'roadmaps' and 'blueprints', outlining 'the way forward' for Europe. But what do European leaders and bureaucrats have in mind when they speak of 'political union'? A closer look at the blueprints produced by the European Council and the Commission reveals that the 'new Europe' envisioned by the European establishment is based on the same flawed assumptions as have underpinned the entire EU response to the crisis. The main one is that the fiscal profligacy of governments and lack of competitiveness of certain countries, rather than the recklessness of banks – and in more general terms, the systemic imbalances created by 30 years of financial deregulation and neoliberal policies, further exacerbated by the hyper-financialised architecture of the EMU and beggar-thy-neighbour policies pursued by some countries – are at the root of Europe's problems, and thus that governments need to be straitjacketed and weaker countries need to be made more 'competitive'. Meanwhile all that Europe's financial sector needs is tighter supervision, not systemic reform.

The two main pillars of the European Council's plan for a more tightly integrated and centralised Europe are a 'banking union', which in turn should pave the way to the direct recapitalisation of troubled banks through a new resolution fund financed directly by the private sector (known as the 'single resolution mechanism', or SRM) or through the existing European Stability Mechanism (ESM); and a 'fiscal union', which in turn should pave the way to various alleged 'solidarity mechanisms', such as the so-called 'growth pact' and a debt redemption fund. Let us now take a closer look at the specifics of the Roadmap's two main pillars.

The Banking Union

In its fullest incarnation, the banking union will provide a Europe-wide integrated supervisory structure for all the continent's 7,000 banks (or at least its largest ones). Under the current plan, it will cover only banks worth €30 billion or more, or those holding assets greater than 20 per cent of their country's gross domestic product, which means in practice about 130 banks, representing about 85 per cent of bank assets in the eurozone. This Single Supervisory Mechanism (SSM), operating under the aegis of the ECB, is scheduled to be operational by mid-2014. Once in place, it will allow the privately funded SRM or the ESM to directly recapitalise troubled banks. This means that the cost of dealing with banking crises would be borne by the whole eurozone rather than by national governments.[5]

The direct recapitalisation of banks would certainly represent a leap forward for the eurozone. If such a system had been in place at the time of the 2008 financial crisis, European governments would not have seen their public debt go through the roof as a result of having to individually bail out their hugely indebted banks, and many of the problems that followed would have been avoided. But although this would be an improvement over the present architecture of the EMU, it still presents a number of troubling issues.

First and foremost, by focusing solely on supervision rather than reform and regulation, it does not do much to prevent financial crises from recurring. It is widely agreed that the reliance on supervision and self-regulation (rather than reform and regulation) was one of the main contributing factors to the 2008 crisis. The principal areas of regulatory failure, according to a study by the Institute of Global Economics and Finance (IGEF) of the Chinese University of Hong Kong, were:

- unwillingness and inability to restrain irrational exuberance, which leads to economic and financial bubbles
- excessive leverage of financial institutions (as well as some non-financial firms) and of the financial sector as a whole
- off-balance-sheet activities, also known as the 'shadow banking system'
- excessive reliance on credit rating agencies
- failure to control moral hazard, also known as the too-big-to-fail problem.[6]

The IGEF's conclusion is not that supervision failed because the regulators failed to do their job (although to a large extent they did) or had insufficient powers – which would imply that it is simply a question of improving the efficiency of supervisory agencies or granting them additional powers – but that financial supervision alone is destined to fail in the absence of radical systemic reforms, restraints and regulations. Simply put, the financial system has become too complex, powerful and fast-paced to be supervised effectively.

Unfortunately the proposed European banking union does not address any of the issues raised by the IGEF (or other, potentially even more serious ones such as the problems posed by derivatives and high-frequency trading). Once again it makes the mistake of relying solely on supervision rather than reform and regulation. In short, despite ample demonstration of the financial system's inability to self-regulate itself, and despite the fact that the main cause of the regulatory failure that allowed the global financial crisis to happen was, according to the IGEF, 'the overly strong faith on the part of the US [and European] financial regulators that whatever could go wrong "the market would take care of it"', the European Union's highest institutions are once again relying on the banks to see the error of their ways. This is a telling demonstration of the extent to which neoliberal ideology – and in particular the myth of the self-regulating market – permeates such institutions.[7]

The SSM also raises a number of potentially even more troubling issues. A core one is regulatory capture: the process in which a regulatory agency, purportedly created to act in the public interest, instead advances the commercial or special concerns of interest groups that dominate the industry or sector it is charged with regulating. According to the IGEF, this was a second fundamental cause of the 2008 regulatory failure.[8] From this perspective, granting the ECB such sweeping powers of supervision over Europe's largest institutions seems a very bad idea.

Europe's central bank suffers from a very serious lack of transparency. The ECB's handling of the Goldman Sachs–Greece swap deal, and its consistent refusal to disclose internal documents concerning that deal (or any other sovereign derivative deal) proves this all too well. There are worrying links between the European Union's top brass and the financial industry (beginning with Mario Draghi, the president of the ECB, himself a former Goldman Sachs employee), and there is the wider, and yet unresolved, issue of financial lobbying at the EU level.

This is related to the wider issue of the accountability (or lack thereof) of the ECB. In many ways, complaining about the 'unaccountability' of the ECB is naïve, since (as was discussed in Chapter 3) Europe's central bank is staunchly independent – and thus largely unaccountable – by its very nature. Even if we accept the debatable proposition that the monetary policy of countries (or groups of countries, in the case of the EMU) should be managed by institutions that are entirely independent of democratically elected institutions, since the start of the euro crisis the ECB has evolved into something very different from a 'normal' central bank (if it ever was one). It has gone well beyond its purely monetary prerogatives and has taken on the form of a 'full-blooded political actor engaging in a strategy aimed at forcing EU political leaders to embrace fiscal rectitude', as Jacob Funk Kirkegaard, research fellow at the Peterson Institute for International

Economics, writes.[9] As EU policy analyst Protesilaos Stavrou puts it, the ECB is more akin to a 'dealer of last resort' than to a lender of last resort.[10]

Thus, Europe (and in particular the eurozone) already finds itself in a situation of serious democratic deficit, in which policies are decided and dictated by institutions lacking any democratic accountability or legitimacy. This would be worrying in itself, even if the policies of the ECB and other EU institutions had proven to be a form of 'enlightened dictatorship'. But there has been nothing enlightened about the policies pursued by the EU elite – and in particular the ECB – since the start of the euro crisis.

By taking on the role of single supervisory agency for the entire eurozone, the ECB will become an exceptionally powerful institution, with the right to intervene directly in any part of the area under its jurisdiction, in the context of the supervisory powers conferred by the SSM. As Protesilaos Stavrou writes, '[d]emocratic or not, the ECB shall represent, at least in relative terms, the most federal institution in the EU edifice.'[11] This is particularly worrying if we consider that the implications of the SSM go far beyond the ECB itself, and will have important ramifications in various parts of the EU architecture. It will in effect profoundly change the institutional morphology of the European Union, in what amounts to nothing less than 'bring[ing] "federal Europe" in through the back door', according to Bela Galgoczi, senior researcher at the European Trade Union Institute in Brussels.[12] The banking union 'would clearly reduce sovereign risk, but at the same time also the sovereignty of the sovereign', deepening the European Union's democratic deficit, he says.

There is potentially a positive side to all this: that the SSM should, in turn, pave the way to the direct recapitalization of troubled banks through the 'single resolutions mechanism' (SRM). The SRM is a fund based on, or augmented by, contributions from the financial sector itself, through levies imposed both before and when the funds are required.[13] This would be a major development for the eurozone, since it would break once and for all the 'death embrace' between banks and states, and force the financial sector to bail itself out in the event of a crisis. Regrettably, as of mid-2013 there is still much confusion and controversy over the SRM. The plan seems to be to set up a fund equal to 1 per cent of insured deposits in the banking union, amounting to around €55 billion, built up by bank contributions over the course of ten years.[14] In the meantime, recapitalisation remains reliant on the existing European permanent bail-out fund, the ESM.

Until recently the ESM was only allowed to offer financial stability loans directly to sovereign states. This meant that bank recapitalisation packages were paid to the state (adding to the public debt), tied to requirements for austerity and structural adjustment programmes, and then transferred to the financial sector, as was the case with Spain in 2012. In mid-2013 an agreement was finally reached among the finance ministers of the European Union on the use of the ESM to recapitalise banks directly (to a limited extent), starting from late 2014. In future the funds will no longer count as state debt.

This is certainly an improvement, but it stops short of breaking the 'doom loop' between banks and sovereign states. Before banks can receive direct injections from the shared fund, the requesting government must either provide the capital needed to raise the bank's minimum capital ratio to 4.5 per cent of its assets, or if the institution already meets the capital ratio, make a contribution ranging between 10 and 20 per cent of the ESM contribution.[15] Even more controversially, requesting member states will not be spared the conditionalities – 'including where appropriate those related to the general economic policies of the ESM Member concerned'.[16] In short, the EU establishment is demanding that states whose banks (not governments) run into trouble and thus require financial assistance by the ESM implement the same kinds of austerity and structural adjustment programme – public-sector cuts, wage reductions and so on – as the recipients of sovereign loans have been forced to implement in recent years.

In many ways this is a validation of the book's core theory: that the European elites, and in particular those of core countries, are using any excuse to re-engineer European societies and economies according to a radically neoliberal framework. Moreover, the contentious issue of 'legacy debt' – that is, whether debts incurred prior to the effective establishment of the SSM should be eligible for recapitalisation or not – remains unresolved. The Eurogroup has announced that banks already recapitalised by insolvent states (such as the Spanish and Irish ones) will be dealt with 'on a case-by-case basis' – meaning that legacy losses can be used as a further disciplinary device, as periphery states vie for access to the ESM's limited funds.[17]

More fundamental is the issue of the overall amount that the ESM will be allowed to disburse for all bank recapitalisations. It has been capped at a relatively puny €60 billion (though the limit is allegedly flexible), more or less the same amount expected to be raised through the privately funded SRM.[18] Though a large sum, it is a drop in the ocean compared with the balance sheets of Europe's hyper-leveraged banks. There are around 7,000 financial institutions in the European Union, and as of 2012 they managed around €47 trillion in total assets (of which €33 trillion is in the EMU). This is 366 per cent of the European Union's GDP. 15 megabanks (0.1 per cent of all banks) account for about €20 trillion (up from €7 trillion in the year 2000), equal to 150 per cent of the entire European Union's GDP.[19] As the European Banking Federation (EBF) boasts, the EU banking system is 'the largest in the world, holding consolidated assets three times those of the US system, and almost four times those of the Japanese'.[20] It is also one of the fastest growing in relation to GDP (see Tables 5.1 and 5.2).[21]

These leviathans expose the European economy to huge systemic risks. Not only are they too big to fail – they are too big to bail. The average balance sheets of the European Union's 30 and 15 largest banks (€800 billion and €1.3 trillion respectively) are 13 and 21 times larger than the proposed recapitalisation limit.[22] So it is hard to see how the fund could rescue even one megabank without an additional

Table 5.1 Banking sector assets-to-GDP ratio in the European Union, United States and Japan, 2010

	Total bank sector	Top 10 banks
European Union	349%	122%
United States	78%	44%
Japan	174%	91%

Source: Finance Watch.

huge levy on European taxpayers. It has been estimated that a recapitalisation fund would need around €500–600 billion to provide a viable backstop for a banking sector this size (in line with international comparisons and standards).[23] So the vicious circle between banks and sovereign states, far from being broken, is simply being raised (partly) from the national to the European level. At the same time the implicit guarantee to large banks increases the moral hazard. As the public interest group Finance Watch notes, 'banks need to be simpler in structure, smaller and less entangled if we want them to be "resolvable"'.[24] This means, in short, solving the too-big-to-fail problem once and for all – a point I return to in Chapter 6.

More positively (although it hardly addresses these major issues), European leaders agreed that shareholders and bondholders, and then uninsured depositors with deposits of more than €100,000, would have to face losses before the ESM can intervene, on the model of the Cyprus 'bail-in'.[25] This forces investors to take partial responsibility for their reckless or mistaken investment decisions, instead of putting those losses entirely on states and taxpayers, but it also risks creating divergent responses between solvent and insolvent member states. The former will be able to bail out unsecured depositors, while the latter will have to force losses on deposits above €100,000.[26]

The Fiscal Union

Ever since the euro crisis erupted in 2010, the European Commission and the Council have adopted, behind closed doors and beyond public scrutiny, a complex system of new laws, rules, agreements and even a treaty – the Fiscal Compact – aimed at enforcing austerity, whatever the cost. The result has been a head-on

Table 5.2 Growth of the EU banking sector relative to GDP, 2001–11

	Total bank assets (€ trillion)		EU GDP (€ trillion)	
2001	25		9.6	
2007	38	×1.8	12.3	×1.3
2011	46		12.6	

Source: Finance Watch.

attack on welfare and democracy. The proposed fiscal union basically consists of a strengthening of these new rules, first and foremost the Fiscal Compact. It is aimed at permanently institutionalising on a European scale the supposedly 'emergency' austerity programmes pursued by the EU elite and imposed on member states since the beginning of the euro crisis.

Chapter 2 discussed the provisions of the Fiscal Compact, and its essential requirement that government budgets 'shall be balanced or in surplus'.[27] The new treaty requires member states, for the first time, to transpose a 'balanced budget rule' into national legal systems 'through binding and permanent provisions, preferably constitutional', and to provide for a self-correcting mechanism to prevent their breach. The treaty empowers the European Court of Justice to monitor compliance and impose fines on rule breakers. A state found in breach of its obligations can ultimately be fined up to 0.1 per cent of its GDP. Member states whose debt-to-GDP ratio exceeds the 60 per cent limit are required to reduce it at an average rate of one-twentieth (5 per cent) per year, through massive cost-cutting and austerity measures. Importantly, only countries that have ratified the treaty will be eligible to apply for money from the ESM's permanent bail-out fund. As a joint statement by Corporate Europe Observatory and the Transnational Institute reads, the Fiscal Compact 'will impose even stronger budget austerity than the existing rules, through a permanent regime that will inevitably lead to cuts so deep that it can make the European welfare state history'.[28]

The cornerstone of the fiscal union is the 'two-pack', which adds the final touch to the new system of European economic governance, and is expected to come into force by 2014.[29] Its aim is to make sure that state budgets abide by the new fiscal rules. To this end, member states will be required to submit their budgets to the European Commission and Council for pre-approval. If the budget is not judged to be in line with the EU's obligations, the Commission and other member states can issue corrective 'recommendations' to the member state.

If a member state exceeds the parameters of the Maastricht Treaty, the Commission can decide to place the country in an 'excessive deficit procedure' (EDP), in which case an even stricter system of monitoring and surveillance kicks in. Even more so if a country is forced to seek financial assistance from the European Union, in which case it 'will be subject to tighter monitoring ("enhanced surveillance") by the Commission – in liaison with the ECB – which will go further than the requirements for EDP Member States'.[30]

In other words national budgets, and therefore crucial decisions concerning pension systems, wages, unemployment benefits, economic regulation and other aspects of social policy, are effectively taken out of the control of national parliaments and placed into the hands of the Commission and the Council, which will be able to directly impose their right-wing, austerity-driven agenda on member states and punish those that veer off course. A joint statement by Attac Germany and

Corporate Europe Observatory commented: '[I]t resembles a kind of Troika regime for the eurozone, and not just as a temporary painful economic programme, but as a perpetual model. And with a risk of this model becoming a core mechanism in the whole European Union.'[31]

Another important feature of the fiscal union is 'reinforced economic policy coordination'. This is nothing like the measures needed to ensure that countries with a trade surplus as well as those with a deficit make adjustments (as was argued in Chapter 4). Instead it is a strengthening of trade-side austerity measures (just as the 'two-pack' is a strengthening of budget-side austerity measures). In other words it calls for lower wages, further deregulation of labour markets and an end to collective bargaining. This was reiterated in the call for a 'competitiveness pact' (to supplement the Fiscal Compact) made at the European Council summit of June 2013.[32] As Germany continues to insist, '[e]verybody has to improve competitiveness.'[33] The key word here is 'competitiveness', a telling indication of the plan to transform the monetary union into a huge German-style, export-led economic machine. This would be based on internal devaluation and permanent austerity, in a race to the bottom that is reinforcing centrifugal trends, widening the eurozone's internal imbalances and killing the economies of the periphery – to the sole benefit of Europe's corporate elites and export-based economies.

To make these drastic measures slightly more palatable for the governments and citizens of the weaker countries of the eurozone, EU leaders have also agreed on a series of 'solidarity mechanisms' that are supposed to counterbalance and mitigate the effects of austerity. For starters, countries that have ratified the Fiscal Compact and the other measures of the fiscal union will be eligible to apply for sovereign loans from the ESM. This can hardly be called a 'solidarity' mechanism, though, since the usual austerity requirements will apply. In the words of the Appalled Economists, the ESM is by its very design little more than 'a brutal corrective instrument'.[34]

Then there is the much-debated issue of 'growth policies'. The idea – championed most vehemently by the French president François Hollande, but also by Italy, Spain, and even by the ultra-liberal president of the ECB, Mario Draghi – is that the effects of the Fiscal Compact can be counterbalanced by supplementing them with a 'pro-growth element'. According to this notion, 'the role of Europe is to provide the growth that the states cannot stimulate by themselves, due to a lack of budgetary resources', as Hollande stated.[35]

'Growth' can mean a number of very different things. But to achieve any of them would require an increase in the European budget, and the willingness of the strongest countries of the European Union to act in solidarity with the weakest. Unfortunately Europe seems to be moving in the opposite direction. In mid-2013, EU leaders agreed on the 2014–20 EU budget. For the first time in the European Union's history, the long-term budget was reduced (by about 3 per cent), by shaving spending in areas such as infrastructure, bureaucracy and scientific research.[36] In other words the EU budget, far from being a counterbalance to austerity, has become itself a victim of austerity. The agreed budget amounts to a meagre 1 per cent of Europe's GDP, compared with the 15 per cent of GDP allocated to the federal budget in the United States.

These recent developments show how shallow was the much-touted 'success' of Hollande at the June 2012 European Council. He was widely praised for bringing home a €120 billion 'growth pact' for Europe-wide public investment programmes, but the overall amount is puny in the face of the continent's unemployment levels and recession. The plan has no precise targets for employment or growth, or in terms of national or European strategy. For the most part it reiterates projects that are already under way, mainly inspired by neoliberal policies.

Another much-touted growth-enhancing measure is 'project bonds' (which are also part of the 'growth pact').[37] These are essentially commonly guaranteed loans focused on individual projects. The guarantee is public, but the underlying investment is to be private, following a strict neoliberal logic, so this continues the path of public-private partnerships (PPPs). The bonds could nonetheless breathe some life into Europe's comatose economies if they were well targeted. As of late 2013, though, very few projects had been approved.

Yet another 'solidarity mechanism' currently being studied by the European Commission is a 'European redemption fund' which would pool from each EMU country the public debt in excess of 60 per cent of GDP, and raise money, through commonly guaranteed 'partial eurobonds', to pay it down over a set time period.[38] The scheme was first proposed by the German Council of Economic Experts, an independent economic advisory group. It would save the countries of the periphery a great deal of money (since interest rates would be lower on these loans, although they would keep paying the usual rates on the portion of the debt below 60 per cent) and free up resources for structural investments. As of late 2013, though, there was no sign of an agreement on such a scheme.

The most 'revolutionary' idea proposed – and the only one that would amount to a truly federal 'solidarity mechanism' – is 'full eurobonds with joint liabilities' (usually referred to simply as 'eurobonds').[39] These would replace nationally issued bonds entirely, meaning that member states would not raise money individually any more, but that the EMU would raise money as a whole, at a single interest rate, and then forward it to individual governments, each of which would be fully liable for the entire issuance. This would obviously dramatically lower borrowing rates for the countries of the periphery, as Italy and Greece would enjoy the same interest rates as Germany. It does of course raise the issue of moral hazard, as some countries might let their deficits soar in the knowledge that they will find cheap financing at the European level. Thus, for Germany and the ECB to agree to this form of 'budget federalism', national budgets would have to be under very tight

European control. Moreover, in the absence of a radical democratisation of the European system of governance, the risk is that a commonly raised budget could be used as yet another 'corrective tool' to push through neoliberal reforms, financially rewarding those member states that implement structural reforms and punishing those that don't. In any case, given the very strong political resistance to the issue of eurobonds in the countries of the core, especially Germany, without strong pressure from periphery countries (discussed further in Chapter 6) it is unlikely that these will see the light of day any time soon.

All in all, the various 'solidarity mechanisms' currently on the table are puny tools when compared with the devastating social and economic impact of the Fiscal Compact and other similar measures.

In more general terms, the new European institutional framework outlined in the Council's Roadmap – what we might call 'the coming, or emergent, brave new Europe' – raises a number of worrying issues from both political and economic standpoints. Politically it raises very serious problems of accountability and democratic scrutiny and participation. As we have seen, the top-down 'federal' solution currently being proposed and pursued by the EU establishment consists in a game-changing and unprecedented transfer of sovereignty from the national to the supranational level, in terms of banking supervision (through the banking union) and more importantly, fiscal and budgetary policies (through the fiscal union). From an integrationist perspective, the problem is not the transfer of sovereignty as such; this might indeed be the only way forward for Europe in an increasingly complex and globalised world. The problem is that this transfer of sovereignty is not being paralleled by an analogous and proportionate transfer of democratic legitimacy, accountability and participation from the national to the supranational level (that is, from national parliaments to the European Parliament). In other words the democratic procedure is not being elevated to the European level, it is simply being usurped from the national level. This amounts, in the words of German philosopher Jürgen Habermas, to 'a post-democratic exercise of political authority'.[40]

As EU policy analyst Protesilaos Stavrou writes, we are witnessing 'a rapid and forceful emergence of a technocratic *sovereign* state *within* the EU'.[41] Even though the Council's Roadmap states that '[a]ny new steps towards strengthening economic governance will need to be accompanied by further steps towards stronger legitimacy and accountability' and that '[f]urther integration of policy making and greater pooling of competences must be accompanied by a commensurate involvement of the European Parliament' and an increased 'level of cooperation between national parliaments and the European Parliament', it is clear that 'democratic legitimacy and accountability' is not equivalent to genuine democracy.[42] In this sense, as Stavrou notes, the future role envisaged by the EU establishment for the national and European parliaments is very similar to the role reserved for them in relation to the troika programmes, whereby parliaments labouring under duress were pressured into rubber-stamping decisions taken elsewhere.[43]

Thus, the call for an increased cooperation between the increasingly marginalised national and European parliaments does little to diminish the profound democratic deficit of the European Union, and simply obfuscates the lack of an elected executive and of a genuinely democratic decision-making body at the European level. This leads to the disquieting conclusion that there is nothing intrinsically democratic about federalism. Or, to put it another way, that the European Union is not incompatible with totalitarianism. (By the same token, nor is it totalitarian by nature, as is often simplistically implied, something discussed in Chapter 6.) As Yanis Varoufakis writes, 'a multitude of evils can hide behind the ideological veil of top-down European integration, especially when it is accomplished in the midst of (even by means of) a vicious, asymmetrical recession'.[44]

Protesilaos Stavrou's comparison between the 'post-democratic exercise of political authority' (in Habermas's words) envisioned by the Roadmap and the policies imposed by the troika in bailed-out countries is particular apt. In fact the emerging European Union's democratic deficit, what we might call its political architecture, appears to be closely linked with, and maybe even a precondition for, its economic architecture. We have seen that the fiscal union (and in particular the Fiscal Compact) amounts to a form of perpetual austerity for Europe. Since these reforms are obviously very unpopular, the tactic consists in avoiding democratic discussion of them. To this end, 'automatic correction mechanisms' and quasi-automatic sanctions in the event of non-compliance with the rules are introduced to remove any of element of discussion and/or decision making at either the European or national level, thus accomplishing a lifelong neoliberal dream: the complete separation between the democratic process and economic policies, and the death of active macroeconomic management. As Hugo Radice, life fellow at the University of Leeds, writes:

> These proposals, when fully implemented, will not only enforce a permanent regime of fiscal austerity, but also further remove macroeconomic policy from democratic control .... In essence, it is the politics of depoliticisation.[45]

This process of 'depoliticisation' is also clearly expressed in the Council's and Commission's time-frame for the implementation of the new architecture. 'Immediate priority' is given to the implementation of the rigid fiscal rules (the Fiscal Compact, the 'two-pack' and so on). Then, 'after 5 years', we can start to discuss issues of democracy, and the wider institutional framework of the EMU.[46] Andrew Duff, a liberal MEP and committed federalist, comments: 'What has entirely disappeared from the European Council is the notion of reflection on federal economic government to run things after fiscal integration has eventually been deepened.'[47]

More austerity and neoliberal structural reforms, less democracy, and the increasing 'mezzogiornification' of Europe's periphery – is there any alternative to the bleak, dystopian future envisioned in the Council's Roadmap? Of course there is. When talking of future political scenarios, it is important to understand that the future is not written in stone and does not depend entirely on high-level decisions and unpredictable variables. It depends very much on the choices and actions (and even thoughts, the more spiritually minded would say) of each one of us. In this sense, the scenario outlined above is only the most likely outcome should we, as European citizens, students, workers and activists, remain mostly passive in the face of, and disengaged from, the top-down 'federal' solution currently being proposed and pursued by the EU establishment. In Chapter 6 we shall look at some of the more widely agreed proposals for radical and progressive integrationist reform coming from European social movements, trade unions and left-wing thinkers, and lay out a path for the transition towards a democratic and economically, socially and environmentally sustainable Europe.

CHAPTER SIX

Another Europe is Possible!

Left and Right Views on Leaving the Eurozone

The reactionary involution and neoliberal backlash currently engulfing the eurozone, and the fact that the benefits of being a member of the EMU appear to be shrinking rapidly (especially for periphery countries), have led a number of left-wing economists and thinkers to come to the conclusion that the eurozone – if not the European Union itself – is doomed, and that only its orderly dissolution can save Europe from years of depression and austerity, if not worse.

This is a relatively new development in left-wing circles. Until recently, those advocating an end to the euro and the return, in some form or another, to national currencies have tended to be on the political right, and mostly based in core countries. Their concerns, traditionally focused on the hollowing-out of national sovereignty, have also since the outbreak of the euro crisis been directed at the alleged bailing-out of 'profligate' governments by the 'responsible' countries of the core, and at what they see as an undermining of the ECB's independence. They have now found unlikely allies in a growing number of left-wing, progressive economists, mostly based in periphery countries, who are also openly calling for (or more commonly hinting at) a break-up of the euro and a return to national currencies. Their critique is mainly directed at the plundering of citizens and the assault on the welfare state in the crisis- and austerity-stricken countries of the periphery. I contend that the calls for an end to the monetary union, even if well intentioned, are ill advised, and that – as unlikely and counterintuitive as it may seem – the best hopes for the citizens and workers of Europe lie in a radical reform of the European Union and EMU, not in their rejection.[1]

Curiously, even (some) proponents of the 'default, devalue and exit' strategy acknowledge in principle the benefits of a European cooperative and solidarity-based solution, but they dismiss the notion that the European Union's 'neoliberal authoritarian fortress could be amended and transformed from within' as naïve, 'wishful thinking', unrealistic – if not an outright 'dream'.[2] The underlying assumption is that the European Union, and especially the eurozone, is fundamentally unreformable. No explanation or justification is given in support of this – it is offered as a self-evident truth. But there is nothing self-evident about it in my opinion. In fact, I consider the left's inability to imagine a radically different monetary union and put forward a coherent vision for an alternative European Union/EMU – instead of simply criticising austerity or proposing a return to an imaginary pre-euro 'golden age' (which we all know never existed) – to be a profound failure of the imagination, not to mention a renunciation of the left's historical goal of seizing power to change the political and economic structures from below, above and within.

In this sense, the stance of left-wing anti-euro critics is akin to what we might call an 'anarcho-nationalist' approach to the issue of European integration. I consider this to be one of the main reasons for the left's inability to provide an alternative to the dominant neoliberal and techno-federalist discourse. In a sense, by suggesting that the current system is unreformable, they indirectly lend support to the there-is-no-alternative-to-austerity narrative. I shall now show why I believe the notion of a left-nationalist solution to the crisis to be very problematic from an economically and politically progressive standpoint – and why it should ultimately be rejected. As a benchmark, I shall refer to the work of Costas Lapavitsas, respected progressive thinker and professor of economics at the School of Oriental and African Studies at the University of London, and in particular to a recent study he co-authored with fellow economist Heiner Flassbeck.[3]

The main argument of the progressive anti-euro camp is that a return to national currencies would allow periphery countries to regain monetary sovereignty (that is, the right to print money) and thus boost their exports through currency devaluation, rather than through the more painful and ultimately self-defeating alternative of internal devaluation, or wage compression. At the same time, in breaking free of the eurozone's fiscal straitjacket, they would regain the right to engage in fiscal stimulus programmes. While even the proponents of an orderly exit from the eurozone acknowledge that a violent change of the monetary system would entail high costs for exiting countries, I believe that they underplay the true costs and implications of such a transition.

First of all, there is the issue of the magnitude of the depreciation/devaluation of the new national currency. While a moderate depreciation of the new currency would certainly help boost exports, even Lapavitsas and Flassbeck acknowledge that excessive depreciation would go far beyond what would be warranted to restore the competitiveness of a country's exports and would create huge inflationary pressure. Import prices, particularly energy prices, would surge to unsustainable levels. This would directly affect the consumption basket of workers and others, causing a decline in real wages.[4] In the context of a free-floating currency, this would be a very likely (if not almost certain) outcome, given the power of financial speculators to determine the value of free-floating exchange rates.

The undesirability of a return to a fully flexible currency is well understood by Lapavitsas and Flassbeck:

> In the presence of extremely volatile exchange rates, small and open economies do not have monetary autonomy, because their monetary authorities have to react to the vagaries of the currency market. Under a system of floating exchange rates, the formal freedom of a central bank has no material basis.[5]

This is precisely the problem that led to the creation in 1979 of the European Monetary System (EMS), the fixed-but-adjustable exchange rate regime that preceded the euro – and which Lapavitsas and other euro critics advocate returning to, at least for those countries that wish to leave the common currency. This revised EMS would 'allow countries to peg their new currency at a reasonable rate to the euro' and to regain their monetary autonomy without the risk of excessive devaluation.[6] The authors claim that the European Union has a moral and practical obligation to offer exiting countries such a 'safe way out'.[7]

But as Andrew Watt, head of the Hans-Böckler Foundation's Institut für Makroökonomie und Konjunkturforschung (IMK), notes, it is far from clear why other EMU and EU countries, and/or the ECB, should feel obliged to collaborate actively with periphery countries to allow a realignment of exchange rates.[8] As Watt rightly asks, '[i]f the ECB is not taking effective action now, why should we expect it to do so as part of an attempted orderly break-up?'[9] Moreover, advocates of this path seem to forget that 'in some ways the EMS inhibited national autonomy to a much greater extent than the euro'. The EMS was anchored to the Deutschmark, with the central banks of other European economies essentially shadowing the Bundesbank's monetary policy. When the Bundesbank chose policies that suited Germany's needs but not those of the rest of Europe, as it did in the early 1990s, these countries were pitched into recession, with no recourse via European-level institutions.[10]

Furthermore, the EMS proved unable to defend countries from currency speculators because these could anticipate when a country was about to devalue, causing first the outright departure of one currency (the British pound) and then the ostensibly 'temporary' withdrawal of another (the Italian lira), and ultimately the collapse of the entire system in 1993, following renewed speculative assaults on the franc.[11] Putting an end to currency speculation (by betting on downward adjustments in exchange rates) was one of the reasons that led European countries to create a full-fledged monetary union. The flip side of that, as we now know, is that the relief that currency adjustments provided to domestic economies burdened with overvalued currencies was no longer available. But it is far from clear that a return to the speculation-prone environment of the EMS (even in the unlikely eventuality that EMU countries were to agree to it) would be an acceptable trade-off – especially when we consider that the power of financial markets is today overwhelmingly greater than it was back in the 1990s, as was amply seen in Chapter 1.

Even if periphery countries were somehow able to defend their currencies from speculative attacks, it should be stressed that a solution based on regular currency devaluations is intrinsically un-labour-friendly. It establishes unfettered competition (rather than cooperation and solidarity-based mechanisms) as the sole rule governing trade, resulting in a race to the bottom that is just as toxic in terms of international relations (hence the term 'currency war') and damaging in terms of workers' rights and overall living standards as the process of asymmetric readjustment currently being pursued in the eurozone. In other words, a break-up of the EMU would still result in downward – not upward – convergence, and in workers being pitted against each other. As Andrew Watt observes:

> [T]he transition costs to a new regime are uncertain – after all we have no precedent for the break-up of a monetary union of this type – and probably extremely high. Moreover the return to an EMS has also substantial long-term costs without the promised benefit of facilitating welfare-enhancing social policies.[12]

Likely Problems Accompanying an Exit

An exit from the euro would entail a host of other problems for periphery countries as well. Most obviously, it would create serious problems of public finance. An exiting country would clearly have to default on part or all of its euro-denominated public debt, the real value of which would skyrocket as a result of the new currency's depreciation relative to the euro. As a result, the country would inevitably find itself cut off from international capital markets. At that point, governments would have the option to monetise the deficit to a certain extent, by 'printing' money; but the dangers of resorting to the printing press to pay for government expenses (especially for small and relatively weak countries) are well known.

In the medium term, a country like Greece or Portugal would necessarily have to rely on revenues to finance its expenses, at least until it regained market access. This would obviously require an overhaul of that country's tax system, increasing the tax burden on capital and the wealthy. But in today's context of highly liquid money and high levels of tax evasion (via tax havens), it is far from clear how a single country would be able to single-handedly implement such sweeping reforms without incurring a massive capital flight. Nor is it clear how it would prevent that euro-denominated capital from returning into the country to buy up national assets at fire-sale prices (given the depreciation of the new currency relative to the euro). This would create a bottom-up transfer of wealth of such magnitude as to make the one currently under way pale in comparison.

For the same reason, it is far from certain that a break-up of the euro, or the exit of one or more periphery countries, would halt the 'mezzogiornification' of the periphery and the increased concentration of capital in the hands of core countries.

On the contrary, it is likely to accelerate it, as foreign (and in particular German) capital would be able to scoop up the national assets – banks, businesses and so on – of departed countries at bargain prices, paving the way to an even more dramatic wave of privatisations.[13]

In more general terms, it is not clear why an exit from the euro should lead to anything but a nationalistic, right-wing backlash and a regressive/conservative regime aimed at protecting the existing balance of social forces and characterised by authoritarian rule, continuous devaluations, poor growth, increased inequality and social disintegration – not unlike what happened in Argentina in 2002–03. Some (not all) left-wing anti-euro advocates acknowledge this risk, but their answer appears more 'naïve, wishful and unrealistic' than any possible cooperative and solidarity-based European solution.

The alternative proposed by Lapavitsas and others is a 'progressive exit' (in contrast to the 'conservative exit' described above) based on 'public ownership and control over financial institutions, control over capital flows, income and wealth redistribution, sustained industrial policy to protect employment and ensure growth, and total restructuring of the state in a democratic direction'.[14] In short, nothing less than 'an anti-capitalist turn across the periphery of the eurozone that would lift the neoliberal stranglehold over the EU, thus pushing Europe in an associational, socialist direction'.[15] In the next section, I present my proposal for a set of radical – but, I believe, technically feasible and politically achievable – reforms to deeply transform the European Union/EMU in a democratic and progressive-federalist sense. I shall leave it to readers to decide whether that is more 'unrealistic' and 'politically unfeasible' – and more or less desirable – than an anti-capitalist revolution in one or more periphery countries.

A Proposal for Transformation

To reiterate, it is my belief that the best hopes for the citizens and workers of Europe lie in a radical reform of the monetary union. This would best be achieved by Europeans actively (and more importantly, critically) engaging with the ongoing integration process in order to steer it towards a genuine European supranational democracy. This would allow European citizens to directly influence EU policies and vote out austerity in favour of radical alternatives, such as a continent-wide 'Green New Deal' (GND).

The underlying assumption behind this idea – advocated by those that I would call progressive or realist federalists, a group in which I count myself, which is rooted in the theories of radical 20th-century federalists such as Altiero Spinelli – is that the root of the euro crisis is mainly political, not economic. More specifically, it is an issue of democracy. According to this view, just as no democratic state or country is inherently right-wing or left-wing (even the most ideocratic democracy in the world, the United States, has had rather progressive administrations in the past), the European Union/EMU is neither inherently bad nor good, conservative nor progressive. Or more accurately, it is (and arguably always has been) radically neoliberal (and ideocratic) in its political-economic approach, but only inasmuch as it has always been fundamentally undemocratic and technocratic, and has thus been particularly prone to the influence of corporate interests and neoliberal ideologues.

Thus, the point is not to criticise the European Union as such (which I see at best as a pointless exercise, at worst as a dangerous game that risks playing into the hands of right-wing nationalists and populists) but to work to radically democratise and politicise the European Union and eurozone institutions in order to build a genuine European supranational democracy. This should be based not on a quasi-messianic faith in 'Europe' (as an abstract concept) or ideological aversion to nation states, but on the rational acknowledgement that a democratic, politically united Europe is the best means to forward the interests of citizens and workers, and tame the overwhelming power of global financial and corporate leviathans, thus regaining at the supranational level the democratically legitimated sovereignty that has been slowly but steadily eroded at the national level (or rather usurped by those same financial and corporate powers), and will soon be completely eliminated by the 'fiscal union'.

As Habermas writes, as failed and imperfect as they may be, the existing EU institutions have created the preconditions for:

> realising a more far-reaching goal, namely, the construction of political decision-making capabilities beyond the nation states .... The shattering of neoliberal illusions has fostered the insight that the financial markets – indeed, more generally, the functional systems of world society whose influence permeates national borders – are giving rise to problems that individual states, or coalitions of states, are no longer able to master.[16]

'The fight for democracy must be therefore at the European level', writes the transnational European civil society organisation European Alternatives:

> European politics must become political and democratic, where that means that different political parties and social movements must offer clearly different political programs and have the power to implement them. That means democratic control over the European economy.[17]

Clearly, this differs starkly from the kind of authoritarian or 'executive federalism' (as Habermas calls it)[18] envisioned in the Council's Roadmap. In contrast to this, progressive federalists propose a radically alternative 'federation of citizens', centred precisely around those values and ideals that the European Union's technocratic elite seem intent on destroying, and that – to the extent that we can speak of a

'European tradition' – make up the continent's post-war cultural and political DNA: democracy, human rights, social welfare, workers' bargaining rights and the like.

In many ways, the general aim is to build not only a supranational democracy, but also a 'supranational welfare state' capable of offering those social protections that nation-states seem increasingly unable to guarantee in the face of the overwhelming power of financial markets. In this way we could defend – indeed, improve – the social democratic model that for decades has made Europe a beacon of humanity in the world. This is the essence of the movement's call to arms: 'Another Europe is possible!' Some of the more radical elements of the anti-austerity movement might label this as 'mere reformism', but by criticising austerity they are simply defending that same model – what we might call the status quo – at the national level. In this sense, their stance appears more conservative, in the literal sense, than that of progressive federalists.

As for the question of how to best democratise and politicise the European Union, there are obviously differing views, given the complexity of the matter. But there is a relative consensus among progressive federalists that European democracy should rest upon two institutions. One is a significantly empowered European Parliament, which should be the sole initiator of European legislation (with the exception of inter-governmental treaties, which would be scrutinised by national parliaments). The other is an executive branch: a revamped European Commission with a directly elected president (who would in effect become the president of Europe), alongside a European finance minister, foreign minister and so on. This would ensure national representation through a dual input-based mechanism.

A Commission freely elected by majority vote would transform it from the technocratic (and radically neoliberal-minded) body that it is today into a full-fledged political body, capable of pursuing right-wing or left-wing policies on the basis of an electoral programme chosen by the people. This would allow citizens to choose what Europe they want. It requires the transnationalisation and Europeanisation of European political parties, meaning that elections for both the European Parliament and the European Commission should be organised on a transnational, rather than national, basis. There is talk, for example, of associating every list – the centre-left Alliance of Socialist and Democrats, the centre-right People's Party and so on – with a candidate for the presidency of the Commission. In practical terms, this would mean that citizens in each country could vote for a politician from any country in the European Union.

For some thinkers, though, this is not enough. For Etienne Balibar, radical thinker and professor emeritus of philosophy at Paris Ouest University, for example,

> political Europe, outside of which there is indeed only decline and inability for the people of the continent, will only be legitimate, and therefore possible, if it is more

> democratic than the nations that create it, if it allows them to step beyond their historical conquests in terms of democracy.[19]

In any case, a point that all progressive federalists agree on is that a full-fledged European government should be firmly based on the principle of subsidiarity. The powers exercised at the European level should be confined solely to those issues that cannot be managed effectively at national level, with higher tiers of government acting only when the common interest requires it.[20] Power, in short, should be devolved to the most local institution possible, preventing over-centralisation (the 'super-state' much-feared by eurosceptics) and making the European Union a multi-level system of shared policy making. To this end, in addition to further empowering the European Parliament, national parliaments should be more involved in the European legislative process. Most progressive federalists agree that such sweeping changes to the European Union's architecture should be subject to national referenda, or even better a Europe-wide referendum. (In any case, the treaties arguably require this for changes of such magnitude.)

Having a democratic structure in place is, of course, a (if not *the*) necessary precondition for change, but as we all know it is no guarantee of change. The creation of a European democracy – a huge feat in itself – will not magically eliminate the complex economic, class, ideological, cultural and inter-capitalist struggles that are integral to the euro-crisis. It will simply offer citizens an avenue through which to address these and other issues. So let us now look at some of the more widely agreed proposals for European-level progressive reform coming from the European left.

Financial Reform

As we have seen throughout this book, and as was unanimously accepted before the EU elite began to rewrite history in the wake of the Greek debt crisis, the financial crisis was caused by a bloated, out-of-control, over-leveraged, hyper-deregulated and generally reckless financial system. Not only is finance not serving the real economy any more – it is harming it, as the financial crisis made clear.

It has not always been this way. The original purpose of the financial system was, quite simply, to allocate money to businesses and families and aid the growth of the economy. It should return to do so. And yet little has been done, especially in Europe, in terms of deep structural reforms to rein in and disarm financial markets and avoid a repetition of the 2008 crash. As noted in Chapter 3, the European Union introduced some timid but positive reforms throughout 2012, mostly aimed at tackling speculation on sovereign debt (such as a limited ban on naked CDS trading and tighter controls on credit rating agencies), but these barely scratch the surface of the financial edifice. The prevailing attitude continues to be that of favouring supervision and self-regulation over reform and regulation (despite this being one of the main contributing factors to the financial crisis of 2008), as exemplified by the banking union. As the public interest group Finance Watch notes, 'banks need to be simpler in structure, smaller and less entangled if we want them to be "resolvable"'.[21] This means, in short, solving the too-big-to-fail problem once and for all. There are a number of ways to do that.

Separate Commercial and Investment Banking

In 1999 the United States repealed Roosevelt's Glass–Steagall Act of 1933, which separated commercial banking from investment banking. This led the rise of the so-called European-style 'universal bank': megabanks that participate in many kinds of banking activities and are both commercial and investment banks. Today these banks have become so large and interconnected that they have effectively become too big to fail. That is, their failure would have such disastrous consequences for the economy that governments have to step in and bail them out whenever they run into trouble, at a huge cost to taxpayers. This leads to a situation known as moral hazard, whereby banks are encouraged to take huge risks because they know that the costs of failure will be paid by others.

This kind of deregulation is widely considered to have been one of the leading causes of the financial crisis. And of course of the subsequent euro crisis, as governments across Europe shouldered huge debts to save their failing banks. Despite this, since the crisis governments have done close to nothing to solve the too-big-to-fail issue. In some ways they have exacerbated it. By extending massive support to the banking sector they have created what Mervyn King, former governor of the Bank of England, has called 'the biggest moral hazard in history'.[22] Moreover, in Europe, banks have grown even bigger (in terms of their assets-to-GDP ratio) since the financial crisis. Not only are they too big to fail, they are too big to bail. This means that in the event of a new crisis, the economies of Europe would find themselves even more exposed than they were in 2008. The banking union does little to address this, as we have seen.

This is unacceptable. It is time to address the issue once and for all. Simply put, banks that are too big to fail (or even worse, too big to bail) are too big to exist, and should be broken up. The most obvious way to do this is to separate commercial and investment banking. As Finance Watch notes, breaking up big banks – as well as minimising systemic risks and moral hazard, and facilitating regulatory oversight, making the financial system as a whole more resilient – would have a number of other positive effects. It would show the real economic value and risks of each activity; it would increase competition; it would even stimulate growth.[23]

To date the United States is the only country that has introduced a sort of (very) watered-down version of the Glass–Steagall Act, in the form of the Volcker Rule (see Chapter 1). In Europe, some countries (such as France, Germany and the United Kingdom) are slowly and over-cautiously catching up.[24] These are positive (albeit insufficient) steps forward, but the problem with finance reform of any kind is that it is bound to fail if it is undertaken by any single country, since financial institutions are liquid and borderless by nature. (This is one of the main arguments of progressive federalists in favour of a politically united Europe capable of undertaking sweeping continent-wide financial reform.) In any case, notwithstanding the different views that people may have on the issue of political union, we should vigorously demand EU-wide structural reforms of the financial system, beginning with a simple, no-loopholes separation between commercial and investment banking.

Size Limits on Banks

The separation of retail and investment banking is probably the simplest way to break up the big banks, but it is not the only way. In addition to increased capital requirements and strict leverage ratios, another radical solution, backed also by Andrew Haldane, executive director of financial stability at the Bank of England, is to place size limits on banks, either in relation to the financial system as a whole, or more coherently, relative to GDP. This acknowledges that, as Haldane puts it, 'there is a threshold at which the private-credit-to-GDP ratio may begin to have a negative impact on GDP and, in particular, productivity growth'.[25]

Regulation of Speculative Financial Instruments

Breaking up the big banks is crucial, but it is not enough. Because of the interdependence and interconnectedness of the financial system, and the array of complex speculative financial products at banks' disposal, small banks can pose just as much a threat to the system as big banks.[26] Thus, a serious reform of the financial system must necessarily include the regulation (if not outright ban) of speculative financial instruments, such as securities and derivatives.

As we saw in Chapter 1, securities (such as collateralised debt obligations, or CDOs) and derivatives (such as credit default swaps, or CDSs) played a crucial role in the financial crisis of 2008, and sovereign derivatives and 'naked' swaps had a part in the euro crisis as well (see Chapter 3). Yet despite this, according to conservative estimates (nobody really knows the total value of all the derivatives that are floating out there), the derivatives market has grown in size since the crash of 2008. By the end of 2012 it amounted to $687 trillion – almost ten times the world's GDP – up from 2007's $670 trillion, according to the Bank of International

Settlements.[27] The risk posed by the derivatives market to the global economy is thus higher than ever before.

In recent years, derivative trades were responsible for the failure of US trading firm MF Global (in 2011) and for losses of $6 billion for JPMorgan Chase (in 2012) and at least €3 billion for the Italian bank Monte dei Paschi di Siena (in 2013).[28] Even more worryingly, some commentators believe that 'those incidents were just warm up acts for the coming derivatives panic that will destroy global financial markets'.[29] What is needed, they say, is an outright, across-the-board ban of all derivatives from financial markets.[30] However such a ban is not even being contemplated by regulators and policy makers at the moment. The same argument goes for securities like CDOs, which financier George Soros describes as 'instruments of destruction which ought to be outlawed'[31] – especially given recent reports that European banks have once against started to invest heavily in the same type of high-risk US subprime mortgage as triggered the 2008 financial crisis.[32]

A Financial Transaction Tax

Another way to tackle speculation and rein in finance, and raise significant revenue at the same time, is to introduce a financial transaction tax (FTT). The idea has been around for a long time. John Maynard Keynes advocated it in 1936 in his magnum opus, *The General Theory of Employment, Interest, and Money*. He proposed a small transaction tax on dealings on Wall Street, where he argued that excessive speculation by uninformed financial traders increased volatility – and the idea was later developed by Nobel prize-winner James Tobin (with the 'Tobin Tax').[33] Yet although throughout the years the idea has been backed by such intellectual heavyweights, before the financial crisis of 2008 FTTs were ridiculed as naïve and unrealistic. Today that is no longer the case. In 2011 40 countries made use of FTTs, together raising approximately $38 billion.[34]

A Europe-wide FTT would not only strengthen Europe's finances and reduce the likelihood of crises, it would also raise much-needed revenue. This is probably what prompted the European Commission to propose, in September 2011, to levy by 2014 a tax of 0.1 per cent on the exchange of shares and bonds, and 0.01 per cent on derivative contracts within the 27 member states of the European Union.[35] This would raise approximately €57 billion a year.

There was strong resistance from some non-euro countries, particularly the United Kingdom and Sweden. As a result a group of 11 states – Germany, France, Italy, Spain, Austria, Portugal, Belgium, Estonia, Greece, Slovakia and Slovenia – have resorted to a process called 'enhanced co-operation' to implement the tax in those states that wish to participate. This is a very positive improvement, and should be lauded. Still, there is a serious risk that the proposal will be watered down, that some countries will back out, or that traders will shift to alternative jurisdictions. That is why we must keep the heat on governments on and push for an EU-wide, and eventually global, FTT. As progressive federalists argue, the FTT is a perfect example of how in order to be effective, financial regulation must be enforced by strong, supranational institutions, capable of sidestepping the markets' divide-and-rule strategy.

A Ban on Shadow Banking

Of course no financial reform will be effective if banks are able to avoid regulatory oversight by resorting to off-balance-sheet transactions. Thus, we need comprehensive regulation of – if not an outright ban on – the shadow banking system.

Control Over Money Creation

Finally, we need to kick-start a debate over the pros and cons of private money creation (through fractional reserve banking). At the very least, tools should be developed to limit the quantity of privately created money.

It should be noted that while these proposals might strike some as unrealistic, they are backed by a growing number of senior bankers and key industry figures.[36]

Capital Controls

The issue of financial regulation relates to the wider issue of capital controls (or more precisely, the lack thereof). As we saw in Chapter 1, capital controls are mechanisms or instruments to consciously limit the amount of capital flowing into and/or out of a country. These were an integral part of the post-war Bretton Woods system and at the time were endorsed by most mainstream economists and international institutions (including the IMF), who considered unfettered cross-border capital flows inherently volatile and destabilising. Throughout the 1980s and 1990s, though, all the restrictions limiting movement of capital were lifted, with Europe leading the way.

As a result financial crises started re-occurring with increased frequency, especially in the developing world. Most of these were classic booms gone bust, caused by foreign investors rushing into a country in search of short-term profits, then rushing out when things turned sour. Until recently, however, it was believed that the problem was restricted to poorer and developing nations, and that wealthy economies were somehow immune to the dangers of speculative capital flows, or 'hot money'.

This illusion was brutally shattered by the euro crisis, and in particular by the Cypriot crisis (see page 57). Cyprus became the first eurozone country ever to be authorised by the European Commission to impose a set of radical, temporary capital controls, with limits on credit card transactions, daily withdrawals, money transfers abroad and the cashing of cheques. This caused a global outcry, with commentators and (unsurprisingly) financial industry figures warning that the Cypriot government's decisions would 'blow the euro apart'.[37] Are these criticisms empirically or historically justified?

In the aftermath of similar financial crises, countries such as South Korea, Brazil, Malaysia, Indonesia, Thailand and, in Europe, Iceland chose to re-implement some forms of capital control. Recently even the IMF has cemented a substantial ideological shift (or rather, has returned to its original position) by accepting the use of direct controls to calm volatile cross-border capital flows. It has stated that in certain circumstances 'capital flow management measures can be useful'.[38] It might be asked, then, why the Cypriot government's decision caused such a reaction.

The difference, economists and commentators (even those favourable to capital controls) would almost unanimously retort, is that Cyprus is part of the EMU, and that capital controls are fundamentally incompatible with a currency union.[39] But is that really the case? After all, even the IMF acknowledges that capital controls are particularly useful for countries that have little room for economic manoeuvre, such as those that are part of a fixed exchange-rate system, because they are less equipped to deal with economic shocks (by lowering interest rates or resorting to currency devaluation, for example).[40] What is a currency union if not 'an extreme form of a fixed-exchange-rate regime'?[41]

In this light, it would appear that capital controls in a currency union such as the eurozone – especially if focused on inflows rather than outflows – are not only possible, but necessary (at least in the absence of policies aimed at a true economic convergence). They would arguably have prevented many of the booms-gone-bust that are the root of the huge economic imbalances tearing the single currency apart. As EU analyst Ulrich Machold wrote in 2002, warning against the risks that unfettered financial liberalisation posed for the emerging EMU, 'limited capital controls in times of crisis would not necessarily violate the spirit of the European project and should not constitute an ideological taboo as the integration project continues and in the run-up to enlargement'.[42] Thanks to the crisis in Cyprus, it now looks like the 'ideological taboo' on capital controls has been broken. Thus, we should seize the day and demand that some form of coordinated, cross-border capital control (with a focus on inflows rather than outflows) is introduced across the entire eurozone (at least until the problem of economic convergence, or lack thereof, is resolved).

Cyprus is also paradigmatic of another, potentially even more serious problem: tax havens, which in turn are related to the wider issue of fiscal reform, or tax justice.

Fiscal Reform

To reiterate, tax evasion and tax avoidance together are estimated to cost EU member states €1 trillion a year – enough to repay the total EU deficits in just 8.8 years. These disgraceful practices have exacerbated the deleterious effects on public finances of the anti-redistributive fiscal policies introduced from the 1980s onwards, and have played a crucial role in the systematic plunder of Europe's wealth and pauperisation of its governments. They have contributed massively to Europe's debt crisis, for which ordinary people are now being made to pay.

It is time to put an end to them once and for all. We need to reverse the long-term decline in the taxation of higher incomes, wealth and corporations (especially non-renewable, polluting industries) and throw supply-side economics into the dustbin of history. The FTT is a good step in the right direction but it is not enough. We need to return to a truly redistributive and progressive (or graduated) taxation system. Without drastic taxation of high incomes and wealth there is no possible way out of this crisis. This means reducing the fiscal burden on income from work and increasing it on income from capital.

This must necessarily be part of an EU-wide process of fiscal harmonisation, to put an end to the scourge of 'fiscal dumping'. To put it simply, individuals and corporations must pay the same tax rate in every European country. There are disagreements, even among the left, over what constitutes the optimal tax rate for high earners and corporations, but a good starting point is the pre-1980s tax rates. The top income tax rates in the United States and the United Kingdom were above 70 per cent, and the highest corporate tax rates were around 50 per cent. Whatever rates we decide to adopt – ideally as a result of an open debate amongst all concerned Europeans – even neoliberal-minded organisations like the IMF and the OECD agree that the current rates are too low.[43] To put it in the simplest possible terms, it is time to make the rich pay.

Tax reform, though, has no chance of succeeding if we do not simultaneously tackle the problem of tax havens and tax evasion. This is not only because tax evasion is substantially more important in terms of lost taxes than tax avoidance. The ability of the wealthiest members of society to put their money offshore gives them great power. In recent decades, by threatening to shift their operations offshore they have been able to force governments to eviscerate financial regulation, slash taxes on capital and much more, in a race to the bottom that is destroying the economies of developing and wealthy nations alike. In short, tax reform is bound to fail as long as wealthy individuals and corporations are allowed to hide their money offshore. It would simply provide them with a further incentive to do so. As the Tax Justice Network writes, '[t]he only realistic way to address these problems in a comprehensive way is to tackle them at root: by directly confronting offshore secrecy and the global infrastructure that creates it.'[44] As the TJN explains, there are five clear solutions to the problems caused by tax havens:

- **Country-by-country reporting**. This requires multinationals to break their information down by country of operation – including in each tax haven – so that citizens and authorities can see what corporations are doing in their countries.
- **Unitary tax.** This involves taxing multinational corporations according to the real economic substance of where they do business.
- **Automatic information exchange.** Developing countries – and rich ones – must get the information they need to tax their wealthiest citizens properly.
- **Disclosure of the real life, proper, final, ultimate, actual owners of companies.** We must ensure that the identity of every human who has a stake in a corporate structure – a 'true beneficial' owner – is available in a searchable, low-cost public register. And we should slap severe sanctions on those havens that do not shape up.
- **Making 'wilful blindness' a criminal offence.** We can impose hard penalties on the pinstriped intermediaries who help the tax evaders. The IMF and other bodies dealing with money laundering must officially make tax evasion a money-laundering offence.[45]

In conclusion, this shows that tackling tax havens is not only necessary – it is possible. As with most things, it is 'simply' a question of political will. That is precisely what has been lacking, especially in Europe, for a number of reasons. Vested interests, lobbying, regulatory capture and ideological bias are among them. One thing is clear: no tax revolution will ever come from the top. It will only happen as a result of relentless pressure from below. European citizens need to join forces (if there is a battle that transcends borders, this is it) and force institutions to put the elimination of tax avoidance and tax evasion at the top of the political agenda. These are aberrations that should purely and simply be abolished. It will not be an easy battle. As James S. Henry, senior advisor for the TJN, notes: 'We are up against one of society's most well-entrenched interest groups. After all, there's no interest group more rich and powerful than the rich and powerful.'[46] But it's a battle worth fighting – and one that we cannot afford to postpone any longer.

A Wider and Deeper Transformation

All the proposals thus presented – finance reform, regulation of capital flows, reform of taxation and so on – are different aspects of a wider and deeper transformation that Europe – and especially the EMU – must undergo if it wants to survive, not only as a political project, but also (and perhaps even more importantly) as a cultural and civilisational project. This calls for the reassertion of the primacy of politics, democracy and the state – or supra-state, progressive federalists would say – over markets (and especially finance).

The crisis of Europe is in many ways a crisis of neoliberalism – of the idea that the economy is best left to supposedly self-regulating markets, with the government intervening as little as possible. Over the course of the past 30 years, this has brought about more inequality, insecurity and instability, at the expense of social welfare and labour rights, and it is now tearing apart the very fabric of our democracies and societies, as well as threatening the future of the European integration process. Neoliberalism, free-market fundamentalism, financial deregulation and beggar-thy-neighbour trade policies have caused divergences and imbalances between the European economies (dividing the continent into creditor and debtor countries) that have now reached unprecedented and unsustainable proportions. These in turn are being drastically exacerbated by the continent-wide austerity measures. Thus, if the European integration project is to survive, it must be profoundly revolutionised on the basis of a radically alternative social, economic and political platform.

We need a 'Green New Deal' (GND), in the vein of Roosevelt's post-war New Deal, of which finance and tax reform are crucial but insufficient elements. To resolve the increasing divergence of the continent's economies (exacerbated by centrifugal tendencies at the political level), Europe needs to radically overturn austerity and aim at a genuine economic convergence – not downwards, as it is doing now, but upwards. This requires a cultural as much as a political revolution. It means replacing unfettered competition (which until now has oxymoronically characterised the entire 'integration process') with a true solidarity between the stronger and weaker members of the union. We should do this in the knowledge that these roles are not predetermined and constant in time, but can change according to the ebb and flow of history, as Germans should know better than anyone else – as long as struggling countries are given the means to adequately resolve their momentary crises (something the current European architecture does not provide).

This requires nothing less than a political quantum leap. It will not be enough for democratic institutions to reassert their control over markets through clear rules and regulations. They must, to a certain extent, also regain the levers of economic, industrial and investment policy, and reclaim their right to a certain degree of central planning. The aim should be to address the twin evils currently afflicting the European integration process – unemployment and economic imbalances – even if this means breaking some of the greatest taboos of modern economics. So let us now turn our attention to some of the more widely agreed proposals for social and economic reform coming from progressive thinkers and social movements.

Social and Economic Reform

As we have seen throughout this book, in Europe the economic crisis – as a consequence of the continent's neoliberal architecture and of the austerity policies imposed by the EU elite – has evolved into something much worse. It has become a social crisis, with some countries (such as Greece and Spain) now on the verge of humanitarian disaster. This is exemplified better than anything else by Europe's unemployment levels (see page 99). Such high levels are dangerous and unsustainable. Job creation, and the temporary support of the unemployed, are thus absolute priorities. They must be addressed through both short-term emergency measures and long-term structural reforms.

The easiest solution (technically speaking) in terms of emergency support measures would be a Europe-wide 'joint unemployment fund', an idea strongly advocated by Pierre Moscovici, the French minister of finance.[47] The importance of Moscovici's idea lies in the fact that it would represent an 'automatic stabiliser' capable of offsetting the effects of economic crises and imbalances, as countries facing economic troubles and high rates of unemployment would receive help from better-off countries. As we have seen (in the case of Spain and Greece, for example), unemployment and economic imbalances are two sides of the same coin: solving one problem will positively affect the other, and vice versa. Moreover, as well as having positive social and economic effects, a joint unemployment fund would be a demonstration of solidarity of great symbolic importance from an integrationist perspective. In many ways Moscovici's proposal would be the first step towards a common European welfare state. Of course, in the absence of a European government capable of raising taxes at a federal level, this would require a substantial increase in the contributions of member states to the European federal budget (a point we shall return to).

Unemployment is not the only problem that Europe faces. As we saw in Chapter 1, the share of GDP going to salaries has been continuously decreasing, and that of capital increasing, everywhere in the last few decades. This trend is now being exacerbated as a result of the explicitly class-based policies of austerity and internal devaluation. By forcing countries with sustained trade deficits to lower wages, while ignoring the necessary counterbalancing role of surplus countries, these policies are also widening the core–periphery economic gap. This beggar-thy-neighbour policy, and the long-term decline in the wages-to-GDP ratio, have to stop, and be radically reversed.

A Wage Standard

The most interesting proposal on these lines comes from an Italian economist, Emiliano Brancaccio. He has developed the idea of a European wage standard which simultaneously addresses the interrelated issues of declining salaries and widening trade imbalances.[48] As we have seen, one of the leading causes of Europe's trade imbalances is Germany's decision to adopt a policy of wage deflation despite its systematic current account surplus. To be fully effective, a reform of the monetary union needs to involve measures to reduce the divergence in unit labour costs (ULCs) fuelled – to an even larger degree, relatively speaking, than the rise in ULCs in periphery countries – by the wage moderation policies of surplus countries, and particularly Germany. A European wage standard would address this by establishing a clear set of rules aimed at:

- guaranteeing that the growth of nominal wages in relation to the growth of labour productivity is such as to generate a convergence of wage shares, fostering a tendency towards alignment of wage shares in the EMU in the long term
- linking the growth of nominal wages with respect to labour productivity to the balance of trade, so as to foster a return to equilibrium between countries with trade surpluses and those with deficits, by requiring countries characterised by systematic current account surpluses to accelerate the growth of nominal wages with respect to labour productivity
- establishing a system of sanctions for countries where nominal wages diverge from the dynamics imposed by the standard – in other words, an effective 'excessive surplus procedure'.

Brancaccio's proposal would also represent an important step away from the European Union's current mercantilist, export-led model towards one aimed at increasing domestic demand so as to absorb more imported goods and services.

In this sense, the European wage standard would have the benefit not only of rebalancing the continent's trade surpluses and deficits, and stopping relative wage deflation, but also of highlighting 'a possible link between the general interest in European unity and the interests of European workers' by 'generating potential convergence of objectives among workers from different countries even in the event of divergence in their respective labour productivities', as Brancaccio notes.[49] This, the author concludes, 'is the only logical basis upon which the lost sense of unity can be regained'.[50] Seen in the context of the decades-long neoliberal attack on labour, the wage standard appears nothing less than revolutionary, in that requires a complete rethinking of the role of workers in society, by establishing a strengthening of national collective contracts and their coordination at the European level as the necessary conditions for the determination of a framework.[51]

A Social Compact

As the European Trade Union Confederation (ETUC) states, Europe does not need a Fiscal Compact; it needs a social compact. This must comprise a European wage standard and an EU-wide joint unemployment policy, as mentioned, but also:

- **a defence of collective bargaining and social dialogue:** free collective bargaining and social dialogue are an integral part of the European social model and must be guaranteed at the EU and national level, with the aim of securing decent wages for all
- **a youth guarantee for all young people in Europe,** ensuring the provision of a decent job, or of adequate training opportunities, within four months of losing employment or leaving school
- **measures to improve the quality of jobs**, combat precarious jobs and fight abuses in the practice of part-time, temporary and fixed-term contracts
- **active labour market policies** including initiatives to support people with few or no links to the labour market.[52]

These measures should not be seen as an end in themselves, but as the basis of a radically alternative economic policy in Europe.

Planning for Jobs

Important as it is to support the unemployed and increase the salaries and protections of those who are lucky enough to be employed (especially since this would also help address the trade imbalances within the EMU), we need to go further: we also need to create new jobs. This requires us to put the levers of economic policy firmly back in the hands of our political institutions, and break the taboo of 'central planning'. As we have seen throughout the book, markets have totally failed at regulating themselves – let alone regulating the economy. The crisis of the EMU is paradigmatic of a more general crisis of the global finance-driven regime of accumulation. Markets have blatantly failed to determine prices efficiently and allocate resources between the various sectors of the economy, fuelling huge bubbles which have regularly gone bust (at a huge economic and social cost). We must therefore aim for a new system of production and development in which the role of market prices in determining the level and composition of demand and production is drastically diminished. This means retrieving from the dustbin of history, and updating, the notion of planning.[53] As Brancaccio and fellow economist Marco Passarella write:

> The crisis of the finance-driven regime of accumulation and the subsequent crisis of European unity could, in short, represent a historic opportunity to open up a debate on the need to rebuild the Union around a public engine of economic and social development, based on a modern, dynamic and progressive vision of 'new social and spatial planning'.[54]

This requires a redefinition of the role of political institutions – the state and central bank – as 'creators of new employment'.

More specifically, this 'new social and spatial' planning should take the form of a bold and ambitious Europe-wide public investment scheme in infrastructure, industry, energy, transport, innovation, research, education and natural resources, with the aim of initiating Europe's transition towards a socially and environmentally sustainable economy. The rebirth of Europe and its strategy of job creation cannot be based on outdated concepts of limitless growth and development. It is precisely these ideas that have landed us in the economic, social, ecological and cultural crises we are facing. We need a clean break with the past. Analysing in detail the various (and often conflicting) proposals for a European 21st century industrial and investment strategy is obviously beyond the scope of this book. I shall thus limit myself to summarising some of the more widely agreed elements of this strategy (as presented in the European Green Party's 'Green New Deal' manifesto and on the official GND website):

- **Macroeconomic and fiscal policy**: a truly green economy would promote human well-being and social equality, without placing more strain on the planet than it is able to support. The GND calls for greater financial regulation and a redefinition of the goals of macroeconomic policy, focusing far more on improving the quality of life and reducing our carbon footprint. Ambitious and far-reaching fiscal policies should target the enhancement of public services, and generally be designed to reward sustainable practices and make unsustainable commercial activity and lifestyles disadvantageous from a fiscal point of view.
- **Industry**: industry is a central theme in the GND – because industry touches everything and everyone, from construction and manufacturing to pharmaceuticals and energy. Industry is vital to the global economy, but is a rapacious guzzler of natural resources. Thus, the GND aims to create a modern industrial base making durable, environmentally friendly products that can be maintained and recycled and fed back into the system.
- **Resource and energy revolution**: if we are to avoid dangerous climate change, we need to seriously reduce our greenhouse gas emissions. The European Union should commit to emissions reductions of 40 per cent by 2020 and 80–95 per cent by 2050, based on 1990 levels, in line with the current recommendations of the United Nations Intergovernmental Panel on Climate Change (IPCC). Europe must also play a leading role in forging a binding international climate agreement under the UN framework. A combination of ambitious and binding targets, of incentives and of public investments into green technologies and services would help create millions of green jobs in Europe and tens of millions worldwide, which are much needed at a time of economic slowdown.

- **Transport**: transport is the fastest growing source of human-made greenhouse gas emissions. The European Union needs to work actively to create a sustainable transport system. Ending the direct and indirect subsidisation of inefficient and polluting transport modes, like aviation and road transport, is an important step in ensuring the full environmental costs are taken into account. We need to speed up investment in trans-European railroad connections and networks. Freight must be shifted from roads to rail and inland waterways on a much bigger scale. Affordable public transport and sustainable transport options in our cities, such as cycling and walking, must be promoted.
- **Environment**: climate change, deforestation, desertification and biodiversity loss chart our environmental decline. Important resources are being exhausted. The European Union needs to do more to address the threats to public health, whether related to water-borne or air-borne diseases, noise or toxic substances. Moreover, it has to halt the loss of biodiversity at home and overseas territories.
- **Agriculture**: the growing and cultivation of a huge natural resource – the world's food – has been tainted by intensive farming methods for crops and animals as pressure grows to feed the world. The GND looks to convert current intensive and industrial agricultural practices into greener methods. It envisages a sustainable agriculture and farming infrastructure that produces seasonal, healthy, local food. Green agriculture would provide quality jobs in Europe and allow fair trade with the developing world.
- **Education and research**: finally, the GND calls for massive investment in education, science and research in green, future-oriented technologies to put Europe at the forefront of a global economic revolution.[55]

In short, the GND is about profoundly revolutionising the way we work, move, eat – in other words, the way we live – in the knowledge that the current model is unsustainable not only in environmental terms, but also in social and economic terms, and that a 'good life can only be conceived within a framework where natural limits are accepted and with social justice as a central condition', as the GND manifesto states.[56] It is also about understanding that the entwined ecological and social crises are two sides of the same disaster. Societies have not been able to combat the expanding ecological crisis effectively because it is intimately linked to the social crisis in which the ruling form of capitalism has been organised to impede democratic initiatives. In this sense, solving the ecological crisis depends on disrupting the power of the elites, as French journalist Hervé Kempf convincingly argues in his book *How the Rich Are Destroying the Earth*.[57] We should aim for nothing less. And the GND – especially if coupled with the other far-reaching reforms analysed in this section – goes in the right direction.

Rethinking Work and Income

The transition towards a socially and environmentally sustainable economy – the only possible solution to our current economic, social and environmental crisis – does not only require a profound reappraisal of the crucial role that workers play in society, and more specifically, can and should play in rebuilding European unity and solidarity. It calls also for a reappraisal of the role and nature of work itself. As we have seen, Europe is wealthier than ever before, and yet unemployment and poverty across the continent are reaching record levels. This is in large part an outcome of explicitly class-based neoliberal policies and an inefficient market-driven allocation of capital, but it reflects too the changing nature of labour. Increased automation and mechanisation in manufacturing has made human labour ever more productive (increasing fivefold over the past 50 years) but also increasingly obsolete.[58]

To put it simply, increasingly few workers are able to produce more than ever before. Employees and governments have used this (and the threat of delocalisation) to pressure workers into accepting poorer salaries and fewer rights. Today's global capitalism can be described as a ferociously productive juggernaut that constantly brings a stream of new high-tech products to the marketplace but uses that same technology to ruthlessly divide, weaken and blackmail workers and entire societies. As much as this trend needs to be halted and reversed – by increasing the salaries and protections of those currently employed, and creating new (green) jobs through an ambitious Europe-wide public investment scheme – we also have to acknowledge the fact that technology has most likely made the goal of full employment, in the traditional sense, unattainable.

In light of this, a solution that is gaining rapidly growing support is a Europe-wide unconditional basic income (UBI). This is essentially an income unconditionally granted to all on an individual basis, without a means test or work requirement. It is a form of minimum income guarantee that differs from those that now exist in various European countries in three important ways. It is paid to individuals rather than households; it is paid irrespective of any income from other sources; and it is paid without requiring the performance of any work or the willingness to accept a job if offered. Many studies have demonstrated that UBI is financially feasible. It has the potential not only to eradicate misery, but also to herald a new era for humankind, in which work is not a requirement any more.[59] This would not only allow human beings and societies to develop to their full potential by encouraging non-market-oriented work, such as that of artists, parents and volunteers; it would also constitute a powerful incentive for the search for jobs for all those people who lost them because, unlike the conditional benefits that exist today, it would not disappear with the receipt of a salary. As the best-selling British author George Monbiot writes, '[e]conomic survival becomes a right, not a privilege'. Of course, he says, '[t]hese ideas require courage: the courage to confront the government, the opposition, the plutocrats, the media, the suspicions of a wary electorate. But without proposals on this scale, progressive politics is dead.'[60] As is any hope of rebuilding Europe, and the European welfare state, on a progressive and sustainable basis, we might add.

Working Less

Another proposal that goes in the same direction – in acknowledging the structural unfeasibility of full employment and moving towards a more socially and environmentally sustainable economy and less work-oriented society – is to reduce working hours. Juliet Schor, professor of sociology at Boston College, writes:

> That may seem counter-intuitive in a period when the mainstream message is that we are poorer than ever and have to work harder. But the historical record suggests it's a smart move that will create what economists call a triple dividend: three positive outcomes from one policy innovation.[61]

First, reduced working hours would cause a significant reduction in unemployment (and have been used successfully to that end in the past). Second, they would partly decouple the unemployment problem from GDP growth, which in the current context is not reconcilable with responsible emissions levels. Finally, but just as importantly, the third benefit of shorter hours is time itself, allowing people to build stronger social connections, maintain their physical and mental health, and engage in activities that are creative and meaningful. In conclusion, says Schor, the triple dividend of shorter working hours – reduced unemployment, less carbon emissions, and a better quality of life – shows that those who say we cannot afford to work less have it totally wrong: 'A serious reading of our economic history suggests we can't afford not to.'[62] Thus, we should aim for a Europe-wide reform of the European Union's working time directive aimed at striking the right balance between working hours, wages and employment levels in all countries (and especially those with particularly high unemployment levels).

The European Budget

Many of the progressive measures presented in this section should be understood as federal policies – and thus would require a substantial increase of the European budget. There are two ways to do this.

The first is by replacing nationally issued bonds with eurobonds (see page 158). This should be done in the context of a Europe-wide audit of public debt to assess which parts of the debt are illegitimate and thus should not fall on the shoulders of citizens at either the national or European level, regardless of the interest costs (which would be substantially lowered if national debts were pooled).[63]

The second is by partially (and progressively) replacing nationally collected taxes with a system of federal taxation; in other words, a euro-treasury capable of raising money at the European level through a common fiscal policy. By tackling tax havens and introducing an EU-wide system of redistributive and progressive fiscal harmonisation that targets high incomes, wealth and corporations, we could raise huge amounts of money (up to a trillion euros per year, according to some estimates) and thus both largely finance the restructuring of Europe's economy and significantly lower the fiscal pressure on the working and middle classes.

Since no tax can be introduced without democratic legitimacy (according to the principle of 'no taxation without representation'), many progressive federalists argue that this simply reinforces the need for a politically united Europe: an effective parliamentary representation of the populations, equipped with political control powers at the European level, particularly over the tax base and the use of income tax to support the single currency.[64] In short, in order to create the system of federal taxation necessary to pursue the investment strategies needed to ensure the economic and social cohesion of Europe, we also need to build a supranational government with democratic legitimacy. In this sense, the economic and political dimensions of the European crisis are inextricably linked.

Monetary Reform

There is another dimension to the crisis: what we might call its ideological dimension. In order to pursue a GND, Europe's institutions (in particular the ECB) and some of its more prominent members (first and foremost Germany) will have to abandon their radical anti-inflationary stance, pursue a more expansive monetary policy and minimise the importance given to debts and deficits. If the GND represents the political quantum leap that the continent needs, then this ideological quantum leap represents its necessary corollary. Building a democratic European federation with a common fiscal capacity will provide no solution to the current crisis if Europe remains beholden to the debt-obsessed neoliberal dogmas of austerity and over-restrictive fiscal and monetary policies that are killing the continent's economies.

Since the financial crisis of 2008, the US Federal Reserve and the ECB have reduced their key interest rates to around 0 and 0.25 per cent respectively (as of late 2013). This is the most basic form of monetary policy, and consists of lowering the interest rate at which banks can borrow money from the central bank. Both central banks have also engaged in unconventional forms of monetary policy, known as quantitative easing (QE), by which a central bank directly influences the money supply by creating 'new money' and injecting it into the banking system. The Fed (like most central banks), does this by buying large quantities of mortgage-backed securities and other securities such as government and corporate bonds from private banks. The ECB – whose mandate, as we know, forbids it from intervening in sovereign bond markets (except in exceptional circumstances, and only as an 'emergency' measure) – has resorted to different instruments, such as increasing the maturity of its refinancing operations up to 36 months (basically allowing banks to borrow unlimited funds at exceptionally low interest rates for three years, as long as the banks can provide eligible collateral).

While the QE policies of the ECB and of the Fed differ starkly in their effects on government bond yields and borrowing rates, as monetary policy they are very similar. They are both aimed at stimulating the economy by injecting huge sums of money into the banking system in the hope that the banks will inject it into the wider economy through investments and loans to households and businesses (thus expanding the monetary supply) and bond purchases, in the case of the eurozone. This process (when it works) is known as monetary transmission mechanism.

These forms of unconventional monetary policy, though, have failed to revive the economy. This is disastrously evident in Europe, and to a lesser extent in the United States, where unemployment is effectively declining, but hardly enough to justify the size of the Fed's huge bond-buying programme. In fact, QE has mostly benefited banks and bond traders. The reason, a number of economists argue, is that we are stuck in a 'liquidity trap'. This is a situation described in Keynesian economics, in which injections of cash into the private banking system by a central bank fail to stimulate the economy because the economic and profitability prospects are so dim that banks refuse to lend, and people and businesses hold on to their cash instead of spending and investing (assuming they are lucky enough to actually get a loan). The outcome is to trap the whole economy in a recessionary self-fulfilling prophecy[65]

This essentially leaves central bankers and policy makers with three options. They can do more QE, even though it is failing to stimulate employment or economic growth, especially in Europe. They can do nothing, on the grounds that governments should stop interfering with the economy. Or they can try a radical alternative, which is gaining increased support even in mainstream circles: handing out newly created money, debt-free, directly to governments instead of banks, in what renowned journalist and financial economist Anatole Kaletsky calls 'quantitative easing for the people' (QEP).[66]

QEP is very different from standard QE, where the Treasury is expected to buy the bonds back from the central bank at some point. Under QEP (also known as overt money financing, or OMF), the bond purchases are never intended to be reversed, and thus effectively amount to 'free money'. They are explicitly aimed at an overt increase in the government's fiscal deficit (without, though, adding to the overall debt) through expansionary policies, thus implying a cooperation between fiscal and monetary authorities; and they are subordinated to employment- and/or growth-related targets, as well as inflation targets. In short, if QE consists of injecting liquidity into the banks in the hope that this will percolate into the wider economy, QEP consists of bypassing banks altogether and injecting this money into the non-financial economy of consumption, investment and jobs, either through direct cash hand-outs to citizens (in the form of an unconditional basic income, for example) and tax cuts, or even better, by financing public works. The central bank would in effect be financing the government's expenditures by 'printing' money.

Just as QEP can be used to finance new deficits, it can also be used to write off (part of) the national debt, in a process is known as 'debt monetisation'.[67] Although most people would balk at the idea of printing money and giving it away to governments debt-free – because it is so removed from the current economic and monetary doctrine, especially in Europe – this is not a new idea. In fact, from the 1930s up to the neoliberal counter-revolution of the 1970s, it was one of the few practical points on which Keynesians and free-market economists such as Milton Friedman agreed.[68] Moreover, we should keep in mind that states already create money out of thin air. The only difference is that under the current system they give that money away to private banks (which also create new money themselves in the form of loans). As Martin Wolf writes:

> [I]t is impossible to justify the conventional view that fiat money should operate almost exclusively via today's system of private borrowing and lending .... I fail to see any moral force to the idea that fiat money should only promote private, not public, spending.[69]

Interestingly, the case for OMF was recently made by none other than Adair Turner, member of the UK's Financial Policy Committee and former chairman of the Financial Services Authority, and one of the most influential financial policy makers in the world. In a truly taboo-breaking speech, Turner acknowledged that not only has the standard form of monetary policy – cutting interest rates – failed to kick-start the economy, unconventional forms of monetary policy such as QE have also failed to live up to expectations. He argued that we should 'take the possibility of OMF out of the taboo box' and 'consider whether and under what circumstances it can play an appropriate role'.[70]

QEP/OMF cuts straight to the heart of one of the overarching arguments of this study: the need to reassert the primacy of politics, democracy and the state – or supra-state – over markets (and especially finance). Until now we have argued that democratic institutions need to reassert their control over markets first and foremost through clear rules and regulations, but also to a certain extent by regaining the levers of economic, industrial and investment policy – thus reclaiming their right to a certain degree of central planning. This is already a huge taboo-breaker in itself.

But the growing number of mainstream advocates of QEP argue that we should go even further, and reclaim (a degree of) democratic control over monetary policy itself. This does not mean putting monetary policy at the service of the short-term interests of governments and politicians. Rather, it means rethinking the priorities of monetary policy – which clearly change between leveraging (boom) and de-leveraging (bust) periods – in order that they serve the interests of the wider economy, and society at large. While this would of course require some degree of coordination between fiscal and monetary authorities, it need not necessarily be seen as a threat to central bank independence, as was acknowledged even by the former chairman of the Federal Reserve, Ben Bernanke.[71]

At this point it would be legitimate to ask: if the stated aim of QEP is to inject money directly into the economy through expansionary government spending, why not do this by means of traditional Keynesian revenue- and debt-funded fiscal stimuli? From a technical standpoint, advocates of QEP acknowledge that there are circumstances in which a conventional funded fiscal stimulus – provided the country in question has a central bank capable of keeping, and willing to keep, borrowing costs down (as a standard policy, and not, like the ECB, under the threat of 'conditionality') – could be appropriate. They certainly see it as a better alternative than austerity, which is an option that they do not even take into consideration. They simply consider a debt-free, QEP-funded stimulus to be an even better (and in some cases necessary) option.

From an economic standpoint, advocates argue that QEP is always better than a conventional funded fiscal stimulus because the impact of the stimulus is not offset by public awareness of future debt burdens, self-fulfilling (albeit unfounded) concerns about future debt sustainability and future taxes that will be necessary to reduce the fiscal deficits and debt levels. None other than Milton Friedman, one of the founding fathers of neoliberal economics, argued in the 1940s not only that government deficits should sometimes be financed with fiat money, but that they should always be financed in that fashion, on the basis that such a system would provide a surer foundation for a low-inflation regime.[72]

Moreover, in some cases – such as those in which a country's debt-to-GDP ratio has reached very, very high levels, even by Keynesian standards – QEP might be the only option. An oft-cited example is Japan: with a debt-to-GDP ratio of 230 per cent and rising, many economists, while acknowledging that large Japanese government deficits were, and still are, necessary to avoid a 1930s-style Great Depression, argue that even according to Keynesian theory there is no persuasive explanation of how Japan will ever contain or reduce the growth of its public debt burden relative to GDP – except through monetisation or debt restructuring/repudiation.[73]

In circumstances such as those outlined above, though, the danger is that the level of QEP required to reduce the debt-to-GDP ratio might be so high that it would result in unacceptably high inflation. This leads to the conclusion that if there are conditions in which QEP will eventually be required, it is better to deploy it early and in small amounts, than to allow fiscal debt as a percentage of GDP to accumulate to unsustainable levels. Thus, given the fact that, relative to national income, government debt is now larger in many countries than at any point since the Second World War, and is projected to grow relative to income for years to come, there are good reasons to believe that it is a good time to use QEP/OMF (rather than a funded fiscal stimulus).[74] This holds particularly true in a number of European countries, leading financial experts Pierre Pâris and Charles Wyplosz to conclude recently that 'the only way we can end the crisis' is to 'bury the debt forever' through partial debt monetisation.[75]

More importantly, perhaps, arguments in favour of debt-free rather than debt-based fiscal stimuli are also underpinned by a strong (albeit largely unspoken) ethical-ideological logic. If 'OMF is bound to be at least or more stimulative than an increase in funded fiscal deficits', as Turner writes, why should the burden of the stimulus fall on the shoulders of future taxpayers (through the servicing of the debt) if this can be avoided?[76] This is especially so if we take into account that this burden amounts, in most cases, to nothing less than a shift from the private sector to the public sector.

The main argument against QEP, and expansionary monetary and fiscal policies in general, is that they inevitably lead to inflation – or hyper-inflation, in the case of QEP. Advocates of QEP offer a three-pronged response.

First, the current system – in which states not only 'print' money and give it away to banks through QE, but the banks themselves create most of the digital money in circulation (see Chapter 1) – is just as inflationary as (if not more inflationary than) QEP. More accurately, it is inflationary when it should not be, and is not inflationary when it should be. In short, the ability to create money – in effectively unlimited amounts, through securitisation – gives banks the power to engineer credit-driven booms at will, which in turn leads to soaring prices (especially in the housing market). When these booms inevitably go bust, triggering a crisis, the banks attempt to repair their over-leveraged balance sheets by engaging in excessive de-leveraging, cutting off credit when households and businesses need it the most. This exacerbates the crisis and drives the economy into what economist Richard Koo described as a 'balance sheet recession'.[77] When this happens, because of the way in which fractional reserve banking works, no amount of QE is sufficient to get banks to start loaning again. In such a context, central banks have little influence on the rise and resolution of boom-and-bust cycles, simply because under the current system of fractional reserve banking the money supply is largely out of the central banks' control. It need not be this way, though: 'private credit and money creation are fundamental drivers of both financial and macroeconomic instability and need to be tightly regulated', says Turner.[78]

Second, there is no inherent technical reason to believe that QEP will be more inflationary than any other policy stimulus, or that it will produce hyper-inflation, since the impact on nominal demand and thus potentially on inflation depends entirely on the scale of the operation. Even Friedman believed that a system of money-financed deficits could provide a surer foundation for a low-inflation regime than a debt-based financing system.[79]

Finally, the anti-inflation doomsayers are missing a crucial point: that (a bit of) inflation is precisely what we need, or at the very least is a means justified by the end of employment creation (while maintaining the anchor of commitment to long-term price stability). Most developed countries are trapped in a deflationary spiral: a situation where decreases in prices lead to lower production, which in turn leads to lower wages and demand, which leads to further decreases in prices, which leads to growing unemployment, and so on. In such a situation, not only is a higher inflation rate justified by the prospect of creating jobs, it is also beneficial in itself, as it implies a higher return on investments, producing a more fertile economic environment. It also has the added benefit of alleviating a country's debt burden by eroding the real value of the debt.[80]

This final point is belatedly starting to be acknowledged by central bankers and policy makers around the world (with the notable exception, it goes without saying, of Europe). In the United States, since late 2012 the Fed has committed itself to go beyond 'inflation targeting' (a policy aimed at keeping inflation under a certain limit) by setting a conditional unemployment target of 6.5 per cent as long as inflation does not rise above 2.5 per cent. To this end it has been pursuing an aggressive $85 billion a month bond-buying programme (still ongoing as of late 2013). In the United Kingdom Mark Carney, appointed governor of the Bank of England at the end of 2012, has stated that he will aim for a new policy of 'flexible inflation targeting' – despite the fact that the country has a higher inflation rate that most developed countries, and has been exceeding its 2 per cent inflation target for more than three consecutive years (as of mid-2013). In Japan the new government of Shinz Abe, shortly after coming into office at the end 2012, announced a significant $116 billion public spending programme, with the aim of stemming the decades-long negative inflation rate (despite massive amounts of QE). More importantly, not only did Abe explicitly impose on the Bank of Japan a higher inflation rate, he demanded that it commit to specific actions in pursuit of that target through 'open-ended' (without any termination date) central bank asset purchases: a policy amounting essentially to QEP.

A Programme for the Eurozone

Tectonic shifts are under way in monetary and fiscal policy theory, as a growing number of central bankers and policy makers around the world move towards flexible and/or higher inflation targets, and employment- or growth-related targets. Furthermore, some of them are starting to openly advocate, or covertly implement, overt money financing, or QEP (with some commentators arguing that the United States and Japan are already monetising their debt).[81] And yet in Europe, despite the fact that the continent, like most developed countries, is clearly trapped in a liquidity trap and is heading into a deflationary scenario[82] – and even more importantly, is the region that is suffering the most in economic and social terms – the ECB has consistently refused to follow suit. At the very least it could allow member states to pursue more expansionary fiscal policies by launching a 'normal', non-conditional bond-buying programme to keep borrowing rates down. (It is actually doing the exact opposite.) Instead it is limiting itself to lowering its key interest rates, which as we have seen is bound to fail to revive the economy.[83]

Of course the ECB, lacking a unified government to back it fiscally or authoritatively, is in a much trickier position than other major central banks. From a progressive-federalist perspective, this reinforces the need for a deepening of the integration project. But for this to succeed requires nothing less than an ideological quantum leap, in monetary as well as fiscal and budgetary terms. That may well prove to be the most important step of all, because many of the other proposals presented in this book depend on it. Without a change in the ECB's monetary stance (and in more general terms, in some of its basic ideological tenets), most of the GND-related structural reforms which are required to build a European supranational, progressive democracy on the basis of a socially, economically and environmentally sustainable platform will not be possible.

There are some policies that technically the ECB could pursue in the current inter-governmental context to alleviate the burden of some countries – such as launching a normal, non-conditional bond-buying programme for the countries of the periphery, allowing them to engage in expansionary debt-funded fiscal policies, even if this would inevitably result in a increase in their deficit-to-GDP and debt-to-GDP ratios. It could even monetise part of their debt. But these measures would not resolve the deeper problems inherent in the EMU construct, such as the increasing divergence between the countries of the core and those of the periphery. Here are some of the monetary, fiscal and budgetary reforms that would be necessary in the context of a progressive federalist solution:

- First of all, the future 'European government' should pool the debts of member states and replace nationally issued bonds with eurobonds: federal bonds issued at a determined interest rate by the euro bloc as a whole.
- The pooling of national bonds should happen in the context of a Europe-wide audit of public debts aimed at evaluating their nature and legitimacy, with a particular focus on sovereign derivative deals.
- The ECB should not only become a non-conditional lender of last resort to the future federal government, but should also commit to purchasing eurobonds as part of its standard QE policy, keeping borrowing costs down for the eurozone

as a whole. The ECB must also be made fully accountable to the new European democratic institutions, and must be willing to cooperate with the federal government's fiscal authorities. The OMT programme must be scrapped.

- Under this arrangement, the federal government would raise the money and then forward it to individual governments. At present it is unclear how this system would work from a political-technical standpoint, but one thing is certain: in order for this system to work, the federal government must be willing to engage in revenue-funded and debt-funded expansionary fiscal policies in order to provide finance. This means adopting much more flexible deficit-to-GDP and debt-to-GDP targets, and subordinating these to employment- and/or growth-related targets, and the general attainment of the objectives of the GND. It also means profoundly reassessing the Fiscal Compact.
- The federal government (and especially the countries of the core) must also be willing to engage in a permanent fiscal transfer mechanism between the richer and poorer countries of the union. This is what Europe's economic powerhouses like Germany dread the most, fearing that it will amount to a permanent subsidy by Germany and the core of 'southern inefficiency'. While their concerns are understandable – and appropriate precautions should be taken to ensure that such transfers are aimed at financing proactive structural investments (within the context of the GND) and combating unemployment rather than perpetuating pork-belly politics and crony capitalism – these countries should also come to terms with the fact that fiscal transfers are an inherent and unavoidable trait of any fiscal union. More importantly from their point of view, such an arrangement is more desirable than offering countries in trouble loans that they will not be able to repay. In the United States, for example, some states are more or less permanently in deficit, while others are in surplus, and this is considered perfectly normal, though it is not necessarily a model to aspire to.[84]
- As we have seen throughout this chapter, a large part of the sums necessary to finance the GND (and other measures) can be raised through a tax revolution aimed at taxing capital and wealth, and tackling tax havens.
- Nonetheless, if the federal government needs to engage in debt-funded deficit spending in order to meet its financing needs, the ECB must be willing to support its fiscal stimulus through expansionary monetary policies: that is, asset purchases aimed at keeping borrowing costs down. To this end, it should aim for more flexible employment- and/or growth-subordinated inflation targets.
- In view of recent evolutions in monetary policy theory (and the notion that is better to monetise sooner than later), the ECB should accept debt monetisation in principle and practise QEP- or OMF-style temporary debt monetisation if necessary (to finance expansionary policies without incurring further debt, or to write off a part of the existing debt).

- To this end, we should engage in a Europe-wide debate over the pros and cons of debt-financed versus money-financed government spending.
- A similar debate should be engaged over the pros and cons of private money creation (through fractional reserve banking) versus public money creation. Tools should be developed to limit the quantity of privately created money. (Other measures analysed in this chapter go in that direction.)

Conclusion

In this chapter I have outlined a programme for radical reform of the European Union/EMU. It shows that the construction of a genuine European supra-national democracy, through which to achieve the aim of a progressive and socially, economically and environmentally sustainable society, is not only possible, but is arguably the best means to forward the interests of citizens and workers and tame the overwhelming powers of global financial and corporate leviathans. Throughout the chapter, I have offered an in-depth blueprint for change, consisting a series of interlinked, multi-level and mutually reinforcing reforms. These include:

- The radical democratisation and politicisation of European institutions.
- The overhaul of the financial sector, through such measures as the separation of commercial and investment banking, limitations on the size of banks and their ability to create private money, the regulation of or a ban on speculative financial products, a financial transaction tax, capital controls and other measures discussed.
- A tax revolution: financing the transition to a socially and environmentally sustainable economy by tackling tax havens, ending fiscal dumping and introducing a system of harmonised and redistributive fiscal federalism (in other words, a euro-treasury) aimed at taxing capital and wealth instead of labour.
- A new (macro)economic policy based on the radical rejection of austerity and the reassertion of the primacy of politics, democracy and the state (or rather the supra-state) over markets (and especially finance), through clear rules and regulations but also to a certain extent by regaining the levers of economic, industrial and investment policy. This involves reclaiming the right to a certain degree of central planning, in order to pursue a Europe-wide public investment scheme (the Green New Deal).
- Economic convergence between member states: the idea of a European wage standard to fairly spread the burden of readjustment among deficit and surplus countries, reasserting the crucial role of labour in the promotion of European unity and solidarity; and the introduction of a fiscal transfer mechanism.
- Labour and social reforms, including a European social compact, a joint

unemployment fund and/or EU-wide unconditional basic income, and a reduction in working hours.

- Monetary and budgetary reforms, including the introduction of eurobonds; the transformation of the ECB into a normal, non-conditional lender of last resort to a federal government willing to support expansionary fiscal policies; the adoption of more flexible deficit-to-GDP, debt-to-GDP and inflation targets; the adoption of employment- or growth-related targets; and the opening of a debate over the transition from debt-based deficits to debt-free deficits through a policy of overt money financing.

This programme for a radical, progressive-integrationist Europe-wide 'revolution' irrefutably debunks and discredits the notion that there are no alternatives to a 'new normal' of austerity, mass unemployment and declining living standards within the context of the economic and monetary union. (This is a claim made both by Europe's pro-austerity political-financial elites and by the anti-austerity and anti-euro (and/or anti-EU) advocates of a return to national currencies.) It shows that the realisation of a new and updated European social democratic model might arguably be possible *only* within the framework of a politically united, democratic and cooperationist Europe.

After all, there is little doubt about the fact that many of the reforms proposed in this section – the restructuring of banks and financial markets, the tackling of tax havens, a no-loopholes tax revolution, labour reforms based on workers' solidarity and so on – are only achievable within a politically and economically integrated framework. It is hard to see how any single state would be able to tame the overwhelming (and intrinsically borderless) power of global capital. This is not to say that the notion of a break-up of the euro, or a break-away of certain countries, should be dismissed as naïve, unrealistic and necessarily catastrophic (if not outright impossible). It might indeed prove to be a possible (and maybe necessary) solution if a progressive integrationist project proves politically unfeasible. It simply points to the fact that a progressive integrationist solution to the crisis would be a better option, and that we should do all that is in our power to accomplish it, before considering (or allowing, through inaction) a political and economic break-up of Europe.

This struggle will necessarily have to be a multi-level one. At a grassroots level, it will require the creation of a broad pan-European network of social and workers' movements, civil society organisations, NGOs and progressive thinkers. They will need to highlight the commonality of interests and struggles of all European citizens and workers (especially those of the core countries, to overcome the core–periphery division engineered by the financial-political elite) and to build a broad social consensus for a platform of radical integrationist change.

At an institutional level, somewhat paradoxically (but only apparently so), it will require the political elites of the periphery countries to acknowledge the reality of the core–periphery division (and the wider inter-capitalist struggles under way in Europe) and create a common front to exert pressure on Germany (and the other countries of the core) to shoulder part of the burden of redressing the intra-euro trade and economic imbalances, and in the shorter term agree to some much-needed institutional changes. To that end, they must gain some leverage over the countries of the core. I believe that the only way to achieve that is for periphery countries to aim strategically for a radical reform of the EMU (which is ultimately in their best interest). At the same time – I realise that this may seem to contradict my previous arguments – they must declare themselves to be (and genuinely be) ready to exit the EMU and default on their debt if their demands for a symmetric readjustment are not met.

Periphery countries have a lot to lose from a break-up of the eurozone, in my opinion. But core countries arguably have more to lose, especially if the departing countries default on their debt (a large part of which is held by core countries) and impose capital – and possibly trade – regulations to control dealings with the surplus countries. This is arguably the periphery countries' strongest negotiating advantage, and one they should not be afraid to use – assuming they are able to find a common voice. Paradoxically, the survival of the European Union/EMU might depend on it. As Lapavitsas and Flassbeck write, '[p]rovided they recognize their individual weakness and their collective power, a coalition of the debtor countries threatening the end of EMU may be the best way to force Germany to change its economic model.'[85]

Another negotiating strategy – advocated most notably by George Soros – is for periphery countries (and possibly less orthodox core countries, such as France) to band together and threaten Germany with exclusion from the euro club. This would arguably be a much less painful solution for periphery countries. As Soros explains:

> Since all the accumulated debt is denominated in euros, it makes all the difference which country remains in charge of the euro. If Germany left, the euro would depreciate. The debtor countries would regain their competitiveness. Their debt would diminish in real terms and, if they issued eurobonds, the threat of default would disappear. Their debt would suddenly become sustainable. Most of the burden of adjustment would fall on the countries that left the euro. Their exports would become less competitive and they would encounter stiff competition from the euro area in their home markets.[86]

In any case, whatever strategy they decide to adopt, a radical change of the EMU hinges necessarily on the citizens and leaders of periphery countries understanding that one of the principal reasons why Germany has been able to pursue its own (legitimate, to a certain extent) national interests so impressively – chiefly through beggar-thy-neighbour trade policies – is that its intra-euro trade partners did not pursue theirs. Lapavitsas and Flassbeck again explain: 'It is an integral part of Keynesian theory that beggaring one's neighbours may be a successful strategy as long as the trading partners accept this economic imperialism and do not undertake retaliatory action.'[87] In this sense, retaliatory action could (and should) take the form of short-term unilateral relief measures, undertaken by one or more countries, the most urgent of which is arguably to break free of the ridiculous and self-defeating constraints of the Fiscal Compact.

This means, very simply, putting an immediate stop to the troika-imposed budget cuts in bailed-out countries and engaging in emergency fiscal stimuli (higher spending and lower taxes on labour) aimed at boosting employment and demand, even if this means surpassing the 3 per cent deficit-to-GDP ratio (where it has not been surpassed already). At the same time, the issue of the patent unsustainability of the current levels of interest on periphery country debt should be addressed head-on. This can be done by stating in clear terms that a long-term solution must be found at the European level (through eurobonds and a Europe-wide audit, or debt monetisation) or some countries will be forced to default on part or all of their debt in the near future.

If it was to take this course, a country in economic difficulty would gain some much-needed economic breathing room – the reforms outlined in this chapter cannot be implemented overnight, while citizens and workers need immediate relief – as well as leverage at the negotiating table. This is necessary too, since it is desirable for these rebellious measures to be part of a longer-term (and multi-country) strategy aimed at exerting pressure on core countries rather than an end in themselves.

The reactions would be hysterical. Brussels diplomats and core-country elites would threaten reprisals, the markets would jitter, commentators would scream that the end is nigh. Periphery countries need not fear, though. As we have seen, they have more power than they generally realise. The future of the euro – and potentially of Europe – rests in their hands; they just have to become aware of it.

These rebellious measures, while aimed at long-term institutional change, should also focus on short-term cooperative solutions that can be introduced immediately and within current European law and treaties, as outlined in the 'modest proposal' penned by economists Yanis Varoufakis, Stuart Holland and James K. Galbraith.[88] Their proposal is centred around four major policies:

- the handing over of troubled banks to the ESM, which should be given the power to directly, fully and unconditionally recapitalise or restructure them
- a limited debt conversion programme, whereby the ECB offers member states the opportunity of converting the portion of their debt below the 60 per cent debt-to-GDP limit to a lower interest rate

- an investment-led recovery and convergence programme, whereby the European Investment Bank (EIB) and the European Investment Fund (EIF) jointly issue bonds to finance investments in social and environmental domains without adding to state debt
- an emergency solidarity programme to guarantee access to nutrition and basic energy needs for all Europeans, funded by the European Commission using the interest accumulated within the European system of central banks, profits made from government bond transactions and, in the future, other financial transactions or balance sheet stamp duties that the European Union is currently considering.

As the authors argue, the 'modest proposal' aims at tackling simultaneously the main aspects of the euro crisis – the banking crisis, the debt crisis, underinvestment, unemployment, and more generally the human, social and political emergency – by Europeanising various area of economic activity without the need for new institutions, new rules and new treaties. Notwithstanding the need (in my opinion) for deeper integration to assess Europe's deeper structural problems, these proposals would certainly offer the continent some much-needed breathing space. More importantly, though, they highlight the fact that while the long-term strategy should be aimed at achieving change at the European – to some extent, post-national – level, this will only be attained through progressive change at the national level. However we look at it, the struggle starts from the bottom up.

Europe has been hijacked. It's time to take it back.

Notes

Preface

1 George Soros, 'How to save the European Union', *Guardian*, 9 April 2013.
2 David Marsh, 'Euro zone needs a truth, reconciliation commission', MarketWatch, 22 July 2013.

Chapter 1

1 Andrew Clark, 'Goldman Sachs: Fabrice Tourre defends his "Frankenstein products"', *Guardian*, 27 April 2010.
2 Margareta Pagano, 'Goldman "bet against securities it sold to clients"', *Independent*, 25 April 2010.
3 Zaid Jilani and Brad Johnson, 'Wall Street recession cost 1.5 million times more than the cost of securing Occupy protests', ThinkProgress, 23 November 2011; International Labour Organization (ILO), press release: 'Unemployment reached highest level on record in 2009', 26 January 2010.
4 *BBC News*, 'Bank crisis impact bad as world war, Andrew Haldane says', 3 December 2012.
5 Nouriel Roubini and Stephen Mihm, *Crisis Economics: A Crash Course in the Future of Finance*, London: Penguin, 2011, p. 128.
6 Roubini and Mihm, 2011, p. 128.
7 Roubini and Mihm, 2011, pp. 127–8.
8 Andrea Baranes, *Finanza per indignati*, Milan: Ponte alle Grazie, 2012, p. 114.
9 Baranes, 2012, p. 115.
10 UK: *Guardian*, 'Interest rates cut to 4.5% as Brown unveils £500bn bank bail-out', 8 October 2008; Germany: *Spiegel Online*, 'Fighting the financial crisis: stocks surge as EU nations unveil bailout packages', 13 October 2008; France: Henry Samuel, 'Banking bail-out: France unveils 360bn package', *Telegraph*, 13 October 2008; Austria: Federal Chancellery of Austria, 'Bank rescue package: green light given by EU Commission', 15 December 2008; Netherlands: ThinkAdvisor, 'Dutch bailouts of ING, ABN Amro "large errors": committee', 11 April 2012.
11 US Government Accounting Office (GAO), *Federal Reserve System: Opportunities Exist to Strengthen Policies and Processes for Managing Emergency Assistance*, July 2011, p. 131.
12 William Greider, 'The AIG bailout scandal', *The Nation*, 6 August 2010.
13 Interview on RTÉ One, 2007 (day/month unspecified), viewable at www.youtube.com/watch?v=7inIiXeROpU.
14 Unless noted otherwise, all EU statistics are taken from the Eurostat statistics database.
15 Commission of Investigation into the Banking Sector in Ireland, *Misjudging Risk: Causes of the Systemic Banking Crisis in Ireland*, March 2011, p. i; Michael Lewis, 'When Irish eyes are crying', *Vanity Fair*, March 2011.
16 Lewis, 2011.
17 Lewis, 2011.
18 Lewis, 2011.

19 Guido Fawkes, 'Anglo-Irish bondholders should take the losses. Is the ECB forcing Ireland to protect German investments?', author's blog, 15 October 2010.
20 Lewis, 2011.
21 Jubilee Debt Campaign, *The State of Debt: Putting an End to 30 Years of Crisis*, May 2012, p. 29.
22 Quoted in Lewis, 2011.
23 Lewis, 2011.
24 Quoted in Leslie Crawford, 'Boomtime Spain waits for the bubble to burst', *Financial Times*, 8 June 2006.
25 Euro Challenge, *An Overview of Spain's Economy*, 2012.
26 IMF, *Spain: Financial Stability Assessment*, June 2012, p. 10.
27 Crawford, 2006.
28 Crawford, 2006.
29 Reuters, 'Timeline: Spain's banking crisis', 8 June 2012.
30 *Economist*, 'The Spanish bail-out: going to extra time', 16 June 2012.
31 *Economist*, 16 June 2012.
32 *BBC News*, 'Eurozone debt web: who owes what to whom', 18 November 2011.
33 Harold Heckle, 'Spain goes from boom to bailout in a decade', Associated Press (AP), 9 June 2012.
34 Fondo de Reestructuración Ordenada Bancaria (FROB), *Fund for Orderly Bank Restructuring (FROB)*, April 2013, p. 27.
35 J. Eric Ivester and Bradley G. Wilson, 'Icelandic bank crisis offers insight into global financial meltdown', Chicago: TMA, 15 September 2010.
36 Fjármálaeftirlitsins (FME), 'New Landsbanki takes over domestic operations of Landsbanki Islands hf', press release, 9 October 2008.
37 Quoted in *Wall Street Journal*, 'Excerpts: Iceland's Oddsson', 17 October 2008.
38 Paul Krugman, 'The path not taken', *New York Times*, 27 October 2011.
39 IMF, 'IMF Survey: Iceland's unorthodox policies suggest alternative way out of crisis', 3 November 2011.
40 Speech by Mervyn King to the Worshipful Company of International Bankers, London, 17 March 2009, viewable at http://www.bis.org/review/r090319a.pdf.
41 For an in-depth overview of how fractional reserve banking allows banks to 'create money out of thin air', see the work by the UK-based non-profit group Positive Money at www.positivemoney.org.
42 Positive Money website, 'How we got here' and 'How banks create money'.
43 Speech by Adair Turner at the South African Reserve Bank, 2 November 2 2012, viewable at http://www.fsa.gov.uk/static/pubs/speeches/1102-at.pdf.
44 Institut für Makroökonomie und Konjunkturforschung (IMK), *Financialization of the U.S. Household Sector*, June 2010, p. 55.
45 Hyman P. Minsky, 'Securitization' (1987), in Hyman P. Minsky Archive, paper 15.
46 Quoted in John Cassidy, 'The Wisdom of King', *New Yorker*, 27 October 2009.
47 Investor Dictionary website, 'Predatory lending'; Giles Tremlett, 'Immigrant cleaner leads revolt against Spanish mortgage trap', *Guardian*, 11 December 2011.
48 Quoted in James Fallows, 'Dr Doom has some good news', *The Atlantic*, 1 July 2009.
49 Roubini and Mihm, 2011, p. 15.
50 Baranes, 2012, p. 47.
51 Roubini and Mihm, 2011, p. 62.
52 Luciano Gallino, *Finanzcapitalismo: La civiltà del denaro in crisi*, Turin: Einaudi, 2011, p. 258.
53 J. G. Palma, 'The revenge of the market on the rentiers: why neo-liberal reports on

the end of history turned out to be premature', *Cambridge Journal of Economics*, Vol. 33, No. 3, 2009, p. 2.

54 Gallino, 2011, p. 167 (author's translation).
55 *Economist*, 'Reforming derivatives: heavy lifting', 15 August 2013.
56 BIS, *Triennial Central Bank Survey: Report on Global Foreign Exchange Market Activity in 2010*, December 2010, p. 7; Executive summary of Bernard Lietaer, Christian Arnsperger, Sally Goerner and Stefan Brunnhuber, *Money and Sustainability: The Missing Link*, Brussels: Club of Rome – EU Chapter, 2012, p. 11.
57 David C. Korten, 'Life after capitalism', presentation for Edmonton, Calgary and Saskatoon, November 1998.
58 Adair Turner, 'How to tame global finance', *Prospect*, 27 August 2009.
59 Quoted in John Cassidy, 'What good is Wall Street?', *New Yorker*, 29 November 2010.
60 Quoted in John Arlidge, 'George Soros on the coming U.S. class war', Daily Beast, 23 January 2012.
61 Roubini and Mihm, 2011, p. 46.
62 Roubini and Mihm, 2011, p. 40.
63 Pierre Larrouturou, *Svegliatevi!*, Milan: Piemme, 2012, p. 15.
64 Larrouturou, 2012, p. 15 (author's translation).
65 Nouriel Roubini, 'Economic insecurity and inequality breed political instability', in Janet Byrne (ed.), *The Occupy Handbook*, New York: Back Bay Books, 2012, p. 159.
66 Roubini and Mihm, 2011, p. 191.
67 Peter Coy, 'Lessons from the Credit-Anstalt collapse', *Bloomberg Businessweek*, 20 April 2011.
68 Niall Ferguson and Nouriel Roubini, 'The perils of ignoring history: this time, Europe really is on the brink', *Spiegel Online*, 12 June 2012.
69 See Oxfam's report *Be Outraged: There are Alternatives*, May 2012, pp. 10–12.
70 Adam Przeworski and Michael Wallerstein, 'Democratic capitalism and the cross-roads', in Thomas Ferguson and Joel Rogers (eds), *Political Economy: Readings in the Politics and Economics of American Public Policy*, New York: M. E. Sharpe, 1984, p. 339.
71 Roubini, 2012, p. 161.
72 Encyclopedia of Nations website, 'The International Labour Organization (ILO) – purposes'.
73 Roubini and Mihm, 2011, p. 24.
74 Gérard Duménil and Dominique Lévy, 'The neoliberal (counter-)revolution', in Alfredo Saad-Filho and Deborah Johnston (eds), *Neoliberalism: A Critical Reader*, London: Pluto Press, 2005, p. 12.
75 This is the definition used in Roubini and Mihm, 2011 (p. 32).
76 Ronald Reagan's first inaugural address, January 1981.
77 Rawi E. Abdelal, *Capital Rules: The Construction of Global Finance*, Cambridge, Mass.: Harvard University Press, 2007, p. 57.
78 See Article VI, section 3 of the IMF's Mandate, which recognises the right of members to 'exercise such controls as are necessary to regulate international capital movements'.
79 Carmen M. Reinhart and Kenneth S. Rogoff, *This Time Is Different: Eight Centuries of Financial Folly*, Princeton, N.J.: Princeton University Press, 2009, p. 205.
80 Abdelal, 2007, pp. 58–61.
81 Abdelal, 2007, pp. 61–4.
82 Abdelal, 2007, p. 85.
83 Abdelal, 2007, p. 84.
84 Abdelal, 2007, p. 63.
85 IMF, *Systemic Banking Crises: A New Database*, November 2008, p. 5.

86 Introduction to Stephany Griffith-Jones, José Antonio Ocampo and Joseph E. Stiglitz (eds), *Time for a Visible Hand: Lessons from the 2008 World Financial Crisis*, Oxford: Oxford University Press, 2010, p. 1.
87 John Maynard Keynes, *The General Theory of Employment, Interest, and Money*, New York: Classic House, 2008, p. 128.
88 Interview on CBS, September 2008, viewable at https://www.youtube.com/watch?v=vUJ_Qn0AHTU.
89 Interview on the *Daily Show*, April 2009, viewable at www.thedailyshow.com/watch/wed-april-15-2009/elizabeth-warren-pt--2.
90 Edward Harrison, 'How globalisation led to universal banking in America', Credit Writedowns, 13 July 2012.
91 Commission of Investigation into the Banking Sector in Ireland, 2011, p. 59.
92 Gallino, 2011, p. 55.
93 *Economist*, 'Reforming derivatives', 2013.
94 Gallino, 2011, p. 255 (author's translation).
95 Quoted by Raymond Lonergan in *Mr. Justice Brandeis, Great American*, 1941.
96 Mario Pianta, *Nove su dieci. Perché stiamo (quasi) tutti peggio di dieci anni fa*, Bari: Laterza, 2012, p. 60 (author's translation).
97 Pianta, 2012, p. 60.
98 Gallino, 2011, pp. 12, 21–2 (author's translation).
99 Definition by Greta Krippner of the University of California, as quoted in the introduction to Gerald A. Epstein (ed.), *Financialization and the World Economy*, Cheltenham: Edward Elgar, 2005, p. 3.
100 OECD, *Employment Outlook 2012*, 2012, pp. 109–61; Jason Hickel, 'A short history of neoliberalism (and how we can fix it)', New Left Project, 22 October 2012.
101 Hickel, 2012.
102 OECD, 2012, p. 110.
103 European Commission, *Employment in Europe 2007*, October 2007, pp. 237–42 (1970s–1980s average based on EU-15 data); EU annual micro-economic database (AMECO) data.
104 Larrouturou, 2012, p. 80 (author's translation).
105 OECD, 2012, pp. 115—16.
106 John Kenneth Galbraith, 'Recession economics', *New York Review of Books*, 4 February 1982.
107 Hickel, 2012.
108 *Economist*, 'Free exchange: Zero-sum debate', 5 May 2012.
109 OECD, *An Overview of Growing Income Inequalities in OECD Countries: Main Findings*, 2011, p. 40.
110 Gallino, 2011, p. 163.
111 OECD, 2011, p. 22.
112 OECD, *Growing Unequal? Income Distribution and Poverty in OECD Countries*, 2008, p. 128.
113 OECD, 2011, pp. 22, 38–40.
114 OECD, 2011 p. 38.
115 OECD, 2011 p. 22.
116 OECD, 2008, p. 32.
117 Quoted in Ben Stein, 'In class warfare, guess which class is winning', *New York Times*, 26 November 2006.
118 For an in-depth debunking of this and other free-market-related myths, see Ha-Joon Chang, *23 Things They Don't Tell You About Capitalism*, London: Allen Lane, 2010.
119 Capgemini, *World Wealth Report 2008*, 2008, p. 4.

120 Facundo Alvaredo, Anthony B. Atkinson, Thomas Piketty and Emmanuel Saez. 'The top 1 percent in international and historical perspective', *Journal of Economic Perspectives*, Vol. 27, No. 3, Summer 2013, pp. 14–16.
121 Nicholas Shaxson, John Christensen and Nick Mathiason, *Inequality: You Don't Know the Half of It*, London: Tax Justice Network, July 2012, p. 3; James S. Henry, *The Price of Offshore Revisited: New Estimates for 'Missing' Global Private Wealth, Income, and Lost Taxes*, London: Tax Justice Network, July 2012, p. 40.
122 Heather Stewart, 'Wealth doesn't trickle down – it just floods offshore, research reveals', *Guardian*, 21 July 2012.
123 Gallino, 2011, pp. 298–9, 81.
124 OECD, 2011, pp. 26, 40.
125 OECD, 2011, pp. 26, 40. See also Andrew G. Berg and Jonathan D. Ostry, *Inequality and Unsustainable Growth: Two Sides of the Same Coin?*, Washington DC: IMF, April 2011.
126 Isabel Ortiz and Matthew Cummins, *Global Inequality: Beyond the Bottom Billion – A Rapid Review of Income Distribution in 141 Countries*, New York: UNICEF, April 2011.
127 Berg and Ostry, 2011, p. 3; OECD, 2011, p. 40.
128 Hickel, 2012.
129 Hickel, 2012.
130 Roubini, 2012, pp. 156–7.
131 Özlem Onaran, 'From wage suppression to sovereign debt crisis in Western Europe: Who pays for the costs of the crisis?', report prepared for the conference 'Economic Policy: in search of an alternative paradigm', Middlesex University, 3 December 2010.
132 Quoted in James Kirkup, 'Occupy protesters were right, says Bank of England official', *Telegraph*, 29 October 2012.
133 Alvaredo et al., 2013, pp. 320.
134 Robert B. Reich, *The Great Depression, the Great Recession, and What's Ahead*, University of California, 2010.
135 Larrouturou, 2012, p. 57.
136 Thomas Piketty, Emmanuel Saez and Stefanie Stantcheva, 'Taxing the 1%: why the top tax rate could be over 80%', VoxEU.org, 8 December 2011.
137 CEO, 'Finance lobbyists in experts clothing', CEO website, 17 April 2009.
138 Elitsa Vucheva, 'EU governments committed 3 trillion for bank bailouts', EUobserver.com, 9 April 2009.
139 Quoted in Elitsa Vucheva, 'European bank bailout total: $4 trillion', *Bloomberg Businessweek,* 10 April 2009.
140 Quoted in Cassidy, 2009.

Chapter 2

1 Stacy-Marie Ishmael, 'Greece faces a Herculean adjustment task', *FT Alphaville*, 11 March 2010.
2 Reuters, 'German budget expert: not up to EU to save Greece', 15 December 2009.
3 Moneynews, 'Rogoff: wave of public debt defaults coming', 23 February 2010.
4 Statement by the Eurogroup and ECOFIN ministers on Ireland, 22 November 2010.
5 Peter Spiegel, 'Q&A: Irish promises and promissory notes', *Financial Times*, 7 February 2013.
6 Michael Lewis, 'When Irish eyes are crying', *Vanity Fair*, March 2011.
7 Lewis, 2011.

8 Karl Whelan, 'The ECB's secret letter to Ireland: some questions', *Forbes*, 17 August 2012.
9 Quoted in Whelan, 2012.
10 ECB, 'ECB Governing Council welcomes the request of the Irish Government for financial assistance', press release, 21 November 2010.
11 Rich Barbie, 'EU unveils Irish bailout', CNNMoney, 2 December 2010.
12 Lewis, 2011.
13 Presseurop.eu, 'EU & IMF's men in black arrive in Dublin', 18 November 2010.
14 Interview on Vincent Browne's *Tonight Show*, 22 November 2010, viewable at www.youtube.com/watch?v=L29iCbPQm8U.
15 ECB, 'Recommendations of the Governing Council of the European Central Bank on government guarantees for bank debt', 20 October 2008.
16 Wolfgang Schäuble, 'A plan to tackle Europe's debt mountain', *Europe's World*, Autumn 2010.
17 Paul Krugman, *End This Depression Now!* New York: W.W. Norton, 2012, p. 149.
18 *Economist*, 'Greece's economic woes: the labours of austerity', 7 April 2011.
19 *Economist*, 7 April 2011.
20 Eurostat, 'At risk of poverty or social exclusion in the EU27 – in 2010, 23% of the population were at risk of poverty or social exclusion', press release, 8 February 2012.
21 Paul Krugman, 'When austerity fails', *New York Times*, 22 May 2011.
22 *BBC News*, 'Portugal's 78bn euro bail-out is formally approved', 16 May 2011.
23 Robert M. Fishman, 'Portugal's unnecessary bailout', *New York Times*, 12 April 2011.
24 The Portuguese Economy, 'Portugal's bailout: reinventing the wheel', 28 May 2011.
25 *BBC News*, 'ECB told Italy to make budget cuts', 29 September 2011.
26 The letter is viewable in its entirety at www.corriere.it/economia/11_settembre_29/trichet_draghi_inglese_304a5f1e-ea59-11e0-ae06-4da866778017.shtml.
27 Marcus Walker, Charles Forelle and Stacy Meichtry, 'Deepening crisis over euro pits leader against leader', *Wall Street Journal*, 30 December 2011.
28 Elisa Martinuzzi and Chiara Remondin, 'Goldman Sachs says adviser Mario Monti resigns his post at firm', *Bloomberg*, 14 November 2011.
29 Regarding Angela Merkel's involvement, see Walker, Forelle and Meichtry, 2011; regarding the ECB's involvement see Karl Whelan, 'The secret tool Draghi uses to run Europe', *Forbes*, 22 July 2012, and Matthew Yglesias, 'The ECB's disastrous dual mandate', Slate, 18 June 2012.
30 Stephen Foley, 'What price the new democracy? Goldman Sachs conquers Europe', *Independent*, 18 November 2011.
31 UPI, 'Papandreou calls off Greek referendum', 3 November 2011.
32 See for example Wolfgang Schäuble's assertion that Greece should postpone the elections and form a technocratic government: Gerrit Wiesmann and Quentin Peel, 'Berlin split on bail-out for Greece', *Financial Times*, 16 February 2012; or Jean-Claude Juncker's assertion that a win by 'radical leftists' opposed to the bail-out deal would have 'unforeseeable' consequences for the EMU: Reuters, 'Juncker warns Greece not to quit euro zone – paper', 16 June 2012.
33 European Council, Treaty on Stability, Coordination and Governance in the Economic and Monetary Union.
34 CEO-TNI, 'Stop the EU's antidemocratic austerity policies – for a different Europe', CEO website, 8 May 2012.
35 *Wall Street Journal*, 'Q&A: ECB President Mario Draghi', 23 February 2012.
36 Ben Rooney and Chris Isidore, 'ECB loans out 529.5 billion to European banks', CNNMoney, 29 February 2012; Margit Feher and Todd Buell, 'ECB eases collateral standards for loans', *Wall Street Journal*, 22 June 2012.

37 European Commission, *Report on State Aid Granted by the EU Member States – Autumn 2011 Update*, December 2011.
38 IMF, *Global Financial Stability Report*, April 2011.
39 IMF, *Spain: Financial Stability Assessment*, June 2012, p. 12.
40 Quoted in Giles Tremlett, 'One bust bank could bring Spain to its knees, warns prime minister', *BBC News*, 29 May 2012.
41 Patrick Donahue and Brian Parkin, 'Germany prefers permanent fund for Spain, stirring conflict', *Bloomberg*, 11 June 2012.
42 Center for Economic and Social Rights (CESR), 'UN calls on Spanish government to "revise" austerity measures which are harming human rights', press release, 24 May 2012.
43 Vicente Navarro, 'The euro is not in trouble. People are', Common Dreams, 16 August 2012.
44 Navarro, 2012.
45 See for example Reuters, 'Worst of euro crisis is over, Germany's Schaeuble says', 27 December 2012.
46 See for example Alex Politaki, 'Greece is facing a humanitarian crisis', *Guardian*, 11 February 2013, and Suzanne Daley, 'Wave of evictions leads to homeless crisis in Spain', *New York Times*, 11 November 2012.
47 TNI, *The EU Crisis Pocket Guide*, November 2012, p. 5.
48 Floyd Norris, 'Controls on capital come late to Cyprus', *New York Times*, 28 March 2013; Emily Young, 'Russian money in Cyprus: why is there so much?', *Guardian*, 18 March 2013.
49 Norris, 2013.
50 Norris, 2013.
51 Constantinos Stephanou, 'The banking system in Cyprus: time to rethink the business model?', *Cyprus Economic Policy Review*, Vol. 5, No. 2, 2011, pp. 123–30.
52 European Commission, *Country-Specific Recommendations 2013*, 29 May 2013.
53 Peter Spiegel and Scheherazade Daneshkhu, 'EU eases hard line on austerity', *Financial Times*, 28 May 2013.

Chapter 3

1 Sheila Killian, John Garvey and Frances Shaw, *An Audit of Irish Debt*, University of Limerick, September 2011, p. 21.
2 See for example Paul Krugman, *End This Depression Now!* New York: W.W. Norton, 2012a, p. 177.
3 Paul Krugman, 'European crisis realities', *New York Times*, 25 February 2012b.
4 Paolo Mauro, Rafael Romeu, Ariel Binder and Asad Zaman, 'Prudent or profligate', *Finance and Development*, Washington DC: IMF, Vol. 50, No. 2, June 2013.
5 For 2007 data see OECD, *Economic Outlook 2009*, Vol. 1, p. 55; for 2011 data see OECD, *Economic Outlook 2011*, Vol. 2, p. 35.
6 Luciano Gallino, *Finanzcapitalismo: La civiltà del denaro in crisi*, Turin: Einaudi, 2011, p. 15; European Commission, *Report on State Aid Granted by the EU Member States – Autumn 2011 Update*, December 2011.
7 Paul Krugman and Richard Layard, 'A manifesto for economic sense', 2012.
8 IMF Data Mapper – Public Finances in Modern History Database; see also S. M. Ali Abbas, Nazim Belhocine, Asmaa El-Ganainy and Mark Horton, *Historical Patterns of Public Debt – Evidence from a New Database*, Washington DC: IMF, May 2011, pp. 9–10.
9 See for example Appalled Economists, *Manifesto of the Appalled Economists*, 2010.

10 Appalled Economists, 2010.
11 IMF Data Mapper – Public Finances in Modern History Database; see also Appalled Economists, 2010.
12 On the post-war surplus of advance countries see Mauro et al., 2013, chart 4; on the rise of debt-servicing costs see IMF Data Mapper – Public Finances in Modern History Database and Mauro et al., 2013; on the relationship between financial liberalisation and the rise of debt-servicing costs see Francesco Caselli, Alberto Giovannini and Timothy Lane, *Fiscal Discipline and the Cost of Public Debt Service: Some Estimates for OECD Countries*, Washington DC: IMF, April 1998, pp. 17–18; on the overall budget deficit of advanced countries see Danish government, *Denmark in the Global Economy: Competitiveness Report 2010*, 2010, p. 22, figure 32.
13 Appalled Economists, 2010.
14 Appalled Economists, 2010.
15 AP, 'Apple income taxes: company paid only 1.9 percent tax on earnings outside U.S.', 4 November 2012; Avaaz, 'Who are the world's biggest tax avoiders?', 6 December 2012, viewable at http://en.avaaz.org/1202/who-are-the-worlds-biggest-tax-avoiders.
16 Richard Murphy, *Closing the European Tax Gap*, Downham Market: Tax Research UK, February 2012.
17 Financial Secrecy Index, 2011.
18 James S. Henry, *The Price of Offshore Revisited: New Estimates for 'Missing' Global Private Wealth, Income, and Lost Taxes*, London: Tax Justice Network, July 2012; TJN, 'The price of offshore revisited', press release, 19 July 2012, p. 2.
19 Henry, 2012, p. 43; Nicholas Shaxson and John Christensen, 'Time to black-list the tax haven whitewash', *Financial Times*, 4 April 2011.
20 Henry, 2012, p. 36.
21 Henry, 2012, p. 5.
22 TJN, 2012, p. 2.
23 Murphy, 2012, p. 2.
24 Murphy, 2012, p. 14.
25 Murphy, 2012, p. 2.
26 Javier Solana, 'A Europe for the world', Project Syndicate, 18 October 2012.
27 Credit Suisse, *Global Wealth Report 2013*, October 2013, pp. 4-11; Facundo Alvaredo, Anthony B. Atkinson, Thomas Piketty and Emmanuel Saez, 'The top 1 percent in international and historical perspective', *Journal of Economic Perspectives*, Vol. 27, No. 3, Summer 2013, p. 15.
28 Credit Suisse, 2013, pp. 23-24.
29 Credit Suisse, 2013, Figure 3, p. 23.
30 Capgemini, *World Wealth Report 2012*, 2012, pp. 6–7.
31 Gabriel Zucman, *The Missing Wealth of Nations: Are Europe and the U.S. Net Debtors or Net Creditors?*, Paris School of Economics, 25 February 2013, p. 3.
32 The term is from Gustavo Piga, *Derivatives and Public Debt Management*, Zurich: ISMA, 2001.
33 Nick Dunbar, 'Revealed: Goldman Sachs' mega-deal for Greece', *Risk Magazine*, 1 July 2003.
34 Elisa Martinuzzi, Alan Katz and Gabi Thesing, 'ECB rejects request for Greek swap files, citing "acute" risks', *Bloomberg*, 5 November 2010.
35 Dunbar, 2003.
36 Interview on the PBS documentary *Money, Power and Wall Street*, 2012.
37 Reuters, 'FACTBOX – Debt derivatives deals in weak euro zone states', 22 February 2010.
38 Reuters, 2010.

39 Mark Brown and Alex Chambers, 'How Europe's governments have enronized their debt', Euromoney, September 2005.
40 Lorenzo Totaro and Elisa Martinuzzi, 'Italy holds derivatives on $211 billion of debt', *Bloomberg*, 19 March 2012.
41 Nicholas Dunbar and Elisa Martinuzzi, 'Italy said to pay Morgan Stanley $3.4 billion', *Bloomberg*, 16 March 2012.
42 Dunbar and Martinuzzi, 2012.
43 Piga, 2001, p. 123.
44 Orazio Carabini, 'Super regalo a Morgan Stanley', *l'Espresso*, 3 February 2012.
45 Joint Social Conferences, *Resisting Financial Dictatorship – Reclaiming Democracy and Social Rights!*, 2012.
46 WEF, *Global Competitiveness Report 2011–2012*, 2011, p. 15.
47 Krugman, 2012a, p. 173.
48 Krugman, 2012a, p. 173.
49 Markus Sievers, 'Teufelswerk oder erfolgreicher Rettungsplan?', *Frankfurter Rundschau*, 16 August 2012.
50 DIW, *Reallöhne 2000–2010: Ein Jahrzehnt ohne Zuwachs*, 2011, p. 12.
51 Larrouturou, 2012, p. 41.
52 Krugman, 2012a, p. 175; Özlem Onaran, 'From wage suppression to sovereign debt crisis in Western Europe: who pays for the costs of the crisis?', report prepared for the conference 'Economic policy: in search of an alternative paradigm', Middlesex University, 3 December 2010, table 1, p. 19.
53 Federal Statistical Office of Germany (Destatis) data.
54 Destatis data.
55 Heiner Flassbeck and Costas Lapavitsas, *The Systemic Crisis of the Euro – True Causes and Effective Therapies*, Berlin: Rosa-Luxemburg-Stiftung, May 2013, p. 8.
56 Flassbeck and Lapavitsas, 2013, p. 8.
57 Flassbeck and Lapavitsas, 2013, p. 12.
58 Heiner Flassbeck, 'German mercantilism and the failure of the eurozone', Yanis Varoufakis' blog, 21 April 2012.
59 Matthew O'Brien, 'The myth that entitlements ruin countries, busted in 1 little graph', *The Atlantic*, 27 June 2012.
60 Speech by Vítor Constâncio at the Bank of Greece conference on 'The crisis in the euro area', Athens, 23 May 2013, viewable at www.ecb.europa.eu/press/key/date/2013/html/sp130523_1.en.html.
61 OECD data; ECB, Occasional Paper Series, No. 53, October 2006, figs 3–4, p. 16.
62 Victoria Stoiciu, 'Populismul economic neoliberal, lenesii Europei si mistificarile dreptei românesti', *CriticAtac*, 6 February 2012 (translation by Presseurop.eu).
63 James Meadway, 'Greece should shake off the euro straitjacket', London: NEF, 13 September 2011.
64 Daniel Alpert, 'Challenge to austerity deepens, the handwriting is on the wall', EconoMonitor, 6 May 2012.
65 BIS, *Quarterly Review*, March 2010, Table 9B, p. 76.
66 BIS, *Quarterly Review*, December 2010, p. 17.
67 Costas Lapavitsas et al., *The Eurozone Between Austerity and Default*, Research on Money and Finance, September 2010, pp. 23–5.
68 Frank Slijper, *Guns, Debt and Corruption: Military Spending and the EU Crisis*, Amsterdam: TNI, April 2013, p. 11.
69 Helena Smith, 'German "hypocrisy" over Greek military spending has critics up in arms', *Guardian*, 19 April 2012.
70 Roxane McMeeken, 'Less healthcare, but Greece is still buying guns', *Independent*, 6 November 2011.

71 SIPRI data.
72 Slijper, 2013, pp. 11–12.
73 Pratap Chatterjee, 'Bailing out Germany: the story behind the European financial crisis', Common Dreams, 28 May 2012.
74 Simone Foxman, '20 banks that will get crushed if the PIIGS go bust', *Business Insider*, 25 November 2011.
75 BIS consolidated statistics.
76 Gareth Gore and Sudip Roy, 'Spanish bailout saves German pain', *International Financing Review*, 29 June 2012.
77 Gore and Roy, 2012.
78 Gore and Roy, 2012.
79 Quoted in Gore and Roy, 2012.
80 Attac Austria, 'Greek bail-out: 77% went into the financial sector', 17 June 2013.
81 Presseurop.eu, 'Greek aid will go to the banks', 9 March 2012.
82 Presseurop.eu, 9 March 2012.
83 Quoted in Stefan Schultz and Philipp Wittrock, 'Bedrohte Wirtschaftsunion: Aufmarsch der Ego-Europäer', *Spiegel Online*, 12 May 2011 (author's translation).
84 John Whittaker, 'Eurosystem debts, Greece, and the role of banknotes', Lancaster University Management School, 14 November 2011.
85 Stephanie Flanders, 'Greece: costing the exit', *BBC News*, 16 February 2012.
86 *Bloomberg*, 'Hey, Germany: you got a bailout, too', 24 May 2012.
87 *Bloomberg*, 24 May 2012.
88 Robert Reich, 'Follow the money: behind Europe's debt crisis lurks another giant bailout of Wall Street', author's website, 4 October 2011.
89 Reich, 2011.
90 Eric Toussaint, 'Greece–Germany: who owes who? (Part 1)', Liège: CADTM, 1 October 2012.
91 Yanis Varoufakis, 'Monetising the … ECB: the latest insult to be added to Greece's multiplying injuries', author's blog, 20 May 2013.
92 Toussaint, 'Greece–Germany: who owes who? (Part 2)', Liège: CADTM, 6 November 2012.
93 ECB, Statutes of the ESCB and of the ECB.
94 Ronald Janssen, 'Another Europe now!' Social Europe Journal, 14 November 2012.
95 Quoted in Stephen Kinsella, 'Remember: a country is not a company', *Harvard Business Review*, 25 March 2013.
96 Kinsella, 2013.
97 Quoted in Kinsella, 2013.
98 Quoted in Kinsella, 2013.
99 Robert J. Shiller, 'Debt and delusion', Project Syndicate, 21 July 2011.
100 Kinsella, 2013.
101 Krugman, 2012a, p. 182.
102 Appalled Economists, 2012.
103 Sean O'Grady, 'Fear and loathing as the hedge funds take on the euro', *Independent*, 4 March 2010.
104 O'Grady, 2010.
105 Louise Story, 'A secretive banking elite rules trading in derivatives', *New York Times*, 11 December 2010.
106 Stefania Vitali, James B. Glattfelder and Stefano Battiston, *The Network of Global Corporate Control*, ETH Zurich, September 2011, pp. 6, 33.
107 Vitali et al., 2011, p. 8.
108 IMF, *Euro Area Policies 2012: Article IV Consultation*, July 2012, p. 14; Ambrose

Evans-Pritchard, 'Blaming the Spanish victim as Europe spirals into summer crisis', *Telegraph*, 22 July 2012.

109 ECB, 'Technical features of Outright Monetary Transactions', press release, 6 September 2012.

110 Alex Barker, 'EU ban on "naked" CDS to become permanent', *Financial Times*, 19 October 2012.

111 John O'Donnell, 'EU agrees new controls for credit rating agencies', Reuters, 27 November 2012.

112 ECB, 2012.

113 Larry Elliott, 'Mario Draghi rescue plan with more misery at its core will not save euro', *Guardian*, 6 September 2012.

114 IMF, 'Fiscal monitor update: as downside risks rise, fiscal policy has to walk a narrow path', 24 January 2012.

115 Protesilaos Stavrou, *Single Supervisory Mechanism: How it Relates to the Institutional Morphology of the European Union*, author's blog, 7 February 2013.

116 Krugman, 2012a, p. 183.

117 ECB and *Financial Times* market data.

118 ECB and *Financial Times* market data.

Chapter 4

1 Céline Allard and Luc Everaert, 'Lifting euro area growth: priorities for structural reforms and governance', IMF Staff Position Note SPN/10/19, Washington DC: IMF, 22 November 2010, p. 12.

2 Paul Krugman, *End This Depression Now!* New York: W.W. Norton, 2012, p. 149.

3 *Le Monde*, 'Carte – plus de 40 plans de rigueur en zone euro', 21 February 2013.

4 OECD, *Restoring Public Finances, 2012 Update*, 2012a, p. 35; OECD, *Fiscal Consolidation: How Much, How Fast and by What Means?* April 2012b, p. 6.

5 OECD, 2012a, p. 9.

6 Alexis Tsipras, leader of the Greek left-wing party Syriza, quoted in Efty Katsareas, 'Greek opposition: IMF mistake won't ease austerity', AP, 7 June 2013.

7 OECD, 2012a, pp. 136–9.

8 OECD, 2012a, p. 139.

9 OECD, 2012a, p. 139.

10 OECD, 2012a, p. 139.

11 OECD, 2012a, p. 139; also David Stuckler and Sanjay Basu, 'How austerity kills', *New York Times*, 12 May 2013; and Alexander Kentikelenis et al., 'Health effects of financial crisis: omens of a Greek tragedy', *The Lancet*, Vol. 378, Issue 9801, 22 October 2011, pp. 1457–8; and Marina Karanikolos et al., 'Financial crisis, austerity, and health in Europe', *The Lancet*, Vol. 381, Issue 9874, 13 April 2013, panel 2, pp. 1323–31.

12 Adam Gaffney, 'Austerity and the unraveling of European universal health care', *Dissent*, Spring 2013.

13 Zachary Laven and Federico Santi, 'EU austerity and reform: a country by country table', Washington DC: European Institute, April 2012; OECD, 2012a, p. 139.

14 For nominal wages data see ETUI, *Benchmarking Working Europe 2013*, 2013, p. 49; for average salary data see *El Mundo*, 'Estiman que los sueldos griegos bajarán un 23% en 2012, hasta los 13.167 euros', 21 May 2012.

15 ETUI website, 'Wage development infographic'.

16 Eric Toussaint, 'Greece: the very symbol of illegitimate debt', Liège: CADTM, 3 March 2011.

17 Laven and Santi, 2012.
18 Toussaint, 2011.
19 Toussaint, 2011.
20 Toussaint, 2011.
21 Toussaint, 2011.
22 Toussaint, 2011.
23 Toussaint, 2011.
24 Eurostat, *Taxation Trends in the European Union – Data for the EU Member States, Iceland and Norway – 2013 Edition*, 2013, p. 31.
25 Laven and Santi, 2012.
26 Toussaint, 2011.
27 Joseph Zacune, *Privatising Europe: Using the Crisis to Entrench Neoliberalism*, Amsterdam: TNI, March 2013, pp. 9–10 and annex, pp. 1–2.
28 Laven and Santi, 2012; Toussaint, 2011.
29 Toussaint, 2011.
30 Toussaint, 2011; Press TV, '600,000 Greek children living below poverty line: UNICEF', 22 May 2013.
31 Eurostat, 'At risk of poverty or social exclusion in the EU27 – in 2011, 24% of the population were at risk of poverty or social exclusion', press release, 3 December 2012.
32 Eurostat press release, 3 December 2012.
33 Alex Politaki, 'Greece is facing a humanitarian crisis', *Guardian*, 11 February 2013; *Economist*, 'Greece's government: up, but not out', 23 May 2013.
34 Stuckler and Basu, 2013.
35 Judith Sunderland and Hugh Williamson, 'Xenophobia in Greece', New York: Human Rights Watch, 13 May 2013.
36 Politaki, 2013.
37 OECD, 2012a, pp. 223–9.
38 OECD, 2012a, p. 227.
39 OECD, 2012a, p. 227; Gaffney, 2013.
40 Gaffney, 2013.
41 Gaffney, 2013.
42 OECD, 2012a, p. 227; María Luisa Sánchez Simón, 'Back to the dark days', Brussels: Education in Crisis, 16 July 2012.
43 The Real News, 'Educational strike in Spain brings hundreds of thousands into the streets', 24 May 2012.
44 The Real News, 2012.
45 OECD, 2012a, p. 227; OECD, *Restoring Public Finances*, 2011, p. 188.
46 Eurostat, *Taxation Trends in the European Union*, p. 31.
47 OECD, 2012a, p. 227.
48 OECD, 2012a, p. 227.
49 RichesFlores Research, *Spain: Spiraling Downward in Greek Fashion?* 15 July 2012.
50 RichesFlores Research, 2012.
51 Laven and Santi, 2012.
52 Eurostat press release, 3 December 2012; Giles Tremlett, 'Spain: the pain of austerity deepens', *Guardian*, 1 January 2013.
53 Intermón Oxfam, 'España podría alcanzar los 18 millones de pobres en una década si se mantienen las medidas de austeridad y los recortes sociales', press release, 13 December 2012.
54 Instituto Nacional de Estadística (INE), 'Encuesta de Condiciones de Vida', press release, 22 October 2012.
55 Tremlett, 2013.

56 Tremlett, 2013.
57 OECD, 2012a, pp. 203–9.
58 OECD, 2012a, p. 206.
59 OECD, 2012a, p. 207; *Portugal News*, 'Hospitals cut overtime by a fifth', 16 April 2013.
60 OECD, 2012a, p. 207; UNI Europa, *Troika Watch*, May 2013, pp. 5–8.
61 OECD, 2012a, p. 207.
62 UNI Europa, 2013, pp. 5–8.
63 OECD, 2012a, p. 207.
64 Laven and Santi, 2012.
65 UNI Europa, 2013, pp. 5–8.
66 Andrei Khalip and Daniel Alvarenga, 'Portugal adds an hour to public employees workday as part of budget cuts', *Christian Science Monitor*, 4 May 2013.
67 Reuters, 'Troika heading to Lisbon to pore over spending cuts', 6 May 2013.
68 UNI Europa, 2013, pp. 5–8.
69 UNI Europa, 2013, pp. 5–8.
70 OECD, 2012a, p. 208.
71 Barry Hatton, 'Portugal introduced tax hikes despite outcry', AP, 15 January 2013.
72 Hatton, 2013.
73 OECD, 2012a, p. 207.
74 Barry Hatton, 'Portugal's government eyes new income taxes', AP, 24 September 24, 2012.
75 UNI Europa, 2013, pp. 5–8.
76 UNI Europa, 2013, pp. 5–8.
77 Zacune, 2013, p. 12 and annex, p. 3.
78 Klaus Heeger, 'Portugal: the long and painful path of austerity', EurActiv, 9 April 2013.
79 Barbara Spinelli, 'Europa, il sonno della politica', *la Repubblica*, 15 May 2013.
80 Giles Tremlett, 'Portuguese death rate rise linked to pain of austerity programme', *Guardian*, 19 March 2012.
81 Karanikolos at al., 2013, panel 5, pp. 1323–31.
82 Karanikolos at al., 2013, panel 5, pp. 1323–31.
83 Eurostat, 'At risk of poverty or social exclusion in the EU27 – in 2011, 27% of children aged less than 18 were at risk of poverty or social exclusion', press release, 26 February 2013.
84 UNI Europa, 2013, pp. 5–8.
85 OECD, 2012a, p. 166; see also Italian government, *Documento di Economia e Finanza 2012*, 2012.
86 OECD, 2011, p. 143.
87 OECD, 2012a, p. 166.
88 OECD, 2011, p. 143.
89 OECD, 2011, p. 143.
90 Laven and Santi, 2012.
91 OECD, 2011, p. 143.
92 Laven and Santi, 2012; *la Repubblica*, 'Lo Stato incassa 23,7 miliardi dall'Imu. Prima casa, imposta media da 225 euro', 12 February 2013.
93 OECD, 2012a, p. 166.
94 Laven and Santi, 2012.
95 Laven and Santi, 2012.
96 Laven and Santi, 2012.
97 Zacune, 2013, pp. 11–12 and annex, p. 3.
98 Laven and Santi, 2012.

99 RT, 'Millions of poverty-stricken Italians unable to afford heat, meat amid economic crisis', 22 May 2013.
100 RT, 2013.
101 RT, 2013.
102 RT, 2013.
103 Stuckler and Basu, 2013.
104 OECD, 2012a, p. 160.
105 OECD, 2012a, p. 160.
106 OECD, 2012a, p. 160.
107 OECD, 2012a, p. 160.
108 OECD, 2012a, p. 160.
109 OECD, 2012a, p. 160.
110 OECD, 2012a, p. 160.
111 OECD, 2012a, p. 160.
112 OECD, 2012a, p. 160.
113 OECD, 2011, p. 135.
114 ETUI, *Benchmarking Working Europe 2013*, p. 49.
115 OECD, 2012a, p. 160.
116 Laven and Santi, 2012.
117 Zacune, 2013, p. 10 and annex, p. 2.
118 Zacune, 2013, p. 10 and annex, p. 2.
119 Eurostat, 'At risk of poverty or social exclusion in the EU27 – in 2011, 27% of children aged less than 18 were at risk of poverty or social exclusion', press release, 26 February 2013.
120 Irish League of Credit Unions (ILCU), 'Results of the final ILCU 2012 "What's Left" tracker', press release, 17 January 2013.
121 *TheJournal.ie*, '56pc of Irish homes "go into debt to pay essential bills"', 12 February 2013.
122 Central Statistics Office (Ireland), *Survey on Income and Living Conditions*, 13 February 2013.
123 Caroline Carney and Bertrand Maître, *Constructing a Food Poverty Indicator for Ireland*, Dublin: Irish Department of Social Protection, 2012, p. i.
124 OECD, 2012a, pp. 210–15, 216–23, 96–101.
125 OECD, 2012a, pp. 130–3.
126 OECD, 2012a, pp. 122–9.
127 OECD, 2012a, pp. 85–90, 185–90.
128 OECD, 2012a, pp. 243–51.
129 Democracy Now, 'Why austerity kills: from Greece to U.S., crippling economic policies causing global health crisis', 21 May 2013.
130 Quoted in Democracy Now, 2013.
131 Karanikolos at al., 2013.
132 Harald Sander, 'Good news from the Eurozone… or is it?', The Conversation, 19 August 2013.
133 On this point see Ronald Janssen, 'Another Europe now!' *Social Europe Journal*, 14 November 2012.
134 Paul Krugman, 'The big fail', *New York Times*, 6 January 2013.
135 Interview by Elena Polidori in *la Repubblica*, 16 June 2010.
136 Alberto F. Alesina and Silvia Ardagna, 'Large changes in fiscal policy: taxes versus spending', NBER Working Paper No. 15438, Cambridge: NBER, October 2009.
137 IMF, *World Economic Outlook: Recovery, Risk, and Rebalancing*, October 2010, pp. 93–124.

138 IMF, *Fiscal Monitor: Taking Stock – A Progress Report on Fiscal Adjustment*, October 2012a, p. 8; see also Janssen, 2012.
139 IMF, *World Economic Outlook: Coping with High Debt and Sluggish Growth*, October 2012b, box 1.1, pp. 41–3; Olivier Blanchard and Daniel Leigh, *Growth Forecast Errors and Fiscal Multipliers*, Washington DC: IMF, January 2013.
140 Oxford Economics, 'Lessons to be learned from three years of fiscal austerity in Europe', January 2013, pp. 16–18.
141 IMF, 'Greece: ex post evaluation of exceptional access under the 2010 stand-by arrangement', June 2013; 'IMF Document Excerpts: Disagreements Revealed', *Wall Street Journal*, 7 October 2013.
142 IMF, 2013, p. 1.
143 Carmen M. Reinhart and Kenneth S. Rogoff, 'Growth in a time of debt', *American Economic Review*, Vol. 100, No. 2, May 2010, pp. 573–8.
144 Thomas Herndon, Michael Ash and Robert Pollin, 'Does high public debt consistently stifle economic growth? A critique of Reinhart and Rogoff', University of Massachusetts Amherst, 15 April 2013.
145 Arindrajit Dube, 'Guest post: Reinhart/Rogoff and growth in a time before debt', Next New Deal, 17 April 2013.
146 *Economist*, 'Lessons of the 1930s: there could be trouble ahead', 10 December 2011.
147 Quoted in Nouriel Roubini and Stephen Mihm, *Crisis Economics: A Crash Course in the Future of Finance*, London: Penguin, 2011, p. 158.
148 Roubini and Mihm, 2011, p. 158.
149 Roubini and Mihm, 2011, p. 159.
150 Steven Bryan, 'The historical appeal of austerity', Columbia University Press blog, 1 October 2010.
151 Harriet Torry and Margit Feher, 'Nowotny links austerity with rise of Nazism', *Wall Street Journal*, 19 June 2012.
152 Bryan, 2010.
153 Franklin D. Roosevelt's 'Fireside chat', 14 April 1938.
154 Roubini and Mihm, 2011, p. 161.
155 Oxfam, *Be Outraged: There Are Alternatives*, May 2012, pp. 13–15.
156 Oxfam, 2012, pp. 13–15.
157 Oxfam, 2012, pp. 13–15.
158 IMF independent evaluation office (IEO), *Fiscal Adjustment in IMF-Supported Programs*, 2003.
159 IEO, 2003, p. 5.
160 Laurence Ball, Daniel Leigh and Prakash Loungani, 'Painful medicine', *Finance and Development*, Washington DC: IMF, Vol. 48, No. 3, September 2011.
161 John Maynard Keynes, *The General Theory of Employment, Interest, and Money*, New York: Classic House, 2008, p. 26, as quoted in Paul Krugman, 'The demand-side temptation', *New York Times*, 25 January 2011.
162 Vicente Navarro, 'Las causas reales de la política de austeridad', *Nueva Tribuna*, 16 December 2012 (translation by Revolting Europe).
163 Krugman, 2012a, p. 207.
164 European Commission, *European Economic Forecast – Spring 2013*, p. 148.
165 Bryan, 2010.
166 Salvatore Babones, 'European austerity: who should pay?', Inequality.org, 15 May 2012.
167 Paul Hannon and Eamon Quinn, 'Ireland reaches debt deal', *Wall Street Journal*, 7 February 2013; Heather Stewart, 'Irish campaigners demand halt to repayment of Anglo Irish Bank debts', *Guardian*, 18 January 2012.
168 *Assurance of Compliance in the 2nd GRC Programme.*

169 James Petras, 'The new authoritarianism: from decaying democracies to technocratic dictatorships and beyond', Centre for Research on Globalization, 28 November 2011.
170 Michael Burke, 'Cancel the Greek debt', Socialist Economic Bulletin, 16 June 2012.
171 Burke, 2012; ECB and Eurostat data.
172 Karl Whelan, 'For wrong-headed reasons, E.U. leaders are leaning toward a Greek exit', *Forbes*, 13 August 2012.
173 Floyd Norris, 'Banks come first in a Greek rescue plan', *New York Times*, 9 February 2012.
174 Naomi Klein, *The Shock Doctrine: The Rise of Disaster Capitalism*, New York: Picador, 2007.
175 ETUI, 2013, p. 7.
176 CEO-TNI, 'Stop the EU's antidemocratic austerity policies – for a different Europe', CEO website, 8 May 2012.
177 'Five minutes with Noam Chomsky', London School of Economics's EUROPP blog, 3 December 2012.
178 Janssen, 2012.
179 Quoted in Ian Traynor, 'Germany to set the terms for saving the euro', *Guardian*, 31 January 2012.
180 Aaron Pacitti, 'Austerity and the consolidation of elite power', Huffington Post, 23 December 2012.
181 Interview by Dean Carroll on Public Service Europe, 1 February 2012.
182 Paul Krugman, 'The 1 percent's solution', *New York Times*, 25 April 2013.
183 TNI, 'The great European fire sale!', TNI website, 19 March 2013.
184 Gaffney, 2013.
185 Gaffney, 2013.
186 Gaffney, 2013.
187 For an comprehensive overview of the privatization plans currently underway in Europe, see Zacune, 2013 and annex.
188 Renaud Honoré and Anne Bauer, 'Olli Rehn, austère gardien de la rigueur budgétaire', *Les Echos*, 8 November 2012.
189 CEO, 'What was discussed during Commissioner Rehn's meetings with Goldman Sachs?', CEO website, 18 September 2012.
190 CEO, 'BusinessEurope and the European Commission: in league against labor rights?', CEO website, 11 March 2013.
191 Frank Slijper, *Guns, Debt and Corruption: Military Spending and the EU Crisis*, Amsterdam: TNI, April 2013, p. 2.
192 Slijper, 2013, p. 4.
193 Slijper, 2013, p. 4.
194 Slijper, 2013, p. 3.
195 Chris Evans, 'Wealth taxes: problems and practices around the world', Centre on Household Assets and Savings Management at the University of Birmingham, April 2013, p. 2.
196 Evans, 2013, p. 2.
197 Richard Murphy, *Closing the European Tax Gap*, Downham Market: Tax Research UK, February 2012, p. 2.
198 Seán Healy, 'Is austerity working?' *Irish Examiner*, 7 August 2013.
199 Salvatore Babones, 'What is austerity, and why should we care?', Inequality.org, 21 May 2012.
200 OECD, *An Overview of Growing Income Inequalities in OECD Countries: Main Findings*, 2011b, p. 40.
201 OECD, 'Crisis squeezes income and puts pressure on inequality and poverty in the OECD. New Results from the OECD Income Distribution Database', 2013, p. 2.

202 OECD, 2013, p. 1.
203 Laurence Ball, Davide Furceri, Daniel Leigh and Prakash Loungani, *The Distributional Effects of Fiscal Consolidation*, Washington DC: IMF, June 2013.
204 ILO, *World of Work Report 2013: Repairing the Economic and Social Fabric*, 2013, p. 27.
205 ETUI, 2013, pp. 50–2; see also ETUI website, 'Wage development infographic'.
206 ILO, 2013, pp. 82–4.
207 Pedersen & Partners, 'Top executive compensation in top 100-companies averages 1.3 million euros', 2012.
208 Pedersen & Partners, 2012.
209 Pedersen & Partners, 2012.
210 Vickie Elmer, 'CEOs in Spain and Italy have the highest pay in Europe', Quartz, 8 June 2013.
211 Tom Fairless, 'EU approves bonus caps for bankers', *Wall Street Journal*, 16 April 2013.
212 For 2010 data see Credit Suisse, *Global Wealth Report,* October 2010, p. 17; for 2012 data see Credit Suisse, *Global Wealth Report 2012*, October 2012, p. 20; for 2013 data see Credit Suisse, *Global Wealth Report 2013*, October 2013, p. 23.
213 ILO, 2013, pp. 79–84.
214 ILO, 2013, pp. 79–80.
215 Pedersen & Partners, 2012.
216 *CNNMoney*, Global 500 list, 2012.
217 TNI, *The EU Crisis Pocket Guide*, November 2012, p. 5.
218 ILO, 2013, p. 79; *Economist*, 'Investment banks: Wall Street is back', 11 May 2013.
219 Emiliano Brancaccio and Marco Passarella, *L'austerità è di destra*, Milan: Il Saggiatore, 2012, pp. 86–7 (author's translation).
220 For nominal wages data see ETUI, 2013, p. 49; for average salary data see *El Mundo*, 2012; for minimum wage data see ETUI website, 'Wage development infographic'; for unit labour costs data see Eurostat statistics database.
221 ECB data; see also ETUI, 2013, p. 49.
222 ABN Amro, 'Daily insight: the periphery's export boom', 19 August 2013, p. 1.
223 European Commission, 'Discussion note: tripartite exchange of views on wage developments', 20 December 2012, p. 3.
224 European Commission, 'Recommendation for a Council Recommendation on the implementation of the broad guidelines for the economic policies of the Member States whose currency is the euro', May 2012, p. 3.
225 James Wilson, 'Germany "pivotal" to rebalancing eurozone', *Financial Times*, 3 July 2012.
226 Paul Krugman, 'Europe's economic suicide', *New York Times*, 15 April 2012.
227 German unit labour costs data taken from the ECB Statistical Data Warehouse.
228 US Department of the Treasury, *Report to Congress on International Economic and Exchange Rate Policies,* 30 October 2013, pp. 24–6.
229 Heiner Flassbeck and Costas Lapavitsas, *The Systemic Crisis of the Euro – True Causes and Effective Therapies*, Berlin: Rosa-Luxemburg-Stiftung, May 2013, p. 17.
230 Valentina Pop, 'Germany estimated to have made 9bn profit out of crisis', *EUobserver.com*, 9 November 2011.
231 Isabelle Couet, 'L'aide à la Grèce ne coûte rien à l'Allemagne', *Les Echos*, 21 June 2012.
232 Hans-Werner Sinn and Timo Wollmershäus, *Target balances and the German financial account in light of the European balance-of-payments crisis*, Munich: CESifo Group, December 2012, p. 16.
233 Remarks at the Festival of Economics, Trento, 2 June 2012.
234 ETUI, 2013, p. 5.

235 Creditreform, *Insolvencies in Europe, 2011/2012*, February 2012, p. 3, as quoted in Emiliano Brancaccio, 'Uscire dall'euro? C'è modo e modo', author's blog, 3 July 2013.
236 Brancaccio and Passarella, 2012, pp. 89–95.
237 Paul Krugman, *Geography and Trade*, Cambridge, Mass.: MIT Press, 1991.
238 Brancaccio and Passarella, 2012, pp. 89–95 (author's translation).
239 Adam Posen, 'Germany is being crushed by its export obsession', *Financial Times*, 3 September 2013.

Chapter 5

1 European Council, 'The European Council agrees on a Roadmap for the completion of Economic and Monetary Union', 14 December 2012.
2 Altiero Spinelli and Enrico Rossi, *Il Manifesto di Ventotene*, 1941.
3 Bela Foundation, *The Way Ahead for Europe*, 2012, pp. 6–10.
4 George Soros, 'The tragedy of the European Union and how to resolve it', *New York Review of Books*, 10 September 2012.
5 European Commission, 'An important step towards a real banking union in Europe', press release, 19 March 2013.
6 Lawrence J. Lau, *Regulation and Supervision Post the Global Financial Crisis*, Institute of Global Economics and Finance (IGEF) of the Chinese University of Hong Kong, 7 September 2010.
7 Lau, 2010, p. 2.
8 Lau, 2010, p. 2.
9 Jacob Funk Kirkegaard, 'The next strategic target: De Gaulle's EU legacy', VoxEU.org, 30 November 2011.
10 Protesilaos Stavrou, *Single Supervisory Mechanism: How it relates to the institutional morphology of the European Union*, author's blog, 7 February 2013.
11 Stavrou, 2013.
12 Bela Galgoczi, 'Banking union – federal Europe through the back door?' *Social Europe Journal*, 14 February 2012.
13 Speech by Mario Draghi, Brussels, 18 February 2013, viewable at http://www.ecb.europa.eu/press/key/date/2013/html/sp130218.en.html.
14 European Commission, 'Proposal for a Single Resolution Mechanism for the Banking Union – frequently asked questions', press release, 10 July 2013.
15 ECOFIN Council, 'ESM direct bank recapitalisation instrument – main features of the operational framework and way forward', 20 June 2013.
16 ECOFIN Council, 2013.
17 ECOFIN Council; see also Yanis Varoufakis, 'The death of direct bank recapitalization: Europe's (newest) day of shame', author's blog, 21 June 2013.
18 ECOFIN Council, 2013.
19 Eurostat data taken from Mats Persson and Raoul Ruparel, 'The eurozone banking union: a game of two halves', Open Europe, December 2012, p. 10; Finance Watch, *The Importance of Being Separated*, Spring 2013, p. 4; and Finance Watch, *Answer to the Public Consultation from the European Commission on the Liikanen Report*, 13 November 2012.
20 EBF, *EU Banking System: Facts and Figures*, 2010, p. 4.
21 Thierry Philipponnat, 'Why we need to reform banking structure in parallel with building a banking union', presentation to DG Markt, 25 October 2012, p. 7.
22 Average balance sheet data taken from Finance Watch, 2012, p. 7.
23 See for example Persson and Ruparel, 2012.
24 Finance Watch, 2012, p. 7.

25 Alex Barker, 'EU reaches deal on failed banks', *Financial Times*, 27 June 2013.
26 On this point see Varoufakis, 2013.
27 European Council, Treaty on Stability, Coordination and Governance in the Economic and Monetary Union.
28 CEO-TNI, 'Stop the EU's antidemocratic austerity policies – for a different Europe', CEO website, 8 May 2012.
29 European Commission, 'Economic governance: Commission proposes two new Regulations to further strengthen budgetary surveillance in the euro area', press release, 23 November 2011.
30 European Commission, press release, 23 November 2011.
31 Steffen Stierle and Kenneth Haar, 'Troika for everyone, forever', CEO website, 2 November 2012.
32 European Council, 'Boosting investment, implementing the Compact for Growth and Jobs', 28 June 2013.
33 See, for example, Wolfgang Schäuble, 'We Germans don't want a German Europe', *Guardian*, 19 July 2013.
34 Appalled Economists, *Europe MisTreated*, 2013, p. 31.
35 Interview on Mediapart, 13 April 2012.
36 European Commission, 'Political agreement reached on MFF 2014–2020', 27 June 2013.
37 European Commission website, 'The pilot phase of the Europe 2020 Project Bond Initiative'.
38 For an in-depth explanation of the proposed redemption fund, see German Council of Economic Experts, *The European Redemption Pact: An Illustrative Guide*, February 2012.
39 European Commission, 'European Commission Green Paper on the feasibility of introducing Stability Bonds', press release, 23 November 2011.
40 Jürgen Habermas, *The Crisis of the European Union: A Response*, trans. Ciaran Cronin, Cambridge: Polity Press, 2012, p. viii.
41 Protesilaos Stavrou, 'The rise of technocracy: full analysis of the Council roadmap for the completion of the EMU', author's blog, 15 December 2012.
42 European Council, 'European Council – conclusions' Brussels, 13-14/12/2012', press release, 14 December 2012.
43 Stavrou, 2012.
44 Yanis Varoufakis, 'Lest we forget: the neglected roots of Europe's slide to authoritarianism', author's blog, 14 March 2013.
45 Hugo Radice, 'Reshaping fiscal policies in Europe: enforcing austerity, attacking democracy', *Social Europe Journal*, 11 February 2013.
46 European Commission, 'A blueprint for a deep and genuine economic and monetary union: launching a European debate', November 2012, pp. 12–13.
47 Andrew Duff, 'Heads of government suffer exhaustion', UEF, 14 December 2012.

Chapter 6

1 On the rise of left-wing euro-scepticism, see Andrew Watt, 'Why left-wing advocates of an end to the single currency are wrong', *Social Europe Journal*, 10 July 2013.
2 Stathis Kouvelakis, 'The end of Europeanism', introduction to Costas Lapavitsas et al., *Crisis in the Eurozone*, London: Verso, 2012, pp. xiv–xxi; Heiner Flassbeck and Costas Lapavitsas, *The Systemic Crisis of the Euro – True Causes and Effective Therapies*, Berlin: Rosa-Luxemburg-Stiftung, May 2013, p. 38.
3 Flassbeck and Lapavitsas, 2013.

4 Flassbeck and Lapavitsas, 2013, p. 38.
5 Flassbeck and Lapavitsas, 2013, p. 5.
6 Flassbeck and Lapavitsas, 2013, p. 38.
7 Flassbeck and Lapavitsas, 2013, p. 38.
8 Watt, 2013.
9 Watt, 2013.
10 Watt, 2013.
11 John Rosenthal, 'Germany and the euro crisis: is the powerhouse really so pure?', *World Affairs*, May/June 2012.
12 Watt, 2013.
13 Emiliano Brancaccio and Marco Passarella, *L'austerità è di destra*, Milan: Il Saggiatore, 2012, p. 94.
14 Kouvelakis, 2012, p. xx.
15 Lapavitsas et al., 2012, p. 135.
16 Jürgen Habermas, *The Crisis of the European Union: A Response*, trans. Ciaran Cronin, Cambridge: Polity Press, 2012, pp. x–xi.
17 European Alternatives, 'European checkmate: democracy at gunpoint', 16 November 2011.
18 Habermas, 2012, p. viii.
19 Etienne Balibar, 'What democratic Europe? A response to Jürgen Habermas', *Social Europe Journal*, 1 October 2012.
20 On this point, see Federal Union website, 'Europe'.
21 Finance Watch, *Answer to the Public Consultation from the European Commission on the Liikanen Report,* Finance Watch website, November 2012, p. 7.
22 Quoted in John Cassidy, 'The Wisdom of King', *New Yorker*, 27 October 2009.
23 Finance Watch, 2012, pp. 8–12.
24 Finance Watch newsletter, March 2013.
25 Andrew G. Haldane, 'Have we solved "too big to fail"?', VoxEU.org, 17 January 2013.
26 On this point see Wolfgang Münchau, 'Politics undermines hope of banking union', *Financial Times*, 16 December 2012.
27 *Economist*, 'Reforming derivatives: heavy lifting', 15 August 2013.
28 Michael Snyder, 'The coming derivatives panic that will destroy global financial markets', The Economic Collapse blog, 4 December 2012; regarding the Monte dei Paschi losses see Gaia Pianigiani and Jack Ewing, 'Monte dei Paschi, venerable Italian bank, yields to change', *New York Times*, 18 July 2013.
29 Snyder, 2012.
30 See for example Alan Kohler, 'Derivatives should just be banned', *Business Spectator*, 22 August 2012.
31 Quoted in Reuters, 'UPDATE 1-Ban CDS as "instruments of destruction" – Soros', 12 June 2009.
32 Esteban Duarte, Maud van Gaal and Heather Perlberg, 'Europe's banks turn to U.S. subprime for salvation', *Bloomberg*, 28 May 2013.
33 John Maynard Keynes, *The General Theory of Employment, Interest and Money*, New York: Classic House, 2008, p. 129.
34 Stephany Griffith-Jones and Avinash Persaud, 'Why critics are wrong about a financial-transaction tax', EuropeanVoice.com, 12 March 2012; see also Stephany Griffith-Jones and Avinash Persaud, *Financial Transaction Taxes*, report produced for the Committee for Economic and Monetary Affairs, February 2012.
35 European Commission, 'Financial transaction tax: making the financial sector pay its fair share', press release, 28 September 2011.
36 For a list of senior bankers and key industry figures calling for the complete separation

of retail from investment banks, for example, see Aline Fares, 'Who are the senior bankers calling for separation?' Brussels: Finance Watch, 26 July 2012.

37 See for example William L. Watts, 'Cyprus capital controls could blow the euro apart', MarketWatch, 28 March 2013.

38 Oxfam, *Be Outraged: There Are Alternatives*, May 2012, pp. 14, 16–17; IMF, *The Liberalization and Management of Capital Flows: An Institutional View*, Executive Summary, 14 November 2012, p. 2.

39 See for example Matthew Yglesias, 'Capital controls in a currency union', Slate, 20 March 2013.

40 M. Ayhan Kose and Eswar Prasad, 'Capital accounts: liberalize or not?', *Finance and Development*, Washington DC: IMF, 28 March 2012.

41 Paul Bergin, 'Monetary union', *The Concise Encyclopaedia of Economics*, 2nd edn, Library of Economics and Liberty.

42 Ulrich Machold, *Capital Controls, EMU and the Crisis of the European Monetary System*, Berlin: European Centre for Comparative Government and Public Policy, 2002, p. 14.

43 OECD, *An Overview of Growing Income Inequalities in OECD Countries: Main Findings*, 2011, pp. 38–9; Andrew G. Berg and Jonathan D. Ostry, *Inequality and Unsustainable Growth: Two Sides of the Same Coin?*, Washington DC: IMF, April 2011, pp. 16–17.

44 Financial Secrecy Index website, 'Overview: Shining light into dark places'.

45 Tackle Tax Havens website, 'The solutions'.

46 James S. Henry, *The Price of Offshore Revisited: New Estimates for 'Missing' Global Private Wealth, Income, and Lost Taxes,* London: Tax Justice Network, July 2012, p. 3.

47 See for example Pierre Moscovici's speech at the Bruegel annual meeting, 7 September 2012.

48 Emiliano Brancaccio, 'For a European wage standard', in Matthieu Méulle (ed.), *Austerity is Not the Solution! Contributions to European Economic Policy*, Brussels: Foundation for European Progressive Studies, 2012, pp. 75–96.

49 Brancaccio, 2012, p. 89.

50 Brancaccio, 2012, p. 90.

51 Brancaccio, 2012,p. 86.

52 ETUC, *A Social Compact for Europe*, resolution adopted by the Executive Committee on 5–6 June 2012.

53 Emiliano Brancaccio and Marco Passarella, *L'austerità è di destra*, Milan: Il Saggiatore, 2012, pp. 119–26.

54 Brancaccio and Passarella, 2012, p. 125 (author's translation).

55 European Green Party, *A Green New Deal for Europe*, manifesto for the 2009 European election campaign; http://greennewdeal.eu.

56 European Green Party, 'Why we need a Green New Deal'.

57 Hervé Kempf, *How the Rich Are Destroying the Earth*, trans. Leslie Thatcher, Hartford, Conn.: Chelsea Green, 2008.

58 On this point see Thomas Schulz, 'Man vs. machine: are any jobs safe from innovation?', *Spiegel Online*, 3 May 2013.

59 See for example Julia Horstschräer, Markus Clauss and Reinhold Schnabel, *Distributional and Behavioral Effects of Basic Income – A Linked Micro-Macro Model for Germany*, Mannheim: ZEW, 2012.

60 George Monbiot, 'Communism, welfare state – what's the next big idea?', *Guardian*, 1 April 2013.

61 Juliet Schor, 'Reducing working hours can benefit the economy and the environment', *Guardian*, 20 June 2011.

62 Schor, 2011.

63 On this point see Eric Toussaint and Damien Millet, 'Citizen debt audits: how and why?' Liège: CADTM, 4 January 2012.
64 On this point see Etienne Balibar, 'What democratic Europe? A response to Jürgen Habermas', *Social Europe Journal*, 1 October 2012.
65 On this point, see Paul Krugman, 'Own horn, tooting of', *New York Times*, 13 August 2011.
66 Anatole Kaletsky, 'How about quantitative easing for the people?', Reuters, 1 August 2012.
67 On this point see Ambrose Evans-Pritchard, 'Helicopter QE will never be reversed', *Telegraph*, 3 April 2013.
68 See for example Adair Turner, 'Debt, money and Mephistopheles: how do we get out of this mess?', speech given at the Cass Business School, 6 February 2013, pp. 3–4.
69 Martin Wolf, 'The case for helicopter money', *Financial Times*, 12 February 2013.
70 Turner, 2013, p. 31.
71 Turner, 2013, pp. 32–3.
72 Turner, 2013, p. 3.
73 Turner, 2013, pp. 23–4.
74 Turner, 2013, pp. 34–6.
75 Pierre Pâris and Charles Wyplosz, 'To end the Eurozone crisis, bury the debt forever', VoxEU.org, 6 August 2013.
76 Turner, 2013, p. 26.
77 Richard C. Koo, 'The world in balance sheet recession: causes, cure, and politics', *Real-World Economic Review*, No. 58, 2011, pp. 19–37; Turner, 2013, pp. 12–14.
78 Turner, 2013, p. 40.
79 Turner, 2013, p. 28.
80 Turner, 2013, pp. 14–18.
81 Turner, 2013, pp. 36–7.
82 On this point see Simon Tilford, 'A dose of inflation would help the eurozone medicine go down', London: Centre for European Reform, 16 May 2013.
83 For a mainstream critical assessment of the ECB's monetary policy, see *Economist*, 'Has anyone seen the ECB?' 4 April 2013.
84 See for example *Economist*, 'America's fiscal union: the red and the black', 1 August 2011.
85 Flassbeck and Lapavitsas, 2013, p. 31.
86 George Soros, 'How to save the European Union', *Guardian*, 9 April 2013.
87 Flassbeck and Lapavitsas, 2013, p. 14.
88 Yanis Varoufakis, Stuart Holland and James K. Galbraith, *A Modest Proposal for Resolving the Eurozone Crisis – Version 4.0*, July 2013.

Index